Advance Praise

A book that brings into the world a rare seeking that is often kept at a distance. A beautiful way of finding oneself, the self that is not limited by the 'I' but rather wanders within and amongst us. The authors have proposed a 'musical composition' that smudges organizational and individual separators, persuading the philosopher and the pragmatist to find each other within themselves.

T. M. Krishna, *Karnatik Vocalist, Writer,*
Social Commentator and Magsaysay Award Winner

Through this book, we are introduced to the Transformative Alignment Map (TAM), which is a profound concept that seeks to explain the relationship between the individual and the system. The high level of clarity that the authors have about the concept has enabled them to treat this complex subject with astounding simplicity. The engaging style of writing makes this book a compulsory read.

R. Seshasayee, *Chairman, IndusInd Bank*

An alchemist is one who transmutes something ordinary into something special. There is an alchemist in each of us waiting to help know and value ourselves. The authors through their sound philosophical foundation and deep research combined with magical insights have created a framework that allows us to discover our inner nature and helps us align within and with others as well as with the context. Read on to discover yourself and enjoy awakening the alchemist in you....

Ravi Kyran, *President, Human Resources, Bajaj Auto Limited*

At a time when more and more individuals search for meaning and alignment in their organizational roles, the authors offer through *Discover the Alchemist Within* a refreshingly new perspective by means of a bold and ingenious synthesis of the essence of Karnatik music and Jungian psychology. Brilliant!

Ganesh Chella, *Vice Chairman and Managing Director,*
Coaching Foundation India (CFI), and Co-author,
HR Here and Now

The TAM, introduced to us through this book, is a refreshing approach to working simultaneously with the layers of self-role in an organizational context. The framework is inviting and yet not definitive in boxing you down. Through a playful yet serious narrative, the authors encourage you to discover and then shape aspects of your stances that contribute to or hinder a more wholesome engagement in multiple roles and systems.

Rosemary Viswanath, *Managing Trustee,*
Group Relations India

This book is for those serious about creating transformation! The authors have combined their extensive research and work with symbols, and insights from Indian music as they explore the self in roles and organizations. Discover the 16 identities around you, as you work your way to create wholesome integration. Having used their self-assessment myself, I am amazed at how much of me it reveals.

Steve Correa, *President, Human Resources,*
Diageo (India) Limited

Discover the Alchemist Within is a book that made me think about the dynamic interplay between multiple individual identities and various roles one plays in organizations. Discovery and deeper understanding of these identities help an individual to find that alignment which could catapult one's effectiveness to newer heights. The state of integration and wholeness is an outcome of perfect alignment in four spaces, namely self and role, role and organization, self and organization, and organization and context. The TAM framework explains this phenomenon. The confluent circle in the TAM model where self, role(s) and organization overlap can be conceived of as the 'sweet spot' where energy, capability, values and strategy come together and are in a state of what the book calls 'transformative alignment'. This is a space that can transform the whole organization and left me thinking if this is the new theory which should be embraced by every organization which aims to become an 'experienced enterprise'.

The other thought-provoking concept is that of 4 psychological worlds and 16 identities, which takes the reader to delve deeper into their own inner worlds and start the journey of self-exploration and personal growth. Moored in the parallels of Indian (Karnatik) classical music and drawing upon rich metaphors from movies, mythology, popular literature and the like, it's a dense yet captivating read.

I found this book eminently illuminating and to be offering deep insights. This is a must-read for everyone who seeks personal exploration and growth and certainly leaders and practitioners chartered with fostering and transforming organizations.

A bold greenfield attempt which succeeds handsomely. Kudos to the trio who made this possible.

Abdul Jaleel, *Vice President, Employee Experience India,*
Adobe India Limited

This book is a lyrical voyage across the psychological worlds of 'connectedness', 'flow', 'autonomy' and 'structure' which reside in each of us. It is an engrossing narration of self-discovery which weaves through multiple signposts ranging from the works of Carl Jung and Joseph Campbell, works of poetry and literature to popular movies, scriptures and stories…and brings one to meet and understand the archetypes of personal transformation. A delightful reading, this book itself is a work of alchemy….

Madhukar Shukla, *Author and Professor, OB and Strategic Management XLRI, Jamshedpur*

Discover the Alchemist Within is a must-read for anyone seeking a rich, meaty, value-added dimension to understand human behaviour. In my 30 years of leadership study, application and teaching, I have rarely encountered a book that has expanded and stimulated me as much as this one. The authors provide fantastic vistas with two paradigm-shifting constructs: the TAM revealing 4 'psychological worlds' and 16 'symbolic identities' or memes. The book reflects the heart of a teacher as it delightfully opens up these vistas for deep dives into refreshing insights that trigger a cascade of epiphanies. This book avoids the boring re-hash of popular and mostly Western-based constructs. By weaving into the reader's journey an Indian context, one is treated to constant perspectives only that context can provide. As a result, the reader is swept into uncharted waters with expansive potential for incredibly broad and deep revolutionary understandings. So enabled, one is given new ideas with the potential to effect substantive, powerful change.

Ed Hampton, *CEO and Managing Member, Performance Perspectives LLC*

This book beautifully draws out learnings for living and working from art forms and philosophies that are timeless and elevating, particularly relevant for today's world of increasing disconnect and discord. In a lilting style, it beckons you to reflect on yourself and recognize your identity/ies, nudges you to be 'more' in your roles and, most importantly, to realize the value of harmony and inclusivity.

Gargi Banerji and Sunil Pillai, *Co-founders, Pragya*

With rapid changes happening in our life and work contexts, our dominant modes of thinking—systematically and analytically—may not deliver results. There is a need to think holistically about our roles, identities and, above all, our purpose. *Discover the Alchemist Within* does this by using dominant archetypes to help us understand ourselves better. The TAM allows us to examine our self, role, organization and contextual realities, and find coherence and resonance.

Vasanthi Srinivasan, *Professor, Organization Behaviour and Human Resources Management, Indian Institute of Management, Bangalore*

DISCOVER THE ALCHEMIST WITHIN

DISCOVER THE ALCHEMIST WITHIN

Taking the First Step Towards Personal Growth

Kartikeyan V.
Rachna Nandakumar
Vishwanath P.

⑤SAGE | Response Business Books

Los Angeles | London | New Delhi
Singapore | Washington DC | Melbourne

First published in 2018 by

SAGE Publications India Pvt Ltd
B1/I-1 Mohan Cooperative Industrial Area
Mathura Road, New Delhi 110 044, India
www.sagepub.in

SAGE Publications Inc
2455 Teller Road
Thousand Oaks, California 91320, USA

SAGE Publications Ltd
1 Oliver's Yard, 55 City Road
London EC1Y 1SP, United Kingdom

SAGE Publications Asia-Pacific Pte Ltd
3 Church Street
#10-04 Samsung Hub
Singapore 049483

Published by Vivek Mehra for SAGE Publications India Pvt Ltd, typeset in 11/14 pts Berkeley by Fidus Design Pvt. Ltd., Chandigarh and printed at Chaman Enterprises, New Delhi.

Library of Congress Cataloging-in-Publication Data Available

ISBN: 978-93-528-0850-2 (PB)

SAGE Team: Manisha Mathews, Alekha Chandra Jena and Ritu Chopra

Illustrations courtesy: Samyukta Kartik

Kartikeyan V.

To the Flute Maestro Dr N. Ramani, who taught me how to love music, and to Savitha, Samyukta, Vinay and Zia, who are teaching me how to love life.

Rachna Nandakumar

To the Universe, for making this happen. To Ravi, Avani and Shakti, for making my world a joyful place and for bringing alive many many parts of myself. To Avalokita and Swara, your smiles light up my heart.

Vishwanath P.

To Geeta, who taught me to be a 'part of the process'. To Anshul, who anchors my world. And to Anvita, who gently reminds me when I am 'off key'.

Thank you for choosing a SAGE product!
If you have any comment, observation or feedback,
I would like to personally hear from you.

Please write to me at **contactceo@sagepub.in**

Vivek Mehra, Managing Director and CEO, SAGE India.

Bulk Sales

SAGE India offers special discounts
for purchase of books in bulk.
We also make available special imprints
and excerpts from our books on demand.

For orders and enquiries, write to us at

Marketing Department
SAGE Publications India Pvt Ltd
B1/I-1, Mohan Cooperative Industrial Area
Mathura Road, Post Bag 7
New Delhi 110044, India

E-mail us at **marketing@sagepub.in**

Get to know more about SAGE

Be invited to SAGE events, get on our mailing list.
Write today to **marketing@sagepub.in**

This book is also available as an e-book.

Contents

Foreword

Kartikeyan, Rachna and Vishwanath have written a unique book.

Tapping into their curiosity and conviction, they have come out with an interdisciplinary framework to study alignment that builds a bridge between Karnatik music and the world of human beings and organizations. From Karnatik music, they have adopted the alignment principles of 'shruti' (pitch), 'layam' (rhythm) and 'bhaavam' (melodic evocation) and applied these to develop a unique framework that they call 'Transformative Alignment Map' or TAM. This enabled them to explore the critical corresponding dimensions of 'resonance', 'coherence' and 'delight' in intrapersonal, interpersonal, intra-systemic and inter-systemic realms. They further applied their thinking to the four critical interfaces of 'Self and Role', 'Roles and Organization', 'Self and Organization' and 'Organization and Context'. They discovered that if these four interfaces could be aligned, it would lead to 'wholesome leadership'.

A long time back, the great master Patanjali expounded the ancient wisdom traditions of India in his seminal work on the 'Yoga Sutras'. He talked about how alignment between the body, breath, mind, intellect and ego (pancha koshas) would make a person achieve balance and transcend all limitations to discover the infinite truth within each human being—PURE BLISS.

This led to the discovery of 'YOGA' which has created well-being in the lives of millions of people all over the world. Kartikeyan, Rachna and Vishwanath's work may be described as the 'Yoga' for organizations. If the 'CONTEXT' is understood in holistic ways, organizations would discover 'PURPOSE' and create compelling 'VISION's that would inspire all their stakeholders.

If people understood how their own vision and values aligned to this purpose, it would create alignment between 'Self and Organization'. If they then listened to the stakeholders with this vision, they would appreciate the important nuances of their roles—thus creating alignment between the 'Self and Role'—and finally when this works in a spirit of enabling the well-being of each other so as to ensure the higher purpose, they would create alignment between 'Roles and Organization'.

Greater alignment creates higher authenticity and whole-someness. It leads to greater integrity and trust and makes such organizations truly 'great'!

This book takes the conversation from the abstract to the practical by enabling readers to explore different 'archetypes' to appreciate themselves and achieve greater alignment and balance in their lives. From learning about the four psychological worlds that create a virtual Mandala of existence, they take you through intimate conversations with sixteen symbolic identities that inhabit and enliven these four worlds. You might revel at the spirit of the MUSE that has the seemingly magical energy that silently lifts you to greater heights, or that of the GUIDE MENTOR that enables you to facilitate the development of others, or the sheer strength and desire of the WARLORD or the tradition-fostering CUSTODIAN. And there are more! Through this book, readers are taken on a joyful journey of 'Self-discovery', the first step towards alignment.

I strongly recommend this book to human beings from all walks of life and in particular to all leaders, consultants, coaches, students, teachers and practitioners who wish to achieve greater harmony that leads to the realization of the full potential of individuals and organizations.

Anil Sachdev
Founder & CEO
School of Inspired Leadership—SOIL

Preface

It finally took the wise words of an eminent flautist to bring it all together.

As corporate leaders turned organizational consultants, we had worked in depth with various frameworks and models aimed at addressing organization and human development over several years. While each tool brought with it its own strengths and nuances, all of them ultimately left us feeling dissatisfied. There was something missing in the equation. A sense that the deeper parts of the human condition still lay untouched. What began as a lament on the unavailability of a truly integrative Organization Development (OD) model quickly intensified into a search for a road map for human and system transformation.

Our quest took us to the doorstep of looking at *alignment* as a process by which fragments could be brought together and transformed into a meaningful whole. Over countless coffees and conversations, we tried to put the pieces together. And yet, the puzzle would not fit. Little did we know that the inspiration had to come from a different space altogether.

Cut to a late rainy November evening in 2014. One of the authors was spending time with his Guru, Padmashri N. Ramani, a flute maestro and musical genius who had held audiences across the world in thrall. Inevitably the conversation drifted towards music and what really creates a great musical experience for the musician and the listeners.

After a long silence, Ramani sir (as his students fondly addressed him) spoke. The words came slowly and haltingly but contained the distilled wisdom that came from decades of playing music.

'Three things, but I will actually say it is ONE thing in three forms. *Ellaame saerndhu irukkanum* (everything has to be aligned). That is the ONE big thing. *Modalla shruti saeranum* (first there has to be resonance with a pitch), *taalam saeranum* (there has to be rhythmic alignment), *kaetkaravaalukku bhaava-maa irukkanum* (the listeners need to feel melodic evocation) ... *Idhu moonum saerndhu illana sangeetham appidingra anubhavame illa* (if these three don't exist in alignment, there is no experience of music)'.

The penny dropped. The 'ONE thing in three forms' was what we had been truly searching for. The idea was elegant in its simplicity and clearly lent itself to looking at the entire spectrum of human experience. It was holistic. It was integrative. And it offered a platform for our deep yearning to create something new and path-breaking which truly belonged to the Eastern tradition in a space typically dominated by largely Anglo-Saxon and/or Abrahamic viewpoints. It took us three years to develop the framework in its entirety. We call it the Transformative Alignment Map (TAM)—a framework that explores and engages with alignment as a process towards human and system transformation.

The canvas of TAM as it grew from there has become a vast one. Most of the philosophical foundations and the meta-framework have been crystallized in the chapter 'An Introduction to the Transformative Alignment Map'. To bring all that alive in one book would be like growing a banyan tree in a flower pot. Thus, this book takes us to just the first part of TAM. In this book, we have tried to unravel the four worlds and the sixteen identities that are core to TAM. This may lead you to taking the TAM-Self assessment for yourself, or you may consider certifying yourself on TAM-Self. The rest of the story, all about TAM Role, TAM Team, TAM Org, Resonances, Dissonances, Coherence, Incoherence, Dissatisfaction, Delight and so on, may perhaps come in the form of other books.

As you read this book, we invite you to bring your curiosity in with you. And yes, you may bring your scepticism along, too! Try and feel how the four worlds resonate with you, to what degree. Read about the sixteen identities as though they are alter-egos of your own self (and many of them might well be so), and add your own thoughts and feelings as you read these. Finally have fun with the play book—it has been created to offer you a playspace within this book so you get more familiar with the framework. And of course, please do take the TAM-Self assessment and schedule a debrief with a TAM coach.

Acknowledgements

There are times when the unconscious whispers to one through the language best known to her— through symbols.

The three of us had been talking about our ongoing work with Transformative Alignment and the idea of a book had been lurking around, daring us some, beseeching us some, then daring us some more and so on. We did the thing that we do best when in doubt, as some of our close friends would attest—draw a Tarot card! The card we drew was of the Magician. The card depicts a Magician, standing with one arm pointed upwards and another downwards and in front of him is a table with a sword, a wand, a pentacle and a cup (chalice). And he stands in front of a garden. An instinctive wave of positive affirmation swept over us as we beheld the image, associating it with the power of communication, conscious action and will. And that is what we feel the unconscious has gifted us through that image—the ability to anchor ourselves in our conviction and announce our perspective. She also gifted us, through the four implements of the Magician, the power of expressing desire, collaboration, creativity and discipline. In an interesting way, these four words bring alive the four worlds of the TAM that you will encounter as you turn the pages of this book. Our gratitude to the unconscious cannot be expressed in words but it can, in commitment and action—to do what we are doing with her gifts and to continue doing so for life.

A lot of people and institutions have supported us through this project. To each of you, we stand up, bow deep and offer you a hug.

You, our family members—Anshul, Anvita, Avani, Ravi, Sam, Savitha, Shakti, Vinay and Zia—have stood by and cheered us along every step of the way. There are times when an event involves commitment of and effort from the whole family. This is one such time. You have laughed with us, sometimes at us, put up with our moods, challenged us, offered us a patient ear, reviewed what we have written and sometimes just watched us. To you, our gratitude and love.

You, our parents, without you, quite literally, we would not be here.

You, our teachers and mentors, Flute Ramani Sir, Ashok Malhotra, Geeta Saxena, P. M. Kumar, Raghu Ananthanarayanan and Sushanta Banerjee—you are giants on whose shoulders we have stood at various times in our lives. To you, our gratitude and commitment to go forward on the paths you have shown us.

You, our many dear friends, members of the TAM Practitioners' cohorts—Heera, Jey, Jeyavelu, Murali, Mustafa, Priya, Ravi, Savitha, Shabari, Sophie, Swasthika, Vinti and the more-than-sixty participants of the various Symbols Labs that we have held over the years—you have affirmed us deeply by sharing spaces we have created and are adding to those. So too, you great musicians T. M. Krishna and Vijay Siva, you have inspired us in more ways than one! To you, our gratitude and offer of continued companionship in your respective unfolding journeys.

You, our publishers and editors, and in particular Manisha Mathews, you trusted us and encouraged us, found meaning and possibilities in the story we wished to narrate. And all of you who have read, critiqued and endorsed our work, we are very touched by your gestures. To all of you, our gratitude and goodwill.

You, the more-than-500 people from various walks of life and the corporates who have taken our TAM assessments and worked out parts of the tapestries of your life with us, we know that there is another story waiting to be told from the patterns and themes your data weaves. To you, our gratitude and commitment to lend an ear to your story as it unfolds.

Rahul, Rashmi, Samyukta and Vinay—your help on our website and assessments, legal matters, illustrations and data analysis have made it possible to get us to where we are. To you, our gratitude and sincere acknowledgment.

And you, dear reader, your picking up this book symbolizes another life that has been touched by TAM. Your presence and willingness to hear what we have to say is a privilege, which we hope the story to follow will do justice to. To you, our gratitude and our deepest appreciation.

1

An Invitation to the Alchemist in You

'This is why alchemy exists', the boy said. 'So that everyone will search for his treasure, find it, and then want to be better than he was in his former life. Lead will play its role until the world has no further need for lead; and then lead will have to turn itself into gold.

That's what alchemists do. They show that, when we strive to become better than we are, everything around us becomes better, too'.

—Paulo Coelho, The Alchemist

There is gold within all of us. The secret goal of alchemy, as Mary-Louise von Franz[1] says, is the search for transformation and wholeness. The alchemist we are inviting you to get acquainted with is us—it is you and those around you—all human beings and human systems. And the alchemy we are inviting you to

---

[1] von Franz, 'Alchemy'.

practise is akin to Carl Jung's idea of individuation. We will unpack our invitation a little bit more, so we can all go about the rest of this book, with the very serious (yet fun) way towards our personal growth.

Jung's view of individuation is the psychic process in which the individual self develops by integrating parts of the psyche that have, over a period of time, either never been accessed by the person or been repressed or suppressed by them. If the process is more or less successful, the 'divided self' or the 'dividual' comes together into a relatively wholesome and integrated entity that is now an 'individual'—hence the term individuation. Coming to the alchemy of individuation, a word of caution—the 'philosopher's stone' that we would like the alchemist in all of us to go after is not a hierarchically superior state of being. Rather, it is in discovering the essence of one's being (the alchemists called this the *quinta essentia* or the quintessence) and in learning to value it in its entirety—in its beauty and ugliness. In fact, and come to think of it, we would not like for you to go *after* anything. Rather, can we enjoin you to go *towards* that gold within?

Jung has likened the process of individuation more sharply with what the alchemist would do, and let us look to the parallels he draws. We will look at colours here. A postmodern deconstructionist's view of colours and the significance associated with them would disable us from proceeding further, so for understanding this part, we will need to stay with certain conventional associations.

The alchemist would start with nigredo, encountering the unconscious and touching the castaway shadow elements. This is the phase that might lead to typical 'black moods'. As we continue to work with the shadow, the repressed elements get cleansed and enter a phase the alchemists would call as albedo (the lighter phase). However, this process by itself is not individuation. The third element—rubedo, the 'reddening' phase—involves the sacred union or coniunctio, where the newly released elements are integrated back into the original entity. Individuation does not happen as an outcome, but it is a process that never ends, perhaps like a slow-moving glacier. This is very resonant with learning about yourself in a Transformative Alignment journey. Going over your TAM-Self instrument with a seasoned and qualified TAM-Self practitioner would show the identities that are in the shadow and the ones consciously being owned up. This process comprises nigredo and albedo. Thereafter, an individual who undertakes mindful work, and works with these consciously attempts to see what he or she is disowning in the shadow elements, and tries to reintegrate them, which leads to a rubedo experience. This process of personal growth to 'get back to yourself' is the essence of the first phase of Transformative Alignment. We say first phase because, as you will see in the next chapter, you can go forward and explore your alignment between your Self and the role(s) you engage in, and thereafter to systems and then to the macro-context outside of the systems you are part of. For the purpose of this book, we will restrict our explorations to 'within the self'.

One last word: What is 'personal growth'? Does not 'growth' imply going towards a 'better' or 'superior' state of something? Are we then contradicting ourselves? Let us turn here to the wise words of Sushanta Banerjee who suggests evocatively that there is no destination, only an ongoing movement. Although he wrote these in the context of 'process work', we are placing this before you here to explicate personal growth, given the considerable resonance between process work and personal growth.

We have all been gifted (cursed?) with a voice within, an eye within, and an ear within which put together overrides the senses and creates a world well beyond the manifest. This vision, contact with the unmanifest, is self-reflexivity. At the first instance, it gives rise to what is called conscience. In its corrupted form this becomes narcissism which in its extreme form gives rise to self-righteousness. In its usual form, it makes us human.

... the next stage of its maturation is to be able to look at oneself and the other with the same eye. When this happens, you find everyone within yourself, from the cheat, the thief, the leper, the magician and.... As I stand today process work is focussed mainly on stimulating this inner spectator and continually fostering its stage wise maturation and *transformation. There is thus no defined destination, only a movement. Like Shri Ramakrishna used to be fond of saying to the disciple caught in any dilemma 'move, man'.*

Our hope is that you will use this book as an opportunity to discover *your* alchemist within yourself.

2

An Introduction to the Transformative Alignment Map

The Transformative Alignment Map (TAM) framework has its origins in the idea of integration and wholeness as available in the Indian music system (particularly Karnatik music) and brings those paradigms into the human development and organization building space. The basic belief here is that the experience of 'being integrated and whole' is healthy for human living. It provides a fertile ground for sustaining one's quality of life as well as fostering striving.

The relevant constructs from the world of Karnatik music that have been taken up for the architecture of TAM are the ideas of 'shruti (pitch)', 'laya (rhythm)' and 'bhaava (melodic evocation)', which explicate phenomenological constructs of 'resonance', 'coherence' and 'delight', respectively. We go on to propose that the absence of these in human beings and human systems implies dissonance, incoherence and dissatisfaction, respectively, which is 'psychological waste'. This waste is all the more toxic and corrosive because it is mostly invisible, intangible and constantly shape-shifting.

We will now unfold the TAM canvas for you in the rest of this chapter but with a point for you to note. The exposition of TAM here is to give you, the reader, an idea of the complete framework of TAM. However, beyond this chapter, the rest of this book will dwell on TAM only as it applies to individuals like yourselves. It is our fond hope that we would have the gift of your indulgence to spur us to write further on the spaces beyond TAM-Self, for example, TAM-Role, TAM-Team, TAM-Organization and so on.

Resonance/Dissonance

You may have noticed that in any Indian classical music perfor-mance, the first thing the musicians do is to align their voices/instruments to a suitable reference point or the *tonic* provided by a standard normal drone (tanpura/tambura). The alignment of the musician's voice/instrument to the reference point becomes the base for the emergence of melody. This alignment in the Indian classical music system is called 'alignment to shruti'. Resonant align-ment leads to melodious music and dissonance in such alignment often leads to odious 'noise'.

At the level of an individual in any system, resonance is experienced when a person's sense of self (broadly conceivable as the drone/pitch) and the role requirements as determined in the system (broadly equivalent to the voice/instrument) are in alignment. This then creates the foundation for the persons to bring in all their psychological energy into finding convergence between the needs of the role and the preferences and proclivities of their self.

The absence of such alignment could lead to pernicious dissonance—mostly manifesting in the form of general disengage-ment, malingering, apathy, indifference and so on. In organizational life, we see this in the form of absenteeism, voluntary turnover and a dipping quality of output.

Coherence/Incoherence

Also central to the idea of Indian music is the concept of 'laya' or rhythm. Laya offers the concept of a steady pattern to which the flowing music adheres. This steady pattern is the experience of how time is structured in music—between notes of a song and across a whole musical presentation. If you have seen musicians beating their hands in a certain rhythmic pattern while presenting music (also called 'taala' or 'taal' in the Indian classical music systems) or the curiously rhythmic 'headbanging' in metal concerts, then you are seeing the manifestation of laya in action.

If the musician's presentation is not aligned with the beat, it will result in an 'out-of-synch' experience, and the taut tension that is required for the gripping effect of the music will go away, resulting in a dissipative experience.

Inside a human system (be it a family, work team or organization), laya is the alignment of multiple roles with the core purpose of the system. Here, the purpose of the system can be conceived of as the central beat to which alignment is sought. If the roles set and the system's purpose are in alignment, the resultant coherence in the system offers an experience of a 'high-capability' system. Likewise, if the roles set does not find an alignment with the purpose of the system, the resulting incoherence drains capability. Manifest phenomena could be missed targets, teaming issues, structural incongruities, blame, infighting, sense of dissipation and so on.

Delight/Dissatisfaction

The creation and expression of music is directed towards the generation of delight, whether in the form of artistic/spiritual unfolding for the artiste or in simply providing wholesome joy to the listener. In this, the key question that is often asked by a musician is—what 'bhaavam' or emotional states did my music evoke and foster?

It can be safely asserted that bhaavam cannot be created without the ingredients of resonant shruti and coherent laya. However, these are necessary but not sufficient conditions for the wholesome experience of delight through bhaavam. This delight is generated when the musician experiences these inside themselves and then expresses them to the 'audience'. The resultant 'jugalbandi' or 'duet' is between the musicians and their audience and not limited to the musicians on the stage creating the music.

In work system terms, we are here talking about stakeholders' delight—is the employee loving it, is the investor happy, is the customer delighted, is the vendor feeling valued, is the regulator satisfied, is the citizen appreciative and so on. When the psychological configuration of the whole system is strategically aligned with the needs of the larger context, a musically equivalent experience of 'sadbhaavam' (good, positive bhaavam) is created.

Similarly, when this alignment does not happen, there is a lack of a strategic fit and 'dissatisfaction' occurs. Examples of such dissatisfaction may be phenomena such as uneasy investors, a dipping customer satisfaction score and net promoter scores, regulatory issues, citizenry unrest, negative press and so on.

Meta-framework of TAM

Taking forward the ideas of alignment towards 'integration and wholeness' and also based on our extensive work/consulting experience, we propose that there are four spaces where alignment is necessary and where waste is likely to occur (if alignment is not attended to). These are as follows:

1. Self and Role Alignment (the space of Energy)—Between each member of a system and their role. This is where the *shruti* of

resonance or dissonance is experienced. High resonance yields greater energy than otherwise.

2. Roles and Organizational Alignment (the space of Capability)—Between any team's collective 'role readiness' and the organization's purpose. This is where a system is experienced as coherent or incoherent, just like in *laya*. Coherence adds to a system's capability to deliver on its promise and incoherence would work against it.

3. Self and Organizational Alignment (the space of Values)— Between the values and preferences of each member in the organization and the whole organization as such. This is where members in a system feel the *bhaavam* of belonging or alienation.

4. Organizational and Context Alignment (the space of Strategy)—Between the organization and its perceived external context. This is the space of the *bhaavam* of delight or otherwise for the context.

TAM helps study alignment or the lack of it using a dynamic framework spanning all the 'spaces' described above. The dynamic nature of the framework suggests that the alignment can vary with time and players in the system. Changes in any one variable in the framework influence changes in the others which are in dynamic interplay—impacting each other and the whole system all the time.

The figure below gives a high-level visual map of the alignment spaces mentioned above. The central space where the spaces of self, role(s) and organization overlap can be conceived of as the 'sweet spot' where energy, capability, values and strategy come together and the whole meta-system is in a state of 'transformative alignment', that is, a space of alignment that can transform the whole organization.

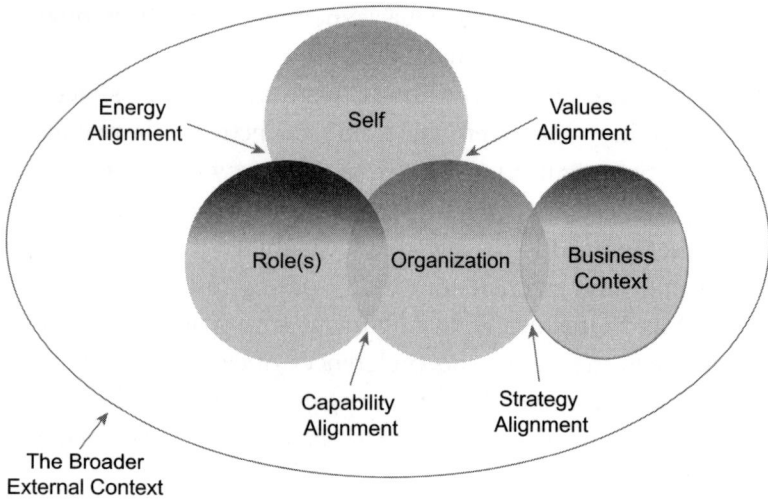

We started by saying that alignment is the process by which parts, pieces and fragments could be brought together to form integrated and wholesome systems. If we take the idea of alignment forward, we also know from sports and dance that alignment is the optimal coming together of body parts such that the muscles do not have to do too much work—this 'coming together' ensures that the outcomes are met with greater elegance, in a streamlined way, and with lesser effort. Savings in effort can lead to additional investment in the existing outcomes or new investment in new outcomes or simply in a greater quality of life and enhanced well-being. It is our hope that families, work teams, organizations and larger human systems of various kinds can indeed acquaint themselves with our vision for transformative alignment and thus move towards greater prosperity and happiness.

The first part of the book explores the first phase of trans-formative alignment in which we look at understanding the nature and quality of that which needs to be aligned. Keeping the above illustration in mind, we then introduce you to four psy-chological worlds. In the next part, we delve deeper into the respective inhabitants of these worlds—the sixteen identities.

Once you have familiarized yourself with the four worlds and the sixteen identities, you are ready to move towards our workbook.

The workbook is intended to provide you a step-by-step approach to exploring your own specific identity configuration and move towards greater alignment between your Self and the various roles that you may be playing.

3

The Four Worlds

In Jungian psychology, the idea of a 'quaternity' is posited. It refers to a fourfold structure. It is usually symmetrical and conveys the idea of 'wholeness'. Given our search for models associated with wholeness and integration, it is little wonder that we look to the quaternity representation. But this is a top-down view. In actuality, when we started working on the Transformative Alignment Map (TAM), one of our primary inspirations came from the work of a Jungian psychologist named Gareth Hill and we started with his thoughts and ideas.[1] However, we also made significant departures from there and came up with the idea of four psychological worlds that all of us human beings and human systems inhabit. This has been explained in Appendix 1—The two axes of orientation.

The four worlds have been opened up in the chapters that follow in no particular order. When you read about a world, you are likely to see a visualization of the world with some examples. We then go on to describe what the world is all about in terms of its pulls, beliefs and stances, gifts, fears and vulnerabilities.

---

[1]Hill, 'Masculine and Feminine'.

We then go on to explicate what we feel might happen if a particular world is 'overdone' or 'underdone' (inhibited) and any other important dynamics that may need to be kept in mind about that world. Finally, we attempt to offer a short peek into what a leader (of any human system) would be like if they were personally steeped in that particular world being described. Every chapter on a world also has an illustrative caselet or a vignette from real life (with actual names being masked where applicable).

As you read the worlds, we invite you to feel into them, and ask yourself how much you resonate with any particular world. And remember—your ruminations may come in handy when you get to the playbook!

4

The World of Structure and Order

... why I like timetables, because they make sure I don't get lost in time.

—Mark Haddon, The Curious Incident
of the Dog in the Night-Time

Visualize a military organization. What do you see?

A clear and non-compromisable hierarchy, for starters, with an explicit chain of command. Roles, responsibilities and relationships that are defined and described to precision. Rules for decision-making and operations are givens. 'Command and control' is operational, so we can experience the exercise of authority and direction by a properly designated role over assigned resources in the accomplishment of a common mission or primary task. Leadership is used to make decisions, translate decision into actions, by synchronizing forces and functions in time, space and purpose, to accomplish missions. There is no space for tolerance of ambiguity. Clarity, predictability and order are the mantras we might hear all around us.

Where else do we see such 'clockwork' features? Assembly lines, surgical units, government departments, the cockpit of an aircraft and an operation theatre are all examples of such organizations. This also shows up in dance and music schools where beginners learn the basic grammar of these art forms. You can add to this list, by thinking of organizations where the reigning deity responds to offerings of structure, control, traditions and the like.

Presenting the world of structure and order (WSO) ...

What Is This World All About?

In all human systems, there exists a psychological pull towards stability, continuity and safety. This pull manifests itself in the world in the form of systems, rules, roles, procedures and the like. Welcome, then, to WSO. In many ways, WSO is like a foundation that enables us to stay in balance and provides order. Robust availability of WSO enables a system to thrive on the ground of norms, practices and traditions and offers the value of dependability, predictability and efficiency to the context.

In terms of basic beliefs and stances, this world believes that all things must serve the 'system' and that all the necessary infrastructure for living comes from the norms, prescriptions and mores of the context, the world and the society. In other words, the belief is that the path is given, and all one needs to do is to follow it faithfully, and all will be well. An individual who operates from this world may often fragment the 'given knowledge' and 'experiential knowledge' and privilege the former. This world is often conceived of as being located 'in the past'—and that is where it gets its fuel for maintaining continuity and traditions. This is a world without much personalized subjectivity even though collective subjectivity would exist in the form of preferences for certain practices and traditions. There is usually no space provided for personal biases, prejudices, whims and fancies here, as this world exalts the objective reality.

The WSO brings many gifts with it. The primary one is the gift of anchorage. Here, you get to see anchorage in order, which provides efficiency. You also witness anchorage in tradition, which yields continuity and answers to most known problems. Anchoring in the system ensures that all gain is for the system and all authority is exercised FOR and ON BEHALF OF the system. Duty and role performance come to the centre of the ring. And the ring itself is expected to be 'the framework' that provides rules, fairness, norms, standards and the base for consistency. Respect and traditions go hand in hand (hand in glove, some detractors of this world might say) and create a sense of solidity.

So, what about the vulnerabilities of this world? Just as each world brings gifts with it, it also carries the burdens of what it is susceptible to. WSO's vulnerability is the fear of potential chaos, discontinuity and loss of control. Perhaps there is an inherent anxiety that the psychic contents of the system would face a situation not unlike mutiny or anarchy and that at an existential level, 'we may not survive'. So, this world may end up tightening up its best features even more to compensate for these fears and this leads us straight to considering what might happen if this world is overplayed.

The Overdone and the Inhibited WSO

'I am wary of the whole dreary deadening structured mess that we have built into such a glittering top-heavy structure that there is nothing left to see but the glitter, and the brute routines of maintaining it'.

—John D. MacDonald, The Deep Blue Good-By

When an individual takes their WSO orientation to the extreme, they may feel a sense of righteousness and may even end up feeling dry and somehow dehumanized. Consider the case of Madhulika, a consultant with a reputed firm. Known to be a stickler for norms, rules and 'the letter of the law', she received a jolt when a 360-degree feedback in her firm revealed that her own team members and peers thought of her as an 'oppressive school teacher' and 'an obdurate patriarch'. This is a classic example of what happens when an individual overdoes the WSO.

In systems where WSO is overdone, you often run into the curious case of 'procedures' being valued more than 'purpose'. A rather cynical quip that is often heard is about how malls in many cities in India employ security staff to elaborately scan the undersides of vehicles and their boots (ostensibly for detecting explosive devices), while when asked, most of the security staff report that they do not know what they are doing—they are just following orders! In overdone WSO systems, human beings may get reduced to the equivalent of bots, unquestioningly carrying out predictable routines.

Let us also take a look at what might happen if WSO is inhibited or underplayed in a system. A survey by Transparency International ranks India at 81 out of 180 countries on the corruption perceptions index in 2017. This only points to a fairly well-accepted fact that cash or favours have often been used to lubricate bureaucratic approvals. This is most often the result of a lack of compliance to rules and legal strictures. As can be seen with countries that lie at the bottom of the rankings, such as Afghanistan or Syria, a muted WSO offers up a spectacle of anarchy and a feeling that 'anything goes'.

When WSO is muted in a system, it can result in systems where boundaries and processes are loosely held leading to chaos and disorganization. This phenomenon is witnessed in the reported urban traffic chaos on most weekdays in major cities of India. When withheld, WSO can lead to insecurity and anxiety in the minds of people, which is why in times of grave collective crises (e.g., natural disasters, terrorist threats, communal flare-ups and so on), it is very important for the rulers of the state to take immediate charge of the situation and reinforce the essential required order and also reassure the citizenry of their safety. Besides these, here is another face of low WSO—sometimes traditions may be disdained and maybe even be dismissed as restrictive or as dogma or as quaint anachronisms. Maybe a classic case of throwing the baby out with the bathwater?

Some Important Dynamics Relating to WSO

If you are a high WSO person, awareness of the dynamics of entrenchment would be helpful in avoiding it. Entrenched WSO can be seen in the compulsive and preoccupied enforcer of structure and order, especially when others in the system do not seem to care as much for these. Such compensation often leads them to be dumped with more and more of the onerous responsibilities in managing the system. And furthermore—they tend to then bask and preen and complain and crib alternatively about having to be so selfless and cross-bearing. Then comes the threat to the well-being of this world when it meets the derision of the context outside—when this world is excluded or ousted for being the 'boring one' or the 'buzzkills' or the inhibitors.

The WSO Leader

The WSO leader focuses on getting things done according to a clearly structured plan. Here, you get the task leader who is oriented towards achieving planned results through known procedures and well-proven methods. The leader here values concrete details and stability, often respecting what is tried and has worked before. This leader is methodical, meticulous, realistic, loyal and respectful of hierarchy. This leader processes decisions in a cautious way, tending to be frugal and comfortable with the familiar.

This leader rarely changes their mind, tending to be risk averse, appreciating benchmarks and 'best practices'. They get put off by tardiness, disorder and the lack of planning, disloyalty and extravagance.

For the WSO leader, systems are essentially to be complied with. They offer the rules and procedures that will yield safety, predictability and efficiency. Eschewing subjective criteria, the WSO leader both creates and follows systems that will help them deal with situations in an orderly manner. The WSO systems would tend to be balanced, clear and would value roles.

A snapshot of their profile is likely to be like this:

People biases	Towards those who comply and uphold
Derailers	Their excessive boundedness
Influence style	Rationalize
Response to change	Resist
Execution style	Guardians/Custodians

An Illustrative Caselet/Vignette: From a Coach's Journal

The first time I met Rahul, the information technology (IT) head of a reputed tech organization, in a leadership retreat, he had struck me as a thoughtful young man with an unruffled, calm demeanour.

So it was with some surprise that I welcomed him on a rainy Friday afternoon, looking decidedly unhappy and agitated. He soon revealed that, what was causing him such grief was the change in the reporting relationship that had come about following an organizational restructuring exercise and how his relationship with his new boss had started to come unstuck. In his role as an IT head, Rahul had always been well regarded in the organization for his meticulous execution and attention to detail. And all that had changed suddenly. Rahul felt that all that he had built was getting questioned and he was not feeling valued in the 'new dispensation'.

As we dug in further, the situation became clearer. Over his career, Rahul had built a name for himself as a responsible, loyal and a diligent manager. His projects ran like a well-oiled machine. Schedules and plans were complied with and for any hiccups, backup plans were in place. Clearly, there was a lot to be thankful for. Projects got executed well. Minutiae were taken care of. Lessons were learnt from scheduled post-mortem sessions and the organization was driven by well-defined metrics. As Rahul himself described his philosophy—'Discipline and structure saves time and brings order. Without structure, productivity deteriorates rapidly'. Things were in order and there was an order to things. Till now.

His new supervisor came from a different organization and had been tasked with changing the entire approach to IT. Suddenly the words transformation, strategic, innovation and change became the currency. All the carefully crafted rules that Rahul had put in place were now open to question. His boss even suggested that he change his entire project execution model. The boss could not see the wisdom of the processes that had worked very well for so long. The final straw had been when his supervisor told him that he needed to change the function's 'culture' which he perceived as slow, bureaucratic and not agile.

Deciding that it was a good time to introduce him to the Transformative Alignment Map (TAM), we approached the situation from a TAM lens. Without any prompting, one could see the dawning revelation on his face. He could see his own pull towards the WSO and sheepishly admitted that he might have perhaps been over-reliant on it. Sure it had its merits, but he could now also see how his relationship with his boss had to do more with each of their preferred worlds than any devaluing of his worth. As a smile crossed his face, he casually mentioned that he now also understood what might be happening in his relationship with his significant other. As we ended the session, Rahul had much more clarity on the world views held by the different pulls and an agenda for his action.

As he discovered that day—while structure and order are key steps towards mastery, chaos is merely order waiting to be deciphered...!

5

The World of Autonomy and Initiative

It will never rain roses: when we want to have more roses, we must plant more roses.

—George Eliot

To date, the Manchester United (MU) football club has won twenty League titles, twelve Football Association (FA) Cup titles, five League Cups, twenty-one Community Shields, three European Cups, one Union of European Football Associations (UEFA) Cup Winner's Cup, one UEFA Super Cup, one Intercontinental Cup and one Fédération Internationale de Football Association (FIFA) Club World Cup. Alongside these victories, many of them records, MU is also the highest-earning football club in the entire world and is widely regarded as having the most supporters across the world for any football team.

At MU, the constellation of human talent spins around a core of agreed ideals. The main one is to win by attacking and subjugating the competition and never letting up. Every individual on the team is expected to imbibe this core and live up to it.

Players are expected to win every game. A fear of losing apparently helps them to be at the top end of their game at all times. In this team, it is not easy to rest and take it easy in life. The drive to constantly stay on top and to win is unmistakably present and pervasive.

Where else have you seen something like this? The Indian cricket team of 2017? Successful broking houses on Wall Street? Tennis stars Federer or Nadal? The small grocer in your neighbourhood who does roaring business, howsoever small? Campus placements in the institutes of management in India? Take your pick, and enter the world of autonomy and initiative (WAI) ...

What Is This World All About?

Moving on from WSO, when we look at WAI, we are first awed by the contrast. Compared to the stable, safety-oriented, balanced WSO, we encounter the face of dynamicity, challenge and heady adventure here. This is the psychological world whose pull is towards owning up and exercising one's strength, power and autonomy. It is in this world that there is an awakening to aspirations, unabashed individualism and a valuing of competence. When this world is awake and alive, it interfaces with the context through goals or causes. The primary driver here would be 'Be strong, and show it!' The WAI, being an agentic world, induces in its occupants the force of competitiveness, independence and achievement orientation.

The WAI would seem to have a basic belief that the self must be asserted on the environment through action. Concomitantly, it also takes on a stance of self-reliance. And of course, pride too! There are two specific consequences that come from inhabiting this world. First, gains are made but there is often low focus on consolidation (consolidation, as you might see, would require a strong WSO as a 'wing') and second, action happens but reflection gets pushed to the background (which would have been helped by a world of connectedness and nurturance (WCN)/world of flow and unfolding (WFU) 'wing'—the next worlds that we will visit). The WAI is essentially 'future' oriented—the quest is towards the tomorrow, to strategize, to gain and to expand for the future. In contrast to the objective 'it' orientation of WSO which moves towards stability, the WAI world is oriented towards the 'I' and tends to engage more with the outer world focused on acquisition and winning. Whims are par for this course, and inner circle/outer circle dynamics can be sensed quite easily in WAI systems (and often lend to much passionate drama). Here, people who will be useful in attaining the goal will form the inner circle, often creating residue and disquiet amongst others.

The gift offered by WAI is courage and belief in oneself. While some people balk at hurdles in life, and some others resign themselves to never being able to cross them, WAI gives you the ability to see such hurdles as thresholds and steps to go forward. In the same vein, cross-roads are seen as 'at least four opportunities' in WAI. Catch the WAI person hesitating! This gift further unfolds as enhanced confidence, high conviction and the ability to impact the world through action.

But let us dig a little deeper. If we were to listen to the inner dialogue of WAI, where fears and vulnerabilities have a relatively free rein, the statements might surprise you—'What if I fail or lose? What if I am powerless, incapable, incompetent, weak? What if I do not create impact on the world? I cannot bear to see the things I have striven for come to naught'. Behind a confident, all-conquering hero lurks an insecure and frightened personality, which then has to assert itself and prove its worth over and over again to the world. Perhaps, there is also the voice of the potentially misunderstood WAI—'what if my authentic accomplishments are seen as just plunder and rapacious pursuits?'

The Overdone and the Inhibited WAI

The WAI when overdone brings up 'counter-dependence', which is defined as the denial of personal need and dependency and may extend to a feeling of omnipotence and refusal of dialogue. This counter-dependence has a voice that sounds like 'I'll go it all alone' or 'I am all powerful' or 'I don't need no dialogue, damn you!' and such. Along with counter-dependence comes high emotional reactivity—quick to respond, often without thinking or reflection. Mercenary tendencies can also begin to make their presence felt—where human loss in the wake of goal pursuit is seen as 'collateral damage'. Adolf Hitler was known to be so focused on the dream of dominating the world with a pure Aryan race that the systemic extermination of Jews was to him an eminently justifiable means to his end.

Here is a physical fact—if you try focusing on a spot or a point on a canvas, very soon, all you will see is that spot or point, all magnified. With WAI overdone, a similar event happens in the psychological domain—this world focuses so relentlessly on a goal (or set of goals) that the context vanishes into irrelevance or is diminished to another collateral.

We are thus speaking of a tonality of being 'unreal', of being intoxicated by one's own power. To have an idea of this, look no further than to the screen villains of any James Bond movie. The essential psychodynamic operating here would seem to be a state of 'action sans reflection'.

Another feature of overdone WAI is the phenomenon of 'burnout'. This is not just stress, it is much worse. Obsessive over-engagement, overreactive emotions, hyperactivity and high anxiety—if any of these seem familiar to you, it may be worth checking yourself (or your work team) for overdone WAI. Finally on this theme, permit us to add something at this stage to the 'insecure and frightened being' that we had introduced earlier—we also believe that at the core of the overdone WAI is a lonely narcissist who has the need for total control of his or her environment, which may include the victimization of others (paradoxically increasing loneliness).

Let us now look at what happens to a being or a system where WAI is underplayed. The first phenomenon we are likely to observe is that of drift. Have you seen a piece of wood on a flowing river? Aimless, stanceless, at the mercy of the waves, sometimes pushed hither and sometimes thither—we hope you get the drift, our warped sense of humour notwithstanding. The drift occurs perhaps because there is no or low conviction in any meaningful pursuit. There is no 'true north', and maybe there is no compass. 'Anything goes' is a phrase that could be applied to such passive WAI. Second, and a different effect of muted WAI, is stagnation in the capability and overall competence of the system. This may also manifest as a reluctance to truly and fully compete and thus an eventual withering away. How can we forget the great Motorola, which in the 1980s and 1990s was a technology giant ahead of its time. However, most of its might got ossified into a limited WSO frame and the company failed to grow its overall core capability even while an agile and high WAI competition blunted its technology edge and blew it out of its pre-eminent perch.

Some Important Dynamics Relating to WAI

For WAI, the wheels need to keep moving and never stop. Progress is the watchword, and things stopping or slowing down can be unimaginable no-nos. A well-known petrochemicals and telecommunications industrialist in India is known to tell his management team to get things done in seemingly impossible timelines. No stopping, no slowing. After all, it is the truly unreasonable people who achieve unreasonably high goals.

The other thing to remember is that this is the world of 'autonomy'—it values its own autonomy, understands the need for autonomy of others and as a corollary dislikes being tied down to the dependency needs of others. So, as long as people function like nodes in a network or as free market agents, it is fine. If people behave like children, or as victims or are 'emotionally needy', WAI is likely to feel pushed back and thus retaliate or ignore these needs completely. This world is also threatened by incompetence or incapability. For it to continue to exist and grow, merit must exist. Mediocrity cannot and will not be tolerated. Mediocrity is likely to be seen as threatening to the very fabric of WAI as is dependency.

The WAI believes that opportunities need to exist or they need to be created. Restrictive practices and denial of opportunities can really provoke this world—either towards working hard to create windows of opportunities or simply exit that arena to go to another place where autonomy and initiative are valued.

An Illustrative Caselet/Vignette

We all know Benjamin Franklin as one of the founding fathers of the United States of America, the man who signed the US Declaration of Independence and the Constitution. Among other things, he was also a renowned polymath, a political theorist, an ingenious scientist and a remarkably witty author.

But the story of his remarkable rise to achieving what he did is absolutely awe inspiring.

Ben was the fifteenth of seventeen children born to a soap and candle maker in 1706. Forced to quit his studies at the age of 10, Ben worked as an apprentice, first under his father and then under his brother James, who ran a print shop. He was entirely self-taught and finally to escape from the punishments meted out by his cruel brother, he ran away to Philadelphia.

That poor, 17-year-old boy walked the pavements and was thankfully able to find work, using his skills as a printer's assistant and his many outstanding traits and talents to make his way in the world. He borrowed money and set up his own printing business. As a businessman, he was hardworking and tireless and soon was running a thriving business. At 21, he founded Junto, a group of 'like-minded group of artisans and tradesman who wanted to improve their life' which spawned many an organization in Philadelphia. A few years later, Franklin conceived the idea of a subscription library, which pooled the funds of the members to buy books for all to read. This was the birth of the Library Company of Philadelphia, which is now a great scholarly and research library.

At the ripe age of 23, he bought a small newspaper, the Pennsylvania Gazette, and turned it into one of the most successful papers.

The list of Franklin's ideas and accomplishments goes on and on, and nothing can do justice to all that he accomplished during his lifetime—some of the greatest ones as a scientist include the lightning rod and the bifocal lenses. As a writer, he is credited with the first political cartoon in the world. He is known to have played three instruments and composed music.

By age 42, Franklin's inventive, industrious nature had brought him from rags to riches, enabling him to devote his next four decades to the revolutionary politics for which we know him best. His fight against the stamp act and subsequent contribution to authoring the Declaration of Independence are beyond compare.

A scientist, a revolutionary, politician, businessman, printer, writer, postmaster and diplomat—Ben was many things but most of all he was one who pursued his goals with single-minded purpose and conviction and courage. And more often than not, accomplished them too. One life—many lifetimes..!

The WAI Leader

The WAI leader seeks and respects laser focus on goals and on growing the system. They are usually strategic, direct, competitive, tough-minded, quantitative and focused. This leader is an analytical thinker, unlikely to change their mind once it is made up, usually highly energetic and may appear impatient. This is also the leader who may get put off by small talk, indirectness, indecisiveness and 'moralistic' statements.

The WAI leader considers systems to be means to an end at best and constraints to work around at worst. To them, systems must make them get to the goals faster and better. Else they are seen as impediments. 'When in doubt, act' would seem to be the motto of such a leader. The WAI leaders tend to be biased towards other people who will help them win, essentially competent, energetic and capable people. When it comes to influencing others, you can see the WAI leader penetratively asserting themselves, usually using strong logic in a cutting and direct fashion. They would drive change in a strong, focussed manner, often brooking no interference.

The table below illustrates some aspects of the WAI leader. You can do a quick check of these against your own style and assess your own WAI-ness. For a more detailed understanding, take the TAM-Self instrument.

People biases	Who can help me win (competence)
Derailers	Excesses/violence/service of self
Influence style	Assert
Response to change	Insist/push for change
Execution style	Drivers

6

The World of Connectedness and Nurturance

Speak not of peoples and laws and
Kingdoms, for the whole earth is
My birthplace and all humans are
My brothers.

—Kahlil Gibran, The Treasured Writings of Kahlil Gibran

What Is This World All About?

Cut to this powerful scene from the movie—Patch Adams. Patch faces charges of practising medicine without a licence and provides this impassioned plea—'Every human being has an impact on another. Why don't we want that in a patient/doctor relationship? That's why I've listened to your teachings, and I believe they're wrong. A doctor's mission should be not just to prevent death... but also to improve the quality of life. That's why you treat a disease, you win, you lose. You treat a person, I guarantee you, you win, no matter what the outcome'. Thus does Patch Adams introduce us to world of connectedness and nurturance (WCN).

The WCN centres around human beings and how they relate with others. This world is about communities, teams, groups and all forms of humans coming together. Key words that are characteristic of this world are relatedness, touch, intimacy, synergy, togetherness, care, healing and so on. The WCN is a like a garden where you come across the fertile soil of 'collective good'. Human beings and human units here are like individual plants and trees. Emphasis here is on living with synergy. Ecological sharing and concern for the 'whole garden' are easily evident here, nurtured by the commitment to relatedness.

The bounty of WCN is visible in what it offers. One distinguishing gift is what we may call 'compassionate inclusivity' and its twin 'meaningful inclusivity'. Let us sit back and contemplate these gifts for a minute. The act of including others can well happen in the other worlds that we have visited so far. In the world of structure and order (WSO), you would likely have such inclusivity driven by the outcome's requirement or by the defined needs of the role or system. In WAI, inclusivity is likely to happen especially if it will drive the achievement of goals or the accomplishment of tasks. WCN's inclusivity has the colour of 'include so the other is not left out' (compassionate inclusivity, accommodativeness as an example) and 'include because the other may have something meaningful to add' (meaningful inclusivity, consensus seeking or polling views or brainstorming as examples). Other than the gift of inclusivity, WCN also brings sharp focus to collaboration (team work, as an example). The emphasis is on deep human collaboration and not role-based cooperation or system-level coordination or choice-less co-option. True collaboration values confrontation and conflict as much as it does helping and burden sharing.

We have talked of other-centredness earlier here or experiencing the world from the perspective of the other. This gift comes in the form of empathy, compassion and a spirit of giving, even sacrificing for the well-being of the other(s) and of the system—in other words, self in service of system. In this respect, it would seem to be like WSO, with the distinction being that the phenomenon of self-in-service-of-system may operate 'for the operational well-being of the system' in WSO; here, it operates 'for the emotional well-being of the people in the system'. Besides these, WCN also brings with it the abundance of generosity of spirit, kindness and gentleness.

When it comes to what this world perhaps fears, there are many lurking around. Among the biggest fears held in this world is the fear of isolation. The WCN is so centred on other people that all it takes to trigger its existential fear is to do 'something' to the 'other people' in the equation—remove them perhaps, or diminish them somehow or even threaten to do either—pull the plug to disconnect and erase so there is nothing to nurture. It would be intolerable for anyone who inhabits this world to end up alone. This is such a potent feeling that many a successful film has been made that centres on this rather dark possibility. If you have seen *I am Legend*, you see the utterly alone-on-earth Robert Neville; in *Castaway*, you emote along with Chuck Noland; in *Gravity*, you yearn for Dr Ryan Stone's safe return to planet earth (another metaphor for WCN).

And while being marooned or cast away might often happen by chance, there is the darker possibility still, of finding oneself alone due to intended human action—we are talking here of being exiled, ostracized, trolled or alienated. In the ancient Greek world, exile or banishment was seen as a fate worse than death, and this theme has often been portrayed with touching emotive content in Greek theatre. The social psychologist Kipling Williams (along with co-authors Forgas and von Hippel) has written extensively on ostracism as a modern phenomenon. He defines ostracism as 'any act or acts of ignoring and excluding of an individual or groups by an individual or a group'.[1] Williams suggests that the most common form of ostracism in a modern context is refusing to communicate with a person. By refusing to

---

[1]Williams et al., *The Social Outcast*.

communicate with a person, that person is effectively ignored and excluded. Nowhere is this more evident today than in social media (cyberostracism). Ignored emails, not 'liking' someone's FB post or simply not picking up someone's calls are common methods of creating nightmares for a WCN-high person.

In a similar vein, trolling is another online phenomenon that publicly 'puts down' another—and this act is like dropping a missile on WCN. Alienation is perhaps a summary phrase— exiling, ostracizing and trolling can all lead to a sense of being alienated, a sense that one does not quite belong—and what could be more antithetical to WCN than *that*?

Then, we come to the other face that haunts WCN—while exile, ostracism, banishment and so on tend to reduce or cut engagement, this other face does quite the opposite—overengage. We are talking here of the nemesis of WCN in the form of war, violence, burning of bridges and nasty confrontation. Extreme aggression and destruction, using force, intentional use of coercive power and leading to injury, death and deprivation—who can argue that these are anti-WCN? As against 'connectedness', we come across defiant agenticity that leads to this.

And lastly, we come across two more significant fears of WCN—one, the fear of loneliness—that I may be in company yet feel no connection—and, the fear of having to let go of the objects of WCN's affection/attention—a clear example being the well-known 'empty nest syndrome'.

The Overdone and the Inhibited WCN

'Smothering' and 'entanglement' are two words that spontaneously come up when we consider what the overdone WCN might be like. You may even put the two words together and say 'smothering entanglement'. The difference between 'mother', a true-blooded WCN identity, and 'smother' would seem to be a matter of extent and intensity. When one is smothered in the tight embrace of overdone WCN, one literally gets asphyxiated. A milder form of this is in creating and fostering excessive dependencies. It can either happen *to* WCN—as, for instance, when one allows oneself to be thoroughly engulfed, enshrouded, absorbed into the other or can be done *by* WCN—when one 'takes over the other's autonomy' however benevolently. An extension of entanglement can be seen in the hapless WCN person who feels stuck in relationships and cannot or will not extricate themselves. The relatedness may have dried out but our WCN-er ploughs on with the relationship. Abuses, arguments, threats and apologies—all these and more notwithstanding, a certain stoicism characterizes our overdone WCN-er.

A different form of overdone WCN can be seen when all communication is laced with highly emotive content, with the spotlight often falling on cloying sweetness and/or deceptively enticing melancholy. Such cloying sweetness often disguises insidious judgements, often about the 'kind of person' or 'character' of the other to who the sweetness is directed. Passive aggressiveness (arising from disowned anger or resentment) is a close cousin of this phenomenon. At a system level, in overdone WCN, the politics and toxicities are glossed over as they may threaten the so-called harmony of the system.

A third and different feature of extreme WCN can come up in what we might call 'victim games'. High WCN is prone to naivete in the name of trust. That segues them right into playing the victim card. If the sacrifice by the victim is further deepened, we also get to see the martyrdom card being played—which is sacrifice to the point of self-destruction. Sometimes the victim WCN can also paradoxically end up becoming the oppressor—when the victim location is hung on to by the WCN-er, they end up oppressing the others for whom they had ostensibly sacrificed. Have you heard the line 'But I am doing all of this for YOU only, how could you do this to me!!'—if you have, that is an example of what we are saying here.

Classic vignettes of overplayed WCN can be seen in the form of the 'sacrificing mother', often seen in Bollywood films of the yore. (The image of the actor Nirupa Roy became a known emblem for this!) So also, we can recall the story of *Devdas*, the quintessential story of many emotion-filled whirlpools, where the lines between 'emotional' and 'maudlin' are blurred irretrievably.

Have you heard the phrase 'being out of touch with reality'? If we twist the phrase around, we discover that extreme WCN tends to be 'out of reality with touch'. And we will leave it to you to figure that one out!

When WCN is relatively underoccupied in a person or a system, we should be ready to see some hesitancy, reluctance and guardedness in valuing the other or in trusting others—self-interest may govern and initiatives to build intimacy may be low. Differentiation, diversity and ecology may be seen as overheads. What comes to mind here is how several WAI-driven companies take up some token attempts to conduct 'diversity initiatives' or 'CSR projects' as the cost of doing business—'get it done and publicize it so we might get on' would seem to be the underlying voice. Another face of low WCN is the 'messy world' syndrome. Feelings and emotions are 'too hot to handle' and so get relegated to the shadows and wounds fester. A further extreme of this would be in the form of disdain or contempt for subjectivity. One of our friends, an expatriate CEO, often quips 'Handle your own issues, don't ask me for tissues'—indicating that he decidedly found deep WCN quite threatening as he was beyond his swim depth!

A third face of low WCN would probably be 'pseudo-collaboration'. In the name of collaboration, mere coordination ensues or, at best, cooperation happens, which is still a relatively objective arrangement when contrasted with authentic collaboration where one wades deep into subjectivity and does not run away from conflicts, hurts, healing and the like. And if the idea of collaboration is not worth entertaining at all, another extreme of this 'dark side of the moon', you can expect to see solo-ism, silo-ism and lone star heroism—where the accent and spotlight is on 'the one' and not 'the many' or 'the us'.

Some Important Dynamics
Relating to WCN

Have you tried to visualize a strifeless world? All connected to all in a cocoon of mutuality and collective interest?

Imagine no possessions
I wonder if you can
No need for greed or hunger
A brotherhood of man
Imagine all the people sharing all the world, you

You may say I'm a dreamer
But I'm not the only one
I hope some day you'll join us
And the world will be as one
(John Lennon, Imagine)

Well, WCN nurtures a somewhat romanticized view of such existence. At heart, WCN is about romanticized idealism—a naive, miscalculated dream of a perfect world without factoring in the flaws that reality would bring. Thus, for instance, when WCN comes to face the *homo economicus*—the utility-seeking consumer and the profit-seeking producer, both of which would pursue their individualistic ends 'come what may'—WCN's worldview gets threatened. WCN gets entrenched in shame of acting for the Self, as if this action would somehow damage the well-being of the collective. Alongside, this world also gets put off by those who do not seem to value collaboration. Thus stuck in romanticized idealism and threatened by alternate realities, WCN often gets frozen and sheds silent tears.

Further, if we look at the pattern of dependencies that characterize WCN, on the one hand, a person in WCN would feel validated by another's emotional dependency on them, and yet such dependency also keeps them stuck. A paradoxical situation gets created and continues, for maybe another stuck belief of WCN may be that the other does not have the capability and/or need to grow beyond the dependency.

And finally, WCN's anger (even if not directly expressed) often rooted in disappointment and unrealized angst lies in the coldness to human touch as displayed by others. Lack of reciprocity, disinterest in its overtures and maybe betrayal of trust, treating of human beings as 'collateral', are all triggers to the threat of WCN's vision for life and living.

An Illustration/Vignette

Love gives naught but itself and takes naught but from itself.
Love possesses not nor would it be possessed;
For love is sufficient unto love.
And think not you can direct the course of love, for love, if it finds you worthy, directs your course.

Love has no other desire but to fulfill itself.
To melt and be like a running brook that sings its melody to the night.
To know the pain of too much tenderness.
To be wounded by your own understanding of love;
And to bleed willingly and joyfully.
To wake at dawn with a winged heart and give thanks for another day of loving;
To rest at the noon hour and meditate love's ecstasy;
To return home at eventide with gratitude;
And then to sleep with a prayer and a song of praise upon your lips.

—Excerpts from Khalil Gibran on Love, *The Prophet*

The WCN Leader

A leader belonging to this world focuses on the human and the community side of the system, looks at the feelings that are generated in the system and considers how they can enable well-being and foster positive/enabling relatedness. The leader here values personal connections and sees how people fit together. The leader here is relationship oriented, empathetic, consensus building, helpful and trusting. This type of leader understands through stories, narrates stories and reads the atmosphere as well as the facts. Aloofness, aggressiveness, bragging and competition may put off this leader.

The WCN leader may create a WCN-centric organization. Sensitivity training (or its variants) would take place in considerable measure, the HR function would be seen as the holder of the human ethos of the organization and in an extreme, the organization itself may appear as a club with no apparent purpose than people being together.

'Systems are meant to facilitate us', thus spoke a WCN leader in a town hall meeting of an organization, where employees were sharing their disinterest in systems, procedures and so on, which they felt were thwarting their attempts to 'get on with real work'. The word 'facilitate' here is an interesting coinage. While WSO might stress on the need to *follow* systems, while WAI leaders may view systems as *things which will help us reach the goal faster*, it is interesting to hear WCN using a humanistic term—'facilitate', for stressing the value of systems. In their all-too-ready collusion, rarely do such leaders see that systems can also be instruments of oppression and dominance!

The WCN leaders often adopt the adage, 'when in doubt, relate'—so if they find themselves beset by a persistent issue or a conflict, what do they do? They walk up to another person, seek some airtime with them and share, unburden, seek advice and guidance—all of which they would sincerely try and implement. Typical phrases that you might hear in the presence of WCN leaders would be 'I care about you'; 'Tell me what you feel'; 'Lets do something together'; 'Let me lend a hand' and so on. Their biases may be towards people that, like them, connect with others and reach out. When it comes to influencing others, WCN-ers play an accommodating or bridging approach. You may hear them say 'Here is what I like about your proposal … and now, if I consider the other side to this, here is something else that may interest you to consider …'. Their execution style is likely to resemble how things might happen in a guild or artisan community. Things would get done in a fraternal and associative way, perhaps like a collegium, an egalitarian community and with high focus on voluntarism.

Please refer to the summary table below for a quick view of some of the likely aspects of the WCN leader.

People biases	Who I relate with; who I like
Derailers	Excessive idealism/sentimentalism/ hyper-sensitivity
Influence style	Avoid/accommodate/bridge
Response to change	Assist/support change
Execution style	Artisans/trade community

7

The World of Flow and Unfolding

Unfinished Poem …
I would love to live like a river flows, carried by the surprise of its
own unfolding.

—John O'Donohue

What Is This World All About?

Depending on whether your preference is for terra firma or terra-aqua, entering the world of flow and unfolding (WFU) can be like entering a forest or jumping into a free and rapidly flowing river. Let us take the forest metaphor—no apparent organization, spellbinding diversity of flora and fauna, vibrant and verdant. At the same time, it is dark and dense—a twist here and a turn there and you can get rather hopelessly lost. Jump into the river now and what do we see—free flow, rapids here and a cascade there, beguilingly deceptive placidity at times with strange and unpredictable currents—home to many never-seen-before marine creatures, and equally, a space of depths that can drown us.

The WFU is the world of curiosity, creation, expression and disruptiveness and the transformation that comes as an outcome of these forces. Think of children exploring the space all around them with wonder. Think of a jazz musician engaged deeply in improvising. Think of the mystic who can access spaces seemingly outside of usual consciousness. We should now be getting a glimpse of this kaleidoscopic world. 'Radical' can be another word that we can use to describe this world. This brings up the idea of being on the edge and extreme and questioning or challenging accepted or traditional norms.

In chemistry, a radical (more precisely, a free radical) is an atom, molecule or ion that has at least one unpaired valence electron. With some exceptions, these unpaired electrons make free radicals highly chemically reactive, unstable and capable of spontaneous and often abnormal actions and reactions. Most such radicals are reasonably stable only at very low concentrations in inert media or in a vacuum. Springing from a radical self-concept and world view, the WFU-er has a deeply personalized and subjective idea of bliss and will follow it, come what may.

To get an idea of such 'bliss following', do look up the intriguing image of The Fool, as it appears in many standard Tarot card decks. In these decks, The Fool is seen walking towards the edge of a cliff, seemingly lost in himself and to the world (following his bliss!). There is no saying what might happen if and when The Fool crosses the precipice, but for The Fool, there is no caring either—and this is no 'foolishness' but 'foolness' (rhymes with 'coolness', do you think?) and who knows—beyond the precipice, there might be death (and maybe the possibility of a new life), or a magical entry to another realm or he might simply sprout wings. Who knows if we don't try! So, WFU's mantra might well be 'Well, we don't know, but let's give it a shot' (think Silicon Valley here, try and fail fast!). The greatest attraction that WFU holds is that of opportunities to experiment and explore, to create new things and all this with an ability to embrace uncertainty and ambiguity.

The pull to explore the 'never before' outweighs the fear of the unknown—at times with great outcomes and at times with loss. But for the WFU, the process matters more than outcomes. If you have watched the 2012 film *The Flight*, you would be familiar with William 'Whip' Whitaker Sr, an airline pilot who miraculously crash-lands his plane after it suffers an in-flight mechanical failure, saving nearly everyone on board. The manoeuvres that he adopts in an emergency would make a WSO-er gag but are quite the things to do for WFU (and we are not talking yet of Whitaker's lifestyle which incidentally brings up some of the dark sides of WFU, and that is for later in this narrative).

The key questions for WFU would seem to be 'what if' and 'why not'. And these questions capture the same spirit that we see in hackers, gamers and at another end in witchcraft and shamanism. You will remember that in the world of connectedness and nurturance (WCN), we had talked about *romanticized idealism*. In WFU, we come across romanticism, and often we find *idealized romanticism* somehow as if inspiration, subjectivity and primacy of the individual are all that need to matter. Quite simply, the pull to WFU is in that it offers a certain quality of dynamism that is quite feminine—an expression-oriented yet curiously nurturing spirit of aliveness, arousal and vibrant restlessness. You will recall that the same pulls exist in the world of autonomy and initiative (WAI) but with a distinctly masculine hue of 'assertive and penetrative'.

The WFU bears the gift of expression and the ability to play. It ushers in the ability to be creative and innovative—in particular, the ability to both create and experience sensory joys. Very often, the output of WFU is in the form of artefacts that provoke, offer enjoyment and 'transport' us to other realms—such as through music and dance, paintings, sculpture, good food, cinema and poetry—the list can go on. The play offered up by WFU would be liberally endowed with spontaneity and often, such play would be at the edge of creation and/or disruption. If you have watched improvisation theatre, as an example, the famous TV show *Whose Line Is It Anyway*, you will have an idea of this. And is there a deeper sense of conviction behind all the play and spontaneity that WFU gives us? The jury will be out on this one, but the probability is high, we aver, that such is the case (except when we encounter overdone WFU, which you will read later in this chapter). The WFU also gives us the gift of what we call 'psycho-olfactoriness'—the ability to sense and smell the underlying human dynamics in any situation—a gift valued by many facilitators, process workers and coaches. This gift is all the more embellished when we get to understand that WFU is a world that readily embraces the postmodern view and the hyperflex frames of our emergent world—the world of alt facts, post-truth and such.

If we look within WFU, at the 'dark side of the moon', as it were, what fears are we likely to see? Having to conform, for one. Some parts of the legend surrounding Krishna, the Hindu God, have it that as a child he was so playful and mischievous that his mother had to literally tie him down to a stone block to ensure some conformity and submission out of him (and yet she did not succeed as we are told). WFU-ers hate any pressure to conform, and equally, they fear stuckness, stagnation and dried-up flow. What if dreams come to nought, is the worry. Stephen King has written eloquently about the phenomenon of writers' block and we have heard of artistes staring desolately at blank canvases, the flow having ebbed, like a dry river bed that we get to see on road trips in the countryside. Alongside and somewhat paradoxically, WFU also fears the opposite—what if we are not able to contain ourselves and we flood rather than flow, overwhelm rather than unfold and inundate rather than irrigate.

The Overdone and the Inhibited WFU

Too much of WFU, and we get a sense of what it might feel like to be addicted to an intoxicant—a sense of permanently being in a haze, and an overpowering feeling of 'I can't live without this' invades and then pervades the person, the system. With this comes a lack of focus and a sense of fragmentation. For the WFU-er, there are so MANY things to go after and try out that staying true to one seems inadequate, a killjoy. When they indulge in such vapid restlessness and faddishness, they end up becoming both fragmented AND they experience a sense of dissipation. At the height of its good days, Motorola was into paging devices, cell phones, two-way radios, network infrastructure, telecom services, semiconductors and satellite phones, to name a few. Although a broad thread of 'communications technology and products' held a core, the company went after so many things that it failed to consolidate and then it fell apart. This is perhaps the 'self-destructive' and 'implosive' tendency of overdone WFU.

Another way of seeing this phenomenon is in the phrase 'what-could-be rules over what-is'. There is always another dream to follow, another castle to build and another journey to travel on. Pragmatics go for a toss. Thoughtless bets are placed, and risks are either downplayed or covered up. Look to the phenomenon of drunken driving. Overdone WFU hovers over the impulsive end. Close to it is another phenomenon—licentiousness—the going beyond customary or known bounds or limits, disregarding rules and indulging in lawlessness. In the utter self-absorption of the extreme WFU, there is a harmful lack of contextual awareness and a tendency to annihilate—both self and context.

The grim eventual outcomes of overdone WFU have been tellingly captured in the 2005 Hindi film *Shabd*, where a writer in the depressive grip of writer's block encourages his wife to pursue a secret relationship so that he can use the unfolding of that narrative to rediscover his writing mojo. The normlessness and caprice that this idea is built on and the dark ending give us a portrayal of WFU 'all the way down', both literally and figuratively. And, normlessness also reminds us of the word 'anomie'. In a society that is anomic, it is frustrating, confusing and even disturbing, to move through everyday life, especially if we are paying attention to what is going on. If we try to unplug, we may distract ourselves for a time but the state of the anomic society comes into play in every area of life. Thus, going off the grid or ignoring what is happening will not result in comfort or relief for long.

Diminished WFU is likely to be observed in safety-seeking behaviour. 'Play it safe', 'Don't talk to strangers' and 'I don't want to say I-told-you-so' are likely statements from here. We may also get to see sepia/monochrome experiences of life and living here rather than vibrant colours. The panorama is not seen, there is relative lack of vividness and flatlands are traversed instead. In the extreme, this can also manifest as boredom, a sense of staleness/stagnation and a general listlessness or lethargy. A relative state of stasis would be seen to prevail (and not a dynamic balance). Many human experiences of loss—death, departures, parting ways in a relationship, empty nest syndrome, loss of a job and so on are some common examples where people report a sense of vitality being drained out from them, sucked out and being placed in a vacuum existence. Fluidity of day-to-day living slows down, unfolding is arrested and the experience of WFU is hindered thus.

Some Important Dynamics
Relating to WFU

Ponder for a moment about the words 'flow' and 'unfolding'. The raison d'etre of WFU is to flow eternally and the operant verb that enables such flow is the process of constant unfolding. Thus, it should come as no surprise that any hindrance to the flow can be a hindrance to the very primary purpose of this world. When overriding forces of conformance come in the way or when WFU-ers are chained to rules, they feel immobilized and stuck, often in helpless resentment.

The other thing to bear in mind here is that given the inherent kaleidoscopic nature of this world, it is accustomed to seeing and beholding a dazzling array of colours, choices, patterns, the abstract, the imaginative, the conceptual and the original. Therefore, anything that the WFU mind interprets as mundane, monochrome, flat, practical and conventional puts it off. Now this may come from an internalized judgementality as well, a feature not unusual for WFU. By extension, WFU is also likely to feel put off by people who do not seem to ask provocative/inquisitive/disruptive questions like 'Why', 'Why not', 'How about', 'How else' and so on.

Excerpts from a Dialogue with the World of Flow and Unfolding

The following is an imaginary conversation between a visitor and the world of Flow and Unfolding. The quotes belong to real people (and are referenced in the notes) and have been arranged in a way to depict how the members experience this world.

V: *Hey, you all seem to be deeply immersed in the work you are doing…*

WFU: *Yes…Being completely involved in an activity for its own sake. The ego falls away. Time flies. Every action, movement, and thought follows inevitably from the previous one, like playing jazz. Your whole being is involved, and you're using your skills to the utmost.*

V: *That sounds interesting. Can you describe to me how that feels…?*

WFU: *There's a hum that happens inside my head when I hit a certain writing rhythm, a certain speed. When laying track goes from feeling like climbing a mountain on my hands and knees to feeling like flying effortlessly through the air. Like breaking the sound barrier. everything inside me just shifts. I break the writing barrier. And the feeling of laying track changes, transforms, shifts from exertion into exultation.*

V: *Seems like you inhabit the present moment, the here and now…*

WFU: *The past and the future*
meet in the eternal now.
I am the eternal now.
I exist.
I am.
I am in the past.
I am in the future.
I am in the now.

V: *Wow, that is deep indeed. But what beliefs do you hold about people and beings?*

WFU: *That we are free spirits. A free spirit is not bound by this, that, matter, materialism or opinion. They sing, dance and flow on the wind—for they are at one with it. They are nothing and everything—void and expanse. Even space and time does not confine or define them.*

V: *How are you able to live like that?*

WFU: *It's a bit like swimming. And you know what swimming is—it's kind of a relaxed attitude with the water. In which you don't keep yourself afloat by holding the water, but by a certain giving to it.*

V: *What then do you aspire for?*

WFU: *I've learned, the hard way, that some poems don't rhyme, and some stories don't have a clear beginning, middle, and end. Life is about not knowing, having to change, taking the moment and making the best of it, without knowing what's going to happen next. Delicious Ambiguity.*

(The WFU statements are all quotes from different authors/ writers and poets listed as follows: Mihaly Csikszentmihalyi, Shonda Rhimes, Raphael Zernoff, Alan W. Watts, Rasheed Ogunlaru, Gilda Radner.)

The WFU Leader

In this aspect of leadership comes the pioneering side—where the leader is looking for variety, possibilities and generating new ideas. This is also that part of leadership wherein we get to see the spontaneous, energetic, novelty seeking, networked and imaginative leader. This leader is receptive to new approaches, open to changing their mind, comfortable using intuition and have a high tolerance (even respect!) for risk. This is also the leader who may get put off by structure, moderation, process, details, repetition, limits and moralizing. The WFU leaders in systems are likely to creatively express themselves, often questioning shibboleths and offering creatively disruptive propositions. One is reminded aptly here of the Hollywood film *The Martian* where astrodynamicist Rich Purnell devises a trajectory to divert the spaceship *Hermes* back to Mars for a daring rescue of a stranded astronaut. NASA rejects his plan, refusing to risk the crew, but another WFU member, Henderson, surreptitiously sends the details to *Hermes*. The crew, knowing that going against orders will likely end their careers as astronauts, unanimously vote for the plan, and NASA—powerless to stop them—resupplies *Hermes* as it uses the Earth's gravity to slingshot back to Mars.

The WFU leaders would tend to adopt a minimalistic approach towards systems. Perhaps they feel that systems bring up the spectre of control which they distance themselves from. Thus, WFU leaders would create 'sandbox' systems where experimentation can freely happen and a ground for flow can be created and tested before production. Being stuck in doubt is not easily welcomed or tolerated by the WFU leader. So, what do they do when in doubt? For one, doubt is a great opportunity for them to create something else. Maybe a good time to question and/or change the existing order. Some others use doubt as a vast playground to play. And while they are about change and play, they are also happy meeting doubt in its own backyard. Why defend a bridge when you can burn it seems to be an often used stance. The WFU leaders tend to be pulled towards and biased in favour of people who provoke/trigger flow, expanding people's and the system's perspectives. The WFU leaders influence in an inspirational way, often through thought-leadership.

They would drive change in a pioneering fashion—dream up the change, inspire the system to make the change happen and then actually make it happen. Typical phrases that you might encounter in a WFU system? 'When all else fails, go back to the drawing board', 'Lets wing it', 'Lets play with that idea' and 'Lets toss that around'.

The table below illustrates some aspects of the WFU leader for your quick reference and to assess your own WFU-ness. For a more detailed understanding, take the TAM-Self instrument.

People biases	One who triggers my flow/lets me unfold; One who provokes; expanders of perspective
Derailers	Excessive fluidity
Influence style	Inspire, thought leadership, appeal to the mind
Response to change	Create, provoke, disrupt
Execution style	Experimenting with new processes, methodologies and tools

8

The Sixteen Symbolic Identities

Worlds are made alive by those that inhabit them. This is true of the physical world we live in, equally so of the psychological worlds that are part of us—either as individual human beings or as groups and communities.

The architecture of the four worlds in the Transformative Alignment Map (TAM) is made up of sixteen specific 'symbolic identities' that have been carefully chosen to represent qualities of:

1. Masculine/feminine
2. Preference for movement and change/preference for stability

All these symbolic identities exist within all of us. We identify with some of these to a relatively greater extent and to some others to a relatively lesser extent.

These identities are neutral, in the sense that they are neither good nor bad and neither desirable nor undesirable. Each of these identities is an energy pattern that exists in human consciousness—which closely parallels the Jungian view of the 'archetype'. For every individual and system, these energy patterns come together to form a unique constellation. The mapping of this is at the heart of the TAM process, which is a suite of assessment instruments designed to illuminate the four alignment spaces described earlier, but more of that in Chapter 26.

Thus, this set of chapters, from Chapters 9 through 24, describe the symbolic identities of TAM in detail. They have been presented here in an alphabetical order, but we invite you to have some fun in reading through an identity and then guessing which TAM world it might belong to!

As you approach these chapters on the identities, you will first be accosted with the question 'Who is "this identity"'. Our response is offered, and we provide you relevant examples from real life. The typical behaviours and actions as well as the likely impact that identity is likely to have on our lives are then explained. We have also tried to share our thoughts on how the respective identities might deal with challenges that come their way.

The inner world of the identity is then explored in depth, looking at the desires, hopes, gifts and vulnerabilities that underlie each. The identity is also sought to be understood in its 'extremes'—for example, what might ensue if an identity is overdone or muted/inhibited. And finally, we have tried to share some thoughts on what leadership behaviours we might see coming from an identity, particularly on aspects of a system such as execution/delivery, people, relationships, strategy and growth, and change and innovation.

Enjoy!

9

The Administrator

So be sure when you step, step with care and great tact. And remember that life's A Great Balancing Act. And will you succeed? Yes! You will, indeed! (98 and ¾ percent guaranteed) Kid, you'll move mountains.

—Dr Seuss, Oh, The Places You'll Go!

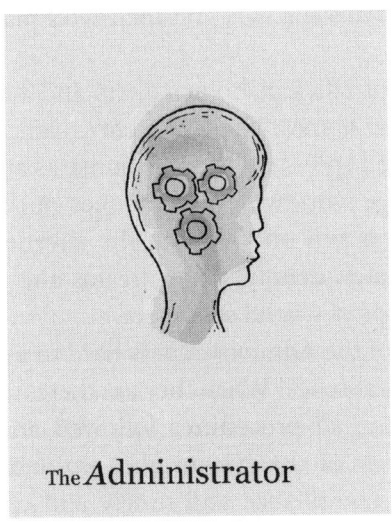

The Administrator

Who Is the Administrator?

Refer to any thesaurus and the words that are associated with the Administrator would be 'functionary', 'organizer', 'executive', 'doer' and so on. The Administrator is one who takes responsibility for the proper running of things in a system, and his or her focus is invariably on efficiency and productivity. They keep things functioning consistently through the cycle of an activity. Operational execution is their mantra, and they are particularly invaluable in throughputs that have multiple variables, aspects and threads. It is no wonder then that they can be quite easily visualized as expert jugglers, juggling many balls in the air at a time with apparently no sign of distraction or fatigue, multitaskers, if you will. They are the people who oil the machines, and maybe they are the oil itself that keeps the machine running!

Walk into the office of a good executive assistant to a CEO and you will get an idea of this identity. They would know the schedules of the CEO at the back of their hand, arrange meetings and minute them. They are great (and that is an understatement) at meticulously following up on deliverables, getting key presentations ready and tooth-combing them for boo-boos. They dot the 'i's and cross the 't's and all in a palpable sense of quiet efficiency. They handle a LOT, yet their workplace is likely to be enviably tidy.

Think also of efficient homemakers and how they manage and maintain their homes. Think of event organizers, of secretaries of associations and sports clubs, of accountants and of programme managers in large worldwide programmes in the IT industry—the list can go on and on. Without the aliveness and vibrancy of the Administrator identity, many dreams might remain dreams or lapse into wisps of wistful sentiment.

The impact of the Administrator is hard to miss—either in its presence or in its absence! When they are there, things get done—quickly, correctly, all procedures followed and without loose ends. Productivity of the system goes up and efficiency rises through proper compliance and timely and complete closure.

They do not let things fall through the cracks. Have you heard of the domino effect—a chain reaction and a cumulative effect that is produced when one event sets off a chain of similar events, like dominoes falling? In the watch of the Administrator, this phenomenon is rather unlikely to occur. All this helps build a dependable reputation for the whole system that they have their footprint on.

The typical behaviours of Administrators are also hard to miss. Because they are so aware of operational things that could go wrong and the effect those may have, they quickly create checks and balances, processes, systems, compliance and monitoring mechanisms. Says Puneet, an executive whose life revolves around meetings, calls, more meetings and more calls, 'I typically create a to-do list, and then I set an alarm to remind me of the to-do list'. They would create standard operating procedures (SOPs) and then comply with them, pushing others also to do so. Some mantras they may chant are standardize, commoditize, get things done, keep accounts, maintain reports, be correct and be sensible.

They are the reliable and dependable, invisible, behind-the-scenes people—women who keep homes and families running, theatre directors, any role that has a finance/security risk, project and programme management, many supervisory roles that depend on maintenance and infrastructure, military/defence, airlines, car manufacturers, law/juridical sciences, surgery and scientists.

They may appear serious (which does not mean that they do not have a sense of humour), as the 'no-nonsense' person, or as the go-to person and as solvers/fixers. When it comes to dealing with challenges and problems, you will find Administrators addressing them dutifully, sequentially and in a carefully considered and deliberative way. They would check and recheck multiple times before execution, especially because they hate errors and bugs. Sometimes it may even appear as though they feel that they have to make up for the carelessness of others.

Lets take the case of the Dabbawalas of Mumbai. Since the late 19th century, dressed in their custom white outfit and traditional Gandhi Cap, an army of more than 5,000 Dabbawalas cater to the lunch needs of almost 200,000 Mumbaikars every single day, transporting home-cooked food from their customers' homes to their offices. Having started with a simple color-coding system, they have now moved to a more complex alphanumeric coding system that enables this process, which would put any complex six-sigma process in high-tech industries to shame. They work on four basic pillars—efficiency, time management, coordination and culture. This is the Administrator at its best, they pull this off with precision, under immense time pressures, in a highly populated city, come rain or shine, every single day.

What Is Their Inner World Like?

The Administrator brings with them the gift of practical action— the ability to get things moving and getting them done. They have the ability to set aside personal comfort and agenda for the 'larger good'. They would wish that the world values the exacting standards that they set for themselves and for others. Their overarching desire is for things to run smoothly, with no nasty surprises and no painful roadblocks either.

But then gifts and desires bring with them fears and sorrows as well, joined at the hip, if you will. In creating their brand of perfection, Administrators also create their personal hell—they come under the embrace of the superego that would like to dictate norms and mores for the others, and their lament is often that the world does not care enough for what they desire, namely a clockwork system. Not only does it not care, it also at times seems to pay taunting lip service to what they value. Sunitha, a homemaker, loves to maintain her kitchen 'just so'. Sana, her daughter who is more an Artiste than an Administrator, does not understand what the fuss is all about. What if the cover cloth on the induction stove is askew? What if the spoons don't go into the shelf meant for them? What if I leave the mixer switch on? Familiar? We suppose so!

And there is something else. Administrators are invisible, and someone else always is always the hero. They thus become the unsung heroes. In addition, their need for predictability and control creates a high level of anxiety, particularly when there are multiple dependencies and moving parts in the system.

We suspect that the Administrator somewhere lives in the fantasy of 'when everything is in order, I will find time and space to do this or do that'. Yet there is a corresponding unwillingness to let go, thereby often placing them in 'poor-me' locations or of having to be viewed as oppressive or uncool. We bet you have heard some conversations like the one below, even if the one below has been exaggerated some, for effect:

Uma: 'I wish I can leave all of this behind and take off on a nice long holiday. Seychelles, the Maldives, maybe even just Coorg!'

Rajan: 'Why don't you do that? I'll stay here and take care of everything'.

Uma: 'No way, you don't even know how to switch off the geyser in the bathrooms. I'll go next year'.

When the 'other' is dutiful and compliant, the Administrator finds a ready fit, a match that can work. Look at it this way—the Income Tax Department (the Administrator) wants you to pay your taxes. You, the citizens, do; you are then the complier, and all is well for the Administrator. It is when you stop being dutiful and compliant and turn 'rogue' that the Administrator's circuit gets all jiggered. Then the Administrator typically does what it does best—enforce all the more. Or turn you into the hands of another identity called the Custodian or the Ruler (you will get to read about the Custodian and the Ruler down the line in this book, but as an example here, it would be the legal system) to deal best with you.

Another likelihood—when the 'other' is a powerful ruler wanting someone to administer their writ, we find another form of resonance.

Take the story of the city of Surat, in Gujrat, India. Surat was the city that led to an exodus of frightened inhabitants due to the plague scare in 1994 and evoked hysterical media coverage the world over.

It was then an old filthy city along the river Tapti. But now it is known as one of the cleanest cities in India. The Surat Municipal Corporation (SMC) has one of the best water-treatment plants in the country, while its solid waste-disposal system is arguably the best in the country, meticulously conforming to the Supreme Court guidelines. The narration can go on, but this is a case of a great Administrator in the form of successive Commissioners of SMC who had the backing of a strong and willing government that helped them along, particularly in the post-plague-scare days.

Now what happens when the ruler is not as powerful and supportive? Or interfering? The Administrator then either hunkers down, waiting for a new ruler, or quits the system especially if they believe that things are not likely to change.

The Administrator in the Extremes

The overdone extreme of the administrator is a rather picky and fastidious character who moralizes about rules and procedures. We may see them as being perfectionists and they may also come across as dry and sarcastic. They may also be perceived as irritable and tense and may seem overburdened. A general lack of spontaneity might be the air around them—thick with no space for change or adaptability. In the eyes of others, they may appear uncompromising, stubborn, irrationally picky and in particular, someone missing the woods for the trees. Do they even feel deserving of comfort or fun or rewards, we might wonder about them.

At the underdone end, we find the one who is unable to multitask or even just keep things moving. Multiple threads might bother them and tie them up in knots, leading to things falling between the cracks in the system. This may then lead to an inefficient use of resources, time and experience and worse—with no apparent scope for corrective action.

Hopefully, the table here will now put things together to give us a quick snapshot of this identity.

Angst	Hope	Gifts	Fear/ Vulnerability
That the world does not value the order and predictability I provide	That the world learns to value what it means to be efficient and productive	Orchestration	Of losing control, things running amok

The Administrator as a Leader in Organizations

- Administrators as leaders would readily take responsibility for the proper running of existing things, focusing on efficiency and productivity.
- When it comes to meeting system objectives, they would be able to dispassionately view people as 'roles' and relationships as 'resources' for task completion. This way, they learn to keep a distance from humanistic thoughts, feelings and attitudes. This helps them in the short term in leading execution but may also end up making their leadership rather instrumental and dry.
- Administrator leaders are likely to be good at driving change projects, even if they do not step up to leading them.
- By focusing in an uncompromising way on driving efficient systems, they build good reputation for delivery and results in the systems they lead, thus contributing to growing and potentially scaling up such systems.
- *Sometimes, their style of leadership can create a sense of boredom, even ennui in the system.*

10

The Artiste

Art is freedom. Being able to bend things most people see as a straight line.

—Overlyxclusive

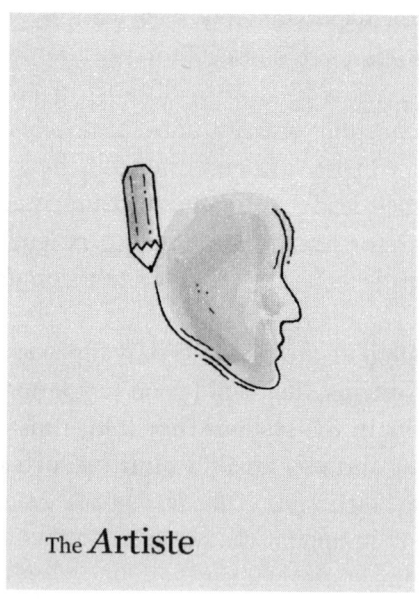

The *Artiste*

*Two years ago, at the Shastri Hall, Mylapore, Chennai, when I heard
TM Krishna sing an elaborate Pantuvarali alapana dripping sowkhya
bhava (the emotive state of repose), my mind became so calm that
I experienced Ananda (bliss), and I wept. Experiencing ananda at
Karnatik concerts happens to me so very rarely these days because an
overwhelming number of vocalists sing in such a way as to excite and
thrill the rasikas' (connoisseur) mind and be suitably rewarded with
loud applause. TM Krishna does quite the opposite: He calms their
mind. One experiences ananda only when the mind is very calm, and
never when the mind is excited. After the concert, I felt so blissfully
happy that I proclaimed, 'It is not possible to sing better than this'.
After that concert, I felt ananda again at three other TM Krishna
concerts, and I said each time, 'It is not possible to sing better than
this!' And here I am, after listening to this video, saying the same thing,
again, 'It is not humanly possible to sing better than this!' It seems like
at each successive concert, TM Krishna reveals a new and improved
version of himself. And, as a result of his refined singing, through
relentless devoted practice, he has transformed 'Aahatha' (external
sound) music that one hears at all the sabhas into 'Anaahatha'
(internal sound) music that our scriptures say only celestial beings
hear in heaven. What we hear in this video, I think, is not ordinary
Carnatic music—it is the extraordinary celestial music. As a Carnatic
vocalist myself, I do not know how he does it, but our ancient treatises
say that through dedicated sadhana, it is possible to accomplish that,
even though only a few have succeeded, I think, in the last hundred
years! TM Krishna is one of them. The way he sang Shree Dikshitar's
Sanskrit masterpiece, 'Soundara raajam upasmahe' (a Karnatik Music
composition), is certainly not from our Earth, but it came down from
the firmament. I think he is in a class by himself. Have you ever flown
in a plane, and looked out of the window when the plane reaches
35,000 feet high? There is just the plane, above the clouds, and nothing
else is around. That is TM Krishna. Alone. All by himself. And no one
else to compare him to …*

—Extract from a Karnatik Music aficionado's posting
on a music listeners' website

Who Is the Artiste?

The word artiste conjures up images of the moody painter in a
studio or a musician in the throes of rendering the composition

finale. Here, we invite you to meet the symbolic identity of the Artiste, a broader and more inclusive view of what constitutes their inner and outer worlds. An Artiste is who you might call the 'ideas person' or the 'creative type'. Operating from an inner world of emotion and evocation, they are forever ready to explore and express. This is an identity that resides in an 'inner landscape'. They are in touch with the fount of their creative expression—a deep, generative well, which they channel into things that can be touched, felt and seen. And their creative expression has the potential to both 'touch and evoke', as well as to 'challenge and provoke'.

Thoughts, ideas and emotions—bring them on, and they are ready to engage with them and do something distinctive with them. You cannot bind them down for long with convention, norm or tradition. They are likely to keep creating things and making them available for others to see, hear, taste, smell, touch and enjoy. And the impact of the Artiste is invariably felt when the world either starts doing new things or continues to do existing things in very different ways. Here is a quick example. When Wikipedia burst on the scene in 2001, they asked us (and eventually got us) to 'imagine a world in which every single human being can freely share in the sum of all knowledge. That's our commitment'.

Consider this phenomenon—'creative imagination' accompanied by an artefact that can be sensorially experienced, and that sensorial experience is accompanied by an experience of that experience, and that creates a mood. If you are in touch with this phenomenon, then you are probably in the presence of the Artiste. Apart from musicians, poets, storywriters, designers, dancers and actors who have a strong probability of being Artistes, they are around us in other forms as well. When Steve Jobs announced the arrival of the iPod before Christmas 2001, he (and Apple Inc) was being the Artiste. When Elon Musk releases the Tesla cars, he is, along with Tesla, being the Artiste. When the analog design team in Texas Instruments India designs an integrated circuit that makes you go 'Wow!' when you view a new home theatre system, they are the Artistes. When the facilitator in a group dynamics workshop creates an exploratory activity on the spot to amplify and allow the group to study a dynamic process operating among them, he or she is being the Artiste. The lovers who create an experience for their loved other, that is, at once intense and profoundly meaningful, they are being the Artistes. In short, Artistes can make you angry, sad, joyful, feel intense love, sorrowful, filled with pathos, and feel several other emotions.

The Artistes' presence opens up new possibilities for the system they are part of, and for the larger context. Working with dreams, reveries, contemplation and visions is part of what Artistes would regularly do—thus they would make the Unconscious accessible to the system as a new (and inexhaustible) resource to draw from. Their impact would be a reframing of 'reality' in a profound way. When the Artiste energy is unleashed and expressed, the system and the world around it are usually transformed in ways that make them fundamentally different than before—in a physical and emotional way. Martin Luther King Jr was indeed being an Artiste (just as his movement was the manifestation of the Warrior–Crusader identity) when he made his famous 'I have a dream' speech. It can be said that they actually reframe consciousness for us—they reach into our normal day-to-day consciousness and do something with it such that we see the same world with different eyes as Marcel Proust would say. And by that expanded consciousness, we become different and we create a different world.

'Explore, create, and manifest change' is the mantra with which the Artiste engages. When you come across them, they are likely to be reflective, immersed yet intensely expressive. They would seem to have psychic eyes, with which they somehow see the yet unmanifest, the possibilities, the subliminal and the invisible. It is likely that questions running through their head might be 'Why can't I' and 'How can I'. Says Srikanth from Chennai—a curious mix of a brilliant stock analyst, film producer, bird photographer and budding educationist (we dropped cricket and golf along the way)—'Whatever I do, it has to be about reinventing. Whether it is about how to make money, or how to make *unusual films, or how to engage young minds in pragmatic learning, I believe in questioning why something is being done the way it is, and more important—how can it be done differently and still generate the same or even better impact'.* They might seem idiosyncratic or quirky, though not necessarily always—perhaps 'distinctive' would be a good word for them. They might destroy the unnecessary and test limits. If you put them through a Hogan Dark Side Assessment, they might check at least four boxes for high candidature for derailment—they would qualify with 'extreme high scores' for being Impulsive, Excitable, Colourful and Imaginative. Yet they are there, not as often derailed as misunderstood in a flat and norm-seeking and norm-promoting ecology!

You are likely to spot an Artiste through their work— when you read, hear, behold something that evokes or provokes you and when you feel a part inside of you stirred. When A. R. Rahman burst on the Indian film music scene in the 1990s, his creations left an indelible mark on an entire generation of music listeners and movie viewers—it was as if a new voice had emerged that could touch and give expression to a modern-day angst that was there but yet not voiced adequately by the music composers that existed before Rahman. It may perhaps be appropriate to add in here, in our characterization of the Artiste, that they would give voice to a prevalent angst, draw it out from its reclusive inner chambers and catacombs, put it out there, even celebrate it and revel in its coming alive. And the world often views Artistes with awe and respect, as much as with indifference and scorn. On the one hand, they are valued for their courage, expression, the beauty they are in touch with and bring to life and their ability to question assumptions and face truths (and push others to do the same) and, on the other, they are also viewed as and chastised for being impractical, irresponsible, disconnected from the realities of life and being intensely narcissistic. M. F. Husain, who in his life was one of India's most well-known painters, was equally vilified. As Uma Nair writes, 'Always concerned with the mysteries of the human panorama, Husain's appropriation and subtle suggestions have fallen on stagnant intellects whose minds are buried under the debris of intellectual and spiritual arrogance'.

When faced with life's challenges and tests, Artistes might wonder about the terms 'challenge', 'test' and so on and note how they are basically problematic. They operate on a wide canvas without binaries and polarities but with possibilities. That said, however, in most life situations, they are likely to take an intensely personal and inside-in view and operate from there. They are very likely to look at what gets evoked for them, what their subjective experience is and express that. And that in itself, often births movements and evokes a groundswell for big change. When Perumal Murugan, the now-famous poet-writer from Tamil Nadu was vilified (as Artistes often are, we have noted) and hounded by several caste outfits for his controversial literary work 'Madhorubagan', he did something outstanding and unusual—he declared the author in himself dead. *'Perumal Murugan, the writer is dead. As he is no God, he is not going to resurrect himself. He also has no faith in rebirth. An ordinary teacher, he will live as P. Murugan. Leave him alone'*, he has posted on his Facebook account. That act by itself was an artistic masterstroke as it went 'viral' and brought him huge support and in many ways (and ironically, for those that were trying to silence him), placed him in the literary spotlight of South India.

What Is the Inner World of the Artiste Like?

Perhaps the Artiste's internal ego state is primarily a depressive one (as described by Melanie Klein), partly 'worked through' in some and raw in others. From this position, deep down, the Artiste's desire may be to mean something special to the context— may be to find expression for their inner world and seek connection for their flow, with a greater/larger something. Their affirmation comes from evidence that their being matters and makes a difference—or that in their absence there would be an impoverishment of the context. The gifts that the Artiste comes in with are their abundant imagination and their ability to create and generate something from their ideas. As Pablo Picasso is known to have famously said, 'Everything you can imagine is real'—and that's a *lot* of realism for Artistes! They also have the gift of feeling viscerally. They can feel their own feelings and the feelings around them—almost like they have an antenna for feelings. Little wonder that many wonderful facilitators of human processes are actually gifted Artistes. Artistes are those beings with a gift that can uniquely honour the spirit of the muse, and they are ones truly capable of surrender. The lover who surrenders to their loved one's being is such an Artiste! Think of the great Sufi poets—are they not truly lovers at heart! Ergo, is the ability to feel love not one of the quintessential characteristics of the Artiste? And what of their hope? Artistes reach within to express themselves. They may believe that by expressing themselves creatively and distinctively, they will be able to understand themselves. That it would—in a virtuous cycle—add to their aliveness. And whether they consciously think of this or not, their aliveness could propel a process of renewal and revitalization of the systems they are part of.

There is also the sorrow of the Artiste—often, they do not know for sure if they really matter. Partly driven by their own doubts and misgivings and partly by the world's seeming preoccupation with itself, they wonder if the world values them. And there is another struggle too. The normal, conventional and all-too-often cognitive frames of the world do not help them understand themselves or navigate their mind adequately. It is here that they turn to their inner explorations with their art—not necessarily only to express for the world but also to help them know and be themselves. And their greatest fear would be of their fount of evocation drying up and feeling blocked: Maybe a sense that inspiration will not come any more and find a channel in them. The common phrase 'writers' block' is an apt expression to help us understand this phenomenon. Moving beyond the fear, we see that an inner contradiction that the Artiste experiences is that of 'feeling special' yet 'feeling part of'. This takes us to one of the discernible shadows that the Artiste casts—that of their own entrenchments. They often expect the context to receive them *in a certain way* and end up digging a pit all around themselves, being accused of destructive narcissism perhaps by an envious or self-protective world and wondering (mostly in private) why the world is at a distance from them. Early on in the journey of this identity, they are often celebrated and indulged for what the world calls their idiosyncrasies. The same bouquets later end up becoming the brickbats that leave them feeling let down and bruised.

For the Artiste identity, great resonance is experienced if the others in the picture are in touch with the 'Admirer' or 'Aficionado' in themselves. However, the difficulty often surrounding this identity is that the Artiste is received mostly with awe or envy or a mix of the two. This makes the others in the presence of the Artiste feel distant and ordinary, if not small. This creates an inflation in the Artiste that in turn throws up another shadow element of the Artiste—a sense of disdain or scorn for those 'ordinary persons'. J. K. Rowling's creation of the term 'mudbloods', used by the dark wizards in her tale to describe non-magical human beings, is an example of such inflation.

The Artiste in the Extremes

As we have seen, the gift of the Artiste is their ability to express themselves in distinctive ways. They are able to reach and touch people and systems from a space of their own inner evocation. And like every coin has an 'other side', the Artiste sometimes suffers from their own abundance. The unfettered Artiste can be like a river in spate. Such an Artiste may prominently display certain idiosyncratic fascinations—this coupled with relatively low contextual sensitivity could lead to chaos and lack of direction—thus paradoxically creating all conditions for the world to distance itself from them. The legendary rock musician Jimi Hendrix could create brilliant music on any given day, yet he could just as easily be destructive and uncontainable at certain times.

If the Artiste's energy is low, there would probably be a pervasive sense of 'ho-hum'. Material that was once creative would start getting rehashed into formulaic productions—and with this, the Artiste gets sold to industry as a 'performer' and 'entertainer' who is expected to bedazzle in order to keep the coffers full. Think of innumerable actors and musicians who fall prey to the lure of the ever-present 'homo-economicus'. Think of great facilitators of human processes who end up looking like what we call 'entertainers'. And so on. Dryness, incrementalism and stuckness—these could be perceivable features of a low Artiste's system.

The table below may help us see some aspects of the Artiste at a quick glance.

Angst	Hope	Gifts	Fear/ Vulnerability
Although I have a need to count for something and to be of consequence, I do not know if I do	That by expressing myself distinctively, I will discover myself	The ability to see things differently and the ability to express creatively and spontaneously	Of feeling 'dry or blocked'

The Artiste as a Leader in Organizations

- They would come up with out-of-the-box solutions and approaches to optimize throughput and create new processes for efficiencies and productivity.
- They would like to relate with people at the level of ideation and thought partnership, seeking constantly to be in shared creative spaces.
- In running businesses, they would look for transformative and disruptive step jumps, preferring to usher in revolutionary change as against incremental growth.

- They would come up with new ideas and ways of expressing them meaningfully.
- Sometimes, Artiste-leaders fall in love with their creativity and creations, like Narcissus, and tend to get defensive and 'overprotective' of their work.

11

The Collaborator

Never doubt that a small group of thoughtful, committed, citizens can change the world. Indeed, it is the only thing that ever has.

—Margaret Mead

The **Collaborator**

Who Is the Collaborator?

The word 'collaborate' comes from the Latin word '*collaborere*'—to 'work together'. And it is with this backdrop that we invite you to meet this identity.

The theme for the 2017 Group Relations Conference (GRC) of Group Relations India and the Human and Institutional Development (HID) Forum—a deeply impactful experiential group learning event—was 'The Courage to Lead—Exploring the Dynamics of Collaboration and Dissent'. The two words 'collaboration' and 'dissent' coming together provides an interesting perspective. For one, it suggests that being the Collaborator is not all about 'being a nice and friendly person'. It is neither about being a cooperative person nor is it about one who is co-opted into a task or one who co-opts another to a task. These are perhaps the misconceptions that underlie this identity. As the directors of that conference stated in their brochure, '… real collaboration and co-creation is possible when leaders have the capacity and courage to invite different views to be aired, differences to be worked with, without getting paranoid or anxious'.

That brings us to the doorstep of the Collaborator. The house of the Collaborator has the courage to invite diversity. It holds the promise of working with differences. Dissent lives in the house of the Collaborator as a blood relative. The energy of this identity is not a containing one—it is expressive and brings a system together through its functions, as we will soon see.

The Collaborators are builder of communities. They are those who create and foster connections with and between people. Through this, a community is built, and the well-being of the system given priority. The Collaborator brings in an intentionality and is not a loose arrangement for people to 'get along' or 'go along with' or 'feel warm'. This intentionality is reflected in the fact that they continue to work towards the nourishment of the system.

The globally renowned group moderation methodology Technology of Participation (ToP) suggests the idea of a task aim and an experiential aim for all groups engaged in an endeavour. The Collaborators straddle both of these—they collaborate AND evoke collaborativeness in others in a way that both aims are met, though we aver that their pull would be primarily towards the experiential aim.

A good example of this is the global commune, Auroville. As their website announces, *'Auroville wants to be a universal town where men and women of all countries are able to live in peace and progressive harmony above all creeds, all politics and all nationalities. The purpose of Auroville is to realise human unity'.*[1] Every part of their intentionality statement vocalizes their experiential aim.

Being naturally endowed with a supportive orientation and an ability to understand the other's condition, the Collaborator makes sure that people within the system are working together effectively. Collaborators could also, if required, fill the role of negotiators within and for a system as they are usually flexible, diplomatic and perceptive. The Collaborator knows the difference between 'fitting in' and 'belonging'. As the GRC brochure referred above indicates, 'Fitting in is about assessing a situation and becoming who you need to be in order to be accepted. Belonging, on the other hand, does not require us to change who we are; it requires us to be who we uniquely are and to be able to bring all of ourselves into work'. The Collaborator builds communities through evoking belonging—including dissent, co-creation, courage, diversity, communion, connections, understanding and supportiveness, to name just a few facets.

Many examples of this identity in the world around us come readily to mind. One has only to look at support groups of various types—Alcoholics Anonymous and the Toastmasters Club are well-known abodes of the Collaborator. So too, in our experience, are institutions of 'process work' like Sumedhas, or Aasthaa, in India. Another example is the Cholamandal Artists' Village, established in 1966, the largest artists' commune in India. It has

---

[1]See www.auroville.org

over 20 resident painters and sculptors, who live as a community and pool their skills. They run the Artists Handicrafts Association, a cooperative which manages the village and sale of works through the permanent exhibition at the complex, which includes paintings, sketches, terracotta/stone/metal sculptures, batiks and handicrafts and so on, making the village a self-supporting entity. The Cholamandal Village is filled with Collaborators, and the Village by itself is a personification of the Collaborator. Another significant Collaborator entity is the Fireflies Intercultural Center in Bangalore, which attempts to surface environmental and ecology issues through workshops, meetings, field action and more. The 2018 edition of the annual Fireflies Dialogues appropriately focused on *Dialogue, Negotiation & Reconciliation*. These dialogues create opportunities for thinkers, artists, activists, students, journalists, policymakers, bureaucrats, scholars and more to create change towards sustainability through knowledge sharing, interaction and participatory processes. Just glance at the words used after we introduced Fireflies to you—dialogue, negotiation, reconciliation, sharing, interaction and participatory—and we should get a vivid snapshot of this identity. The dialogues are remarkable examples of a *Collaborator framework* for the operation of another identity, the Warrior–Crusader.

As we mentioned earlier, many large group facilitation methodologies and technologies like Open Spaces, World Café, ToP and Unconference are also avatars of the Collaborator. These technologies are ways to enable all kinds of people, in any kind of organization, to collaborate to create inspired meetings and events.

Charles Green, the founder of Trusted Advisors Associates LLC, came up with an ingenious approach to 'calculate' trust. His 'trust equation' is a popular one—according to him, one's Trust Quotient (TQ) = (Credibility + Reliability + Intimacy)/Self-Orientation. While we will not go into all the ingredients of this intriguing equation, we will draw your attention to one of them that informs Collaborators directly. We are talking of intimacy. Through their actions, they build a quality of intimacy that would directly grow the level of trust in the system. So, it can be reasoned that wherever the Collaborator is well respected in a system, you will have a good community of trust. And as Lencioni's work and writings suggest, you will see how they lead to a well-performing, vibrant system.

The impact of the Collaborator would be in creating high engagement, cohesion and sharing of responsibilities and resources in a group or a system. They would have a lubricating effect on teams. Morale tends to be better and people seem to work better together when they are around. Another interesting effect of theirs is in lowering the 'degrees of separation' between people, especially when the 'connector' part of the Collaborator is active. And like the Provider of Resources might provide the 'know-how' for a system, the Collaborator offers the 'know-who'.

We like to believe that LinkedIn and Facebook would have offered great spaces for the Collaborator, but we must also sigh and register with you that these social media spaces seem to have become more narcissistic and self-adulatory spaces than spaces for authentic collaboration. Collaborators value both differentiation AND integration. As valuers of differentiation, they are likely to support diversity of thought, views, mindsets and action. They would also create the ground conditions in any system for such to be valued. Equally, they also provide the glue and the integrative effect that holds a system together. We need to go no further than a Karnatik music concert to view this impact of the Collaborator. The singer, the violinist and the percussionist—each brings their own individual (and collectively diverse) skills and abilities to the concert stage. Yet, when they start creating music together, there is a fusion of all of that and a beautiful mandala is created. If we could have astral vision, we might notice the Collaborator right there, making this happen and with a smile of delight on their face.

Let us now place our Collaborators under a microscope and view their likely actions and behaviours.

They are likely to initiate dialogue and provide support to others. In the service of diversity and differentiation, we are likely to see them actually supporting, maybe even encouraging friction and dissent. However, we also feel that in the service of integration, they are likely to be watchful about toxic friction that might come in the way of collaboration. They may head it off, or have offline conversations to make sure it is contained or ask that the community takes a step back and views the matter from distance.

Also (and this complements their pull towards diversity and differentiation)—they would establish and maintain informal networks of communication both within a system and at the interfaces. Like we have said before, they are the glue and the lubricant. They would be Malcolm Gladwell's 'connectors', who would connect different people from different spaces together. They would build deep relationships seamlessly across various boundaries—hierarchical, functional, spatial, vocational, societal, cultural, geographical and so on—and channel these at appropriate points for the well-being of the system. Often, they will be the 'busy communication node' in an organization through whom information flows. They would also know where each individual is at from a personal viewpoint.

We must also not think of the Collaborators as a non-discerning entity. They tend to collaborate with those that they feel would be integral to the primary task of the system and the community. In that sense, they may try people out, see if they will fit in and adapt and then on-board them into the task or the community.

Another aspect of the Collaborator is that once a person is invited into the task or community, they would have their back and look out for them.

Collaborators are also likely to visibly place the system's interests above or ahead of individual interests. We are reminded here of Scrum methodologies, popular and growing in the information technology industry. At times, some Collaborators may behave in a way that might seem anarchic or subversive to the system but in reality, this is in service of the bigger picture of the system's health. An example of this is 'skunkworks', where a small group of people work on a project in an unconventional way, to develop something quickly with minimal management constraints.

You would also find them negotiating on the system's behalf. They are not the hardball negotiators—they do not play the 'good cop bad cop' routine, and they do not use highball tactics or create bogeys. Rather they are the 'integrative negotiators' who would seek to work together with others to expand the pie so that everyone can get a share that is enough for their need.

Here is an example:

Several years ago, young musicians in the Karnatik music world of Chennai came together to start the 'Youth Association for Classical Music', a forum of collaboration whereby it could negotiate with the powerful music 'Sabhas' in the city to provide more platforms to young musicians in return for which the forum instilled a sense of commitment to excellence and camaraderie among the aspiring young musicians on the one hand and also provided the Sabhas with useful advice on which musicians were capable of performing in various formats and themes of the music concerts of Chennai.

And when a system is faced with a challenge, this identity is likely to check for various views, ideas, perspectives, options and so on. Their belief is perhaps that know-who would solve for know-how. Because of an understanding of what different people bring in, they will first figure out who is needed, bring them together and allow the solution to emerge synergistically. And even as this happens, their focus and joy may come from getting people to work together. They are likely to collect and collate viewpoints from both inside the system presenting the problem and outside it.

And having gotten a diverse set of viewpoints (or people in a room), they are likely to quickly press for an integration of voices into a channelled final approach.

What Is Their Inner World Like?

Perhaps the deepest value of the Collaborators is affiliation. Their hope is for mutuality, for win-win approaches to life and work and their belief may be that in synergy, magic will be found. Their hope would also be for a group to be more than a sum of its individual parts and to come together in a deeply connected way.

Latha, a homemaker living in Bangalore, also runs a trust caring for geriatric patients and she mobilizes her neighbourhood community to this end—'I make it a point to know every person in the neighbour-hood. One day it may be the grocer who will send across rice and vegetables to the hospice. Another day, the milkman who will give us free supplies. The people in the residential colony come to me volunteering time, clothes, food, anything they can give—and they do it because I have struck a personal rapport with each of them. Sometimes I get different folks together—the other day the children from the neighborhood joined hands with some carpenters and painters from a nearby under-construction house, and together they painted a wall in the hospice', says Latha, beaming with pride.

Their gift as you can see is the ability to bring people together AND hold them together. The metaphors of the orchestra AND that of a jazz ensemble both come to mind. The Collaborator can do either and both. The structured role-bound collaboration of the orchestra is as accessible to them as is the free-flowing format of a jazz band. Refer to the website www.friendsofpeter.net, and we may all get an idea of what the Collaborator is endowed with. *Friends of Peter* (FoP) is taglined as 'good people helping good people'. Started by Peter Strople in 2008, this endeavour brings business and community leaders together to effect 'Instant Change' as it relates to the critical business and social needs of a community or country. The gift that Peter has is to simply make connections and the ability to bring people together and to keep them together. It is also about the ability to see skills, value and talent in others. The Collaborator is also gifted with the extra-ordinary ability not simply to care about others but to actually do something meaningful for them. In their collaborativeness, they also manage boundaries between themselves and others quite well. This ability allows them to be less prey to the responses of others. Hence, transactional non-collaborativeness from the other would not knock them off balance.

'Will the community be torn apart?' would perhaps be the worry of this identity. Their fear may be that of deep dissonances in the collaborative spaces they have helped set up. Their sorrow and angst are likely to be that, at the end of day, they discover that people in the world are highly individualistic and that human ecologies do not perhaps matter much to others. If the Collaborator has not learnt to value the world of structure and order, they may be prone to control through elaborate protocols of collaboration—try getting membership into some social clubs, for instance! If the world of autonomy and initiative is not developed in our Collaborator, they may, in the name of collaboration, actually end up controlling the group. *Mahita runs an initiative inviting volunteers to save stray dogs in a community in Bangalore. Once she formed her group, she exercised her power, assigning roles and imposing limits on what others in the initiative can or (mostly) cannot do. But her group members live with it both because of the cause they have come together for and that behind her power need, Mahita is actually a warm and generous friend to many of them!*

The Collaborator in the Extremes

The 'excessive' Collaborator would perhaps leave no scope for autonomy or create a cloying and false togetherness—a pseudo-community. Non-confrontational and non-direct, such seeming collaboration may end up infantilizing the system and treating each other with kid gloves. Decisions may not get made because consensus or approval become bottlenecks towards moving ahead. Everyone can say No, but no one can say Yes and move things forward. Make-believe issues get created and differences fester. These stances often lead to surface-level cooperation or mostly compromises but not real collaboration. Coalition governments in India often go through such an 'extreme Collaborator' syndrome. At times, you also have cases of extreme Collaborator and extreme Strategist in a person or system—leading to heavy networking. They would be in all conferences and seminars, and they would proudly hand out and collect business cards. The belief perhaps is that 'the network will do the work for us'. Alas, if only!

Very low or an under-energized Collaborator in a system may be like a garden of weeds—anything can grow anywhere, with no coherence of efforts. Efforts may be 'solo' and resultant structures may be 'silos'. Very often so-called team-building programmes in corporates espouse the bringing in of the Collaborator energy. But what they end up with (and often with the collusion of consultants) is spending time with weak Collaborator energy—so there is no real valuing of differentiation and diversity, no confrontation, conflicts are papered over, 'feel good' is generated and everybody goes home calling themselves 'energized' and 'euphoric'—and all is well—till the inevitable tests of team character break out in the next conflict or escalation of issues.

The Collaborator is one identity that can actually resonate and work with any of the others given their ability to see their gifts and bring them in as per the needs of the system.

Now look at the summary table below:

Angst	Hope	Gifts	Fear/ Vulnerability
No matter what, the world is an individualistic place and perhaps people prefer to be atomized units	That a human ecology can be fostered	The ability to bring and hold people together	That we will all be lone islands. That communities will be torn apart or never get created

The Collaborator as a Leader in Organizations

- Collaborator–leaders would have a map of the whole system and orchestrate tasks and people—making sure that tasks are done synergistically.
- They would create connections with and between people and would make themselves available for others and invest time in the activities of others.
- They would willingly assist change efforts being driven by others and would try and create spaces where people can come together to visualize and drive change.
- They would willingly join and enlist resources for the system's task. And they would work towards a win-win even while growing and expanding the system.
- On the flip side, sometimes they tend to be excessively consensus seeking or 'viewpoint seeking' and these actions may tend to lower momentum and slow system tasks down—giving the impression of some indecisiveness and leading to effort/resource wastage overall.

12

The Curious Child

The important thing is not to stop questioning. Curiosity has its own reason for existence. One cannot help but be in awe when he contemplates the mysteries of eternity, of life, of the marvelous structure of reality. It is enough if one tries merely to comprehend a little of this mystery each day.

—'Old Man's Advice to Youth: 'Never Lose a Holy Curiosity'.
LIFE Magazine (2 May 1955) p. 64'—Albert Einstein

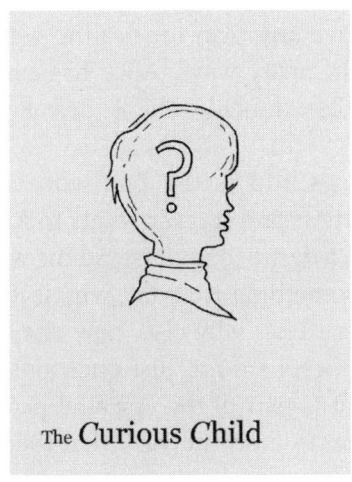

The **Curious Child**

Who Is the Curious Child?

Heard of *Alice in Wonderland*? Alice is a seven-and-a-half-year-old little girl living in an upper-middle-class family in Victorian England. She has an older sister who is too literal minded to play the imaginative games Alice thinks up, a cat named Dinah that she adores, and a nursemaid who looks after her. Just what kind of a girl is Alice? Alice's one defining characteristic is her innate curiosity. She is ready to follow anyone anywhere, as long as they are interesting. Even when she is frightened, just the lure of continuing her exploration helps her conquer her fear. Alice loves strange, previously unexplored territories. She would like to see the beautiful garden of the Queen of Hearts in Wonderland, just as she would love to visit the Eighth Square of the chess board in the Looking-Glass World. She has been taught safety lessons but they are subject to the override clause of her natural inclination to experiment. Show her a strange bottle with a strange liquid in it, and Alice will take a swig to see what it tastes like. Show her a door and she has to get through it, even if it is tiny, locked and labelled 'no entry', and she will walk through it. Tell her about a rabbit hole and she will do what it takes to go in through it, without asking herself how she might get out and back! She does not have any particular reason for the things she does, except that she wants to find out more about the world around her. She also does not have any plan for dealing with the consequences of her actions. In many ways, Alice has curiosity but does not balance it with discernment—she is, dear Reader, the archetypal Curious Child.

The Curious Child is the one who is bubbling with an inner inquisitiveness and forever wants to know more—perhaps insatiably—with a desire to understand the world, understand the *'what is'*. What something is about, why it is so and how it does what it does, what else, why else, how else, why not and so on, these (and like these) are not just questions, they are vectors of wonderment that is part of the essential package of the Curious Child. They seem to hold the view that there is always a gap in understanding or knowing something that is yet to be filled and they seek to operate therefore at the edges and boundaries of knowledge, seeking to know more. That said, it must be borne in mind that this identity is not asking these questions in order to change the world—not at all. Their nature is to *understand* the world (outer and inner) that we occupy and to do that, not inertly but through active inquiry.

And their unbounded curiosity could be evoked by just about anything. A nugget of information heard in passing would take them immediately to Google (their biggest ally these days), or it could be a little phrase that they come across in a newspaper wrapper (never mind if the newspaper is three years old!) while eating *churmuri*. Or it could be eyebrows all knitted and wondering—how can I crack this crossword, how many anagrams can I create of a word, how can I put on this or that and so on. How can I get to know the unknown would perhaps be their single-point agenda. The Curious Children would perhaps embody a paradox—they would want to know everything about everything and they would be disappointed if they did! Their essential energy lies in their perception of a gap which could be either a cognitive gap or a sensory gap. They are the mavens, the *accumulators of knowledge*, as the Yiddish might put it. And their curiosity can take them both deep and broad indeed! Their identity itself carries a natural boundlessness—and it makes one wonder if they are in any way actively concerned about boundaries at all as much as they foster their intense and potent restlessness.

If we take the schema of the Myers–Briggs Type Indicator, popularly known as the MBTI, we may find that our Curious Children have typically an 'extraverted intuitive' preference, with a particular pull towards the facets therein called 'Imaginative' (resourceful, inventive, seeking novelty) and 'Original' (unconventional, new and unusual, different). Their innate curious nature gifts the world enhanced consciousness, and so we may liken this identity to the Greek mythological character Prometheus who steals fire from the Gods so he may gift the world consciousness (and through it, technology and the arts). This identity is the tinkerer, the experimenter and explorer, who is constantly pushing the boundaries of his or her own knowledge. They are also what 99u.com calls 'expert generalists'—who 'develop an appetite for learning and openness' that makes them 'more likely to be able to draw ideas from multiple disciplines'.

Let us look at some examples of the Curious Child. From historic accounts and anecdotes, perhaps Socrates, Kepler, Newton and Galileo, Edison and Leonardo Da Vinci all had some elements of the Curious Child in them. Now take Elon Musk from the contemporary world. He has built four multibillion-dollar companies, each in a different field. And by the looks of it, he has no intention of slowing down. How does he do it? Among other intangible factors, his success comes in part from his approach to learning. He is known to pursue knowledge with an almost religious fervour. He is also known to be a master knowledge transferor—taking knowledge from one field and applying its principles elsewhere. Also consider celebrity chef Heston Blumenthal who has pioneered savoury ice cream encouraged his diners to wear headphones while eating, and even developed recipes for astronauts. He considers his award-winning Fat Duck restaurant as not just as a place for dinner but a place for storytelling—this means the menu is a story. It will have an introduction and a number of chapters and chapter headings that will give you an idea of what is coming. You do not just eat dinner there, you savour a story. A Curious Child combining with an artist to dish out this display..!

From fictional characters, we have the great Sherlock Holmes. Consider quotes from some classics—'My name is Sherlock Holmes. It is my business to know what other people don't know' from *The Adventure of the Blue Carbuncle*, or 'The world is full of obvious things which nobody by any chance ever observes' from *The Hound of Baskervilles* or this famous exchange between Inspector Gregory and Sherlock Holmes in *Silver Blaze*:

Inspector Gregory: 'Is there any point to which you would wish to draw my attention?'

Sherlock Holmes: 'To the curious incident of the dog in the night-time.'
Inspector Gregory: 'The dog did nothing in the night-time.'
Sherlock Holmes: 'That was the curious incident.'

What would happen when the Curious Child's energy is in flow? At one level, they can usher in aliveness, creativity, playfulness, enthusiasm and solution orientation in the system. By pushing boundaries, they can pave the way for new directions to potentially emerge. Their ingenuity may lie in their 'incrementalism'. Unlike the artiste who may be all about paradigm shifts, this identity may locate simple solutions to big problems. In similar vein, while the artiste would act from conviction, the Curious Child would likely act from just curiosity. And while the Artiste's raison d'être would be to express, the Curious Child's would be to receive and play with the world in curiosity. Inspiration for others is likely from the Curious Child, but equally likely is intense irritation—ask Socrates if you can, about the hemlock! Another way of putting this is to say that with the Curious Child, boundaries may be pushed, but they may be violated as well.

If you were to give a small child a box of anything, you may observe that the child might open the box, drop or spill all contents on the floor and then look inside, outside, above and below the box for 'anything else that may be there that's not already on the floor'. That is very characteristic of the Curious Child's behaviour—first check for 'what is there', then check for 'what else is there', then check for 'what else is there' and so on. The Curious Child would playfully take things apart and put them back together. The very essence of a practice called 'reverse engineering' is pretty much all about this. They are willing to try anything and everything at least once. They are usually highly sensorial—looking for experiences to have, foods to taste, things to touch, people to meet and things to understand. The Curious Child would ask a million questions. They are simultaneously detail-oriented and flitting. They often fantasize and indulge in reveries. They would quickly sign up for new experiences to 'figure out' what it is about, question all, 'look under the rock', assemble pieces differently and so on. If we look to the schema of the Big 5 psychometric assessments, you may see the Curious Child embodying the trait of 'originality' (also called 'openness')—the degree of openness to having new experiences or new ways of doing things.

The Curious Children do not have to travel far to meet tests and challenges, they in fact often create them, for they may perhaps look at problems as adventure—something exciting, filled with possibilities and opportunities for learning and discovery. And when such tests and challenges do come up one way or another, they like to meet such with curiosity and wonder, perhaps with a question of 'how has this NOT been done before' (quite unlike the Custodian who might provide a ready reference of 'how has this been done before'). They pack in a lot of imagination—with their persistent questions like what if, how about, why not and so on.

The inventive genius of Thomas Alva Edison comes to mind—who accumulated 2,332 patents for his inventions, including the incandescent light bulb, electrical voice recorder, the phonograph, the motion picture camera and so many more! In today's times, you may see the Curious Child in action in technology companies such as Google, Apple and Samsung or in tech-driven practices such as cryptocurrency trading, driverless cars, chatbots, IOT and more.

Besides, the Curious Child would typically adopt a 'provisionalness'—that any approach or solution is not yet or not quite THE one, often asking what one more twist will yield. They conjure up the image of self-propelled drones—they would typically 'hover' over a situation, never quite landing and allowing the landscape below to shift and reveal more. To them, 'fold-up-and-exit' is not an option—they would believe that there has GOT to be a solution or a way out or forward (even backward would do!).

Another thing that you might see in them, when solving problems, is that they would listen to a view and then deliberately present its exact counterview to elicit deeper search and inquiry. They would both 'fail fast' (i.e., do incremental development to determine whether an idea or approach has value and if it is not working, to cut losses and quickly try something else) and 'fail well' (intelligent failure—acknowledging failure and using it as an opportunity to do 'blameless post-mortem', build skills and grow). And if you noticed, this last statement is indeed a counter-view to the 'fold-up-and-exit' not being an option. What we mean is that they will do their personal best to find a way out of a situation but at the same time, they are not likely to get entrenched or stuck.

A common example of this is the advice often shared among aspirants to the Indian Institutes of Management writing the Common Admission Test which is 'Never get stuck to one problem—try, try again, and try your best. But if you begin to think it is not going anywhere, skip it and go for another—that is indeed a way of your being tested as a future manager—do you get bogged down or are you agile and resilient?'

The Curious Child's presence is likely when there is something unusual and interesting going on. Check them out in labs, research departments, universities, music, films (especially in cinematography and editing), or catch them making experimental movies and music tracks which they put up on YouTube or SoundCloud or see them posting interesting pictures on Instagram. They are also the animated and 'involved' conversationalist who asks a lot of questions, draws you into conversations—maybe even painfully or intrusively so—seeking engagement—they may even exhaust you, extracting more than you may be willing to share!

In that sense, nothing is private or sacrosanct to them and all must yield to their curiosity. They are ones that are both easily interested and easily distracted.

Many years ago, R. K. Narayan, the celebrated novelist of India, wrote a short story about a young boy called Thumbi (Tamil for 'the nectar seeking bee'). The three-year-old, more-than-a-handful of a protagonist was called Thumbi because just like the bee that flits from flower to flower, forever in a buzz, Thumbi would be always on and always restless, often darting from one theme to another before his questions from a previous theme would be fully answered by the harried elders he put to test!

That is the Curious Child for you.

What Is Their Inner World Like?

First, we must step back and endeavour to remind ourselves that we are talking of a very specific identity called the Curious Child who is different from the generic child. 'The child' is more in the nature of an archetypal force with many variants such as the Curious Child, the Wounded Child, the Adapted Child, the Rebel Child and so on. To glimpse into the inner world of the Curious Child, we have to spend a few minutes understanding the psychodynamics of 'playing', an essential characteristic of this identity. J. W. Winnicott, the famous British psychologist, has written quite a bit about this. Playing, says he, is something that happens in the interface between our inner world and external reality. Delving further into his work, we understand that playing happens in that space where our imagination is able to shape the external world without the experience of compliance, there is bearable anxiety and where it is possible to create a non-purposive state of being. The freedom to play would be at the heart of what a Curious Child most desires or hopes for. The ability to play is also the gift that the Curious Child is endowed with.

If this identity had one prayer for life, it may well be that their bucket list should be all done and dusted and that nothing be left incomplete or unvisited. And of course, it is a bucket that gets filled every time something gets completed.

Dare we say that they may wish that age and growth can be transcended? They would hope also that a world built on fancy and whims is treated every bit as valuable as any other, by the world, and that there be no part of the cosmos that may be called 'forbidden' or 'out of bounds'. Their conviction is that whatever they discover would affirm their search—there are no specific goals and no norms to satisfy—what they come across during their search is simply what they were meant to. Interestingly, even if they do not find what they were originally after, they would still feel affirmed as they would find something that would offer them a new thread to pursue as in 'Let's see where THIS fits'.

Complementing their wishes is the gift they come with. We believe that alongside their ability to play comes their polyvalence—that is, their ability to have a pull simultaneously towards many things. So too, given the tendency of the Curious Child to take 'small bets', there is an ease with which they can fail fast, fail well and exit easy—a valuable gift indeed! They would also have a certain richness of vision. Not the kind of longitudinal vision that you might find in the Strategist but richness of the kind you might get in a kaleidoscope. After all, the Curious Child is at best capable of, to borrow from the evergreen Beatles, seeing 'Lucy in the sky with diamonds, tangerine trees, marmalade skies, cellophane flowers, rocking horse people, newspaper taxies, plasticine porters, looking glass ties, and of course the girl with kaleidoscope eyes'. Mavens, again, are typically the Curious Children—forever able to find unusual answers and ask provocative and different questions—they bring depth and detail to even the most 'trivial' things (without trivializing them!), through their constant seeking (as distinct from the Trickster identity, who may do quite the opposite!).

Eventually, the Curious Child realizes that it does have a big fear—of having to grow up, take responsibility, of the seeking having to stop and of encountering a boring and unexciting world. 'Will I, the 'puer' have to end up as the 'senex'', would be the lament! So also, 'Will it be that "law" and "duty" will prevail and my raw vitality one day be replaced by mature wisdom'. Maybe also that 'the world is really a flat, monochrome existence—a dystopia'—and 'The "mainstream" world does not quite get me'.

The Curious Child in the Extremes

In the overly Curious Child, you may see the reckless child, at once defiant, rebellious perhaps with a narcissistic identification with its curious self and thus not grounded in pragmatics and reality. As mentioned earlier, they may also become the intrusive and trespassing being. There would be no closures to their endeavours, no taking of or owning up of responsibility. They would be unable to stay in one place and would likely set up a fantasy world that may well replace the real world (*remember Mall Cobb, the wife of Dominick Cobb in the popular film Inception, and her total and complete identification with the 'Limbo', the dream world that she experiments with and gets trapped in*). It is likely that others might experience the Curious Children as 'pot-stirrers' who do not really achieve much or as those that know a lot about unimportant things. They may also be seen as inspirational and may be eccentric.

Flip the coin to land the other way, the side of the Curious Child being underplayed, and you get one who might accept the 'as-is' unquestioningly, perhaps with indifference even. The shadow of the superego looms large. Status quo is preferred. An absence of libido and movement can be discerned. Thinking is directed, focused, linear and often utilitarian.

Identities that seem to resonate with the Curious Child are 'supportive mentors', 'indulging parents' and perhaps 'awestruck friends and companions'. Identities that might find the Curious Child difficult to deal with could be the 'impatient, action-oriented administrator or task persons' or the 'safety seeker', the custodian and the 'privacy preferror'.

Angst	Hope	Gifts	Fear/ Vulnerability
No matter what, the world does not see, is not interested in seeing anything beyond the obvious and has very little patience for me	That I get to explore all there is to explore	The ability to play, and to value many things simultaneously	That I have to grow up, take responsibility and perhaps stop seeking

The Curious Children as Leaders in Organizations

- When it comes to execution and delivery, the Curious Child leader would display a willingness to try out new processes, methodologies and tools for optimizing system throughput.
- As leaders of people, they would bring in a sense of play and lightness.
- They would willingly pilot or be part of new experiments, change initiatives and prototype developments.
- They would readily bring in and assimilate data, trends and patterns from diverse sources and offer them up for the benefit of the task at hand.
- At times, they may tend to take issues and matters somewhat lightly and not give them the attention that many others may think they deserve!

13

The Custodian

We live in a vast and awesome universe, where, daily, suns are made and worlds destroyed and humanity clings to a clod of rock. The significance of our lives and our fragile realm derives from our own sense of wisdom and courage. We are the custodians of life's meaning.

—Carl Sagan

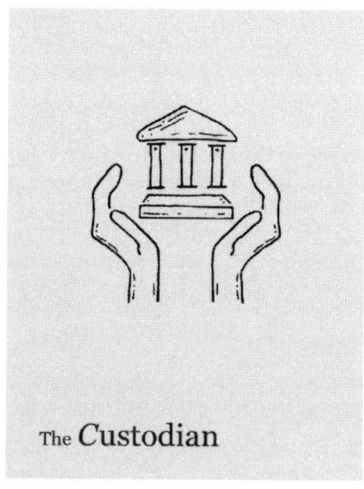

The **Custodian**

Who Is the Custodian?

There once lived a fisherman who had three sons. He sent them out into the world to seek their fortunes and he was curious to learn which one would return as the wealthiest. The sons had learnt about an enchanted castle not far from where they lived, and they were hoping to recover all kinds of treasures from it. On the way, they passed a forest ... the brothers walked in and saw an old man standing in front of them. His long white beard was wrapped around his arm three times. He asked what they wanted. 'We are the sons of a fisherman', they said, 'We came here in search of treasures in the castle'. 'My dear fellows, I am the custodian of the treasures, but I can only give them to a person who can answer three questions. The treasures belong to a princess who lives in a castle high in the mountains surrounded by a lake. There is no chance of finding a way in. She alone has the answers, and without her you won't be able to answer the questions.... The three questions are:

How many fish are in the lake
How many birds are in the land, and
How long has my beard been white.
You have until sundown, not much time....'

and so the story goes.

—*Extracted from the quaint fairy tale Hans Dudledee*

We get a glimpse of this intriguingly powerful identity through this little vignette. Let us now use our magnifying lens to pore deeper and try to understand the Custodian! Straight off the bat, we see that the Custodian is an 'old man'. We understand this to be not necessarily old in the sense of biological age but representing timeless wisdom and tradition. Man again does not mean male but that the Custodian is essentially masculine in the sense that 'he' represents the containing/grounding part of the static masculine (refer Appendix 1). When the brothers walk in, they see the old man standing in front of them. That is to say, that the seeker is invariably accosted by the Custodian. No adventure of value is complete without the seeker getting to know how the context and the system have evolved to where it is now. The Custodian makes no bones about it and he does not hide in the woodworks—he is IN the path of the seeker and accosts them. We next get to hear about his long white beard which is wrapped around his arm three times, but we shall return to this interesting factoid a little later.

Then, he announces himself and also states ground conditions for his support—the seeker has to prove themselves worthy of receiving the Custodian's support—that while he is available as a passive presence to all, his help has to be won. And there is a Standard Operating Procedure (SOP) for winning that—all's fair in the world of structure and order that he inhabits. Fair but not easy. Interestingly, of his three questions, two have to do with the seeker's understanding of the context (the number of fish and birds) and one to do with himself (his beard). What does this mean?

Simply this—the Custodian points to the reality that to understand a person, or a human entity or a human system or process, it is important to understand the context surrounding them AND it is important to understand the 'time-honoured' nature of the distinctive traditions of the person, entity, system or process.

We can, if we wish to, explore more and more nuances and layers beneath this simple vignette, but this much will do for now as an introduction to the Custodian. The Custodian, sometimes also called the Steward or the Guardian, is one who would guard and protect the assets, traditions, ways of life in and norms and practices of the system. They are the caretaker and the 'watchdog' that keep a watch over the system to ensure 'everything is in order and as it should be', and they protect the interests of the system. They are located in the 'past continuous' tense—they are very likely to know what was done and why it was done that way and what needs to be done now to continue the intent of those. They are the guardrails for 'safekeeping' and 'maintaining' what was. The well-being of the system is their primary task.

While consulting with patriarchs of family-owned businesses, we often see this role bestowed with primary emphasis. While they see the business as their playing field, of far greater importance is the fact that they must preserve and nourish the business for it to be passed on to the next generation. Apart from the patriarch, there is usually one or two individuals in the organization, typically the finance head or the company secretary who has worked across generations and will do so even after the next generation has come on board. The primary role of the head finance is then not just doing what the role description says but more importantly of keeping the history of the system alive and safeguarding the system from any harm that can come to it. It has been our experience that the younger generation in their pursuit of 'larger goals' as a warrior or a warlord often has to confront the custodian and prove to be worthy before they get the keys to the kingdom.

Keeping the above in mind, if we start looking for the Custodian in the world, we come across many examples. We can possibly categorize them in three sets—interpreters of symbols and text, preservers of form and upholders of intent/spirit. These are not rigid and mutually exclusive categories but more of indicative clusters.

1. Interpreters of symbols and text—Here you would find scholars in various fields, clerics, the judiciary, storytellers and historians and perhaps the Pope of the Roman Catholic Church.[1]
2. Preservers of form—Musicologists, art curators, traditional dancers, restoration artists, libraries and museums are examples of this.
3. Upholders of intent/spirit—The President of India, the Governor of any state in India, eco-conservationists and the judiciary again.

---

[1]Interestingly, the Pope may be the Custodian and the Ruler rolled into one. At one level, he is expected to preserve the Bible in its pristine form, and yet he has to adapt to the new world order—and thus, for instance, he may have to make laws too, for example, on whether or not the use of contraceptives may be permitted or if abortion may be allowed, or on gay marriage and so on.

The Custodian is likely to bring in a stabilizing and 'past-anchored' effect in the system they are part of. They provide temporal continuity. Now we have said this of the Guide–Mentor (a later chapter) as well, the difference is that while the Guide–Mentor would provide such continuity by focusing their energy on the 'protégé', so that they fit in well into the system, the Custodian would focus their energy on the system and there is no real 'protégé'—there is just the 'other'—who could be an internal or external stakeholder or a bystander.

Custodians are not the norm creators or the rule creators unlike the Ruler. They are more the keepers of the implicit ethos of the system. *As an example, several years ago, the Indian Society for Individual and Social Development (ISISD) had a category of membership called Institutional Members, and this was a membership granted to invited people from a larger pool of general members, and the so-invited Institutional Members were the ones who were expected to be trustees, guardians and custodians of the overall ethos of ISISD and to foster the same mindfully.*

They would strive to create adherence/compliance at one end and also (at the other end) loyalty to the existing values and traditions—again, not blind loyalty but loyalty borne out of having explored convictions at a deep level. The Custodian would create a sense of history and heritage. In that sense, they are like the 'sutradhar'—the 'holder of the thread' or the narrator of the unfolding drama of the system—they would know the history and also be able to offer its riches and treasures in a past continuous sense. One of the very positive impacts of the Custodian is that they contribute significantly to protection of the reputation of the system and so also the valuable intellectual property as well as standards of the system. They are, in effect, the fiduciaries of the system.

We shall now enter the world of the Custodians to see what they might be doing, how they might behave, and their characteristic actions.

The Custodian would interpret actions, events, processes and the like with a clear reference to the context of the system's broader picture, its evolution and past.

The character of Justice Sunderlal Tripathi from the 'Jolly LLB' series comes to mind immediately—in both the movies in this franchise, he is the earthy and eccentric judge, who is the custodian of the law, but the manner in which he seeks to understand the context and nest his interpretation of the letter of the law in the broader context makes for endearing viewing. He is the custodian who sees everything but does not react to everything, and when and if it comes to it, he asserts his authority with no hesitation whatsoever.

Custodians are also the preservers (even if fiercely protective) of family jewels. They would loyally guard the past history, legacy and heritage, including the well-kept secrets of the institution. Bhishma from the great epic *Mahabharata*, Kattappa from the recent film *Bahubali* and Ekalavya from the eponymous film of 2007 come readily to mind as illustrations of this side of the Custodian.

When we say 'loyally', we mean that the Custodians would have a sense of treating certain traditions as sacred—they would demonstrate loyalty to the systems and beliefs that they have sworn such loyalty to, and would prefer to 'go down with the ship' as the quaint maritime phrase has it, than to give up, quit or betray.

Custodians would also diligently build networks of trust. *The banking practices of the Naattukottai Chettiars of Tamil Nadu have been extensively documented and studied. They were the keepers and the trustees of the Chettiars' practice of indigenous credit, financing and moneylending—all of which works on a well-established base of trust, especially within their kith and kin.*

A variant of the 'trust network' is the establishment of the oral and the written tradition—Custodians have been known to preserve and proliferate the institutions' traditions through oral means (prevalent even today in various craft and artisan guilds in India like sthapatis, weavers, smithy and so on) and through careful documentation. The ISISD, as we have mentioned earlier, had, even in the 90s of the last century, published a set of six primers of the process work tradition and practices for their professional and institutional members—these primers were carefully written and edited by the Custodians of the ISISD tradition and are still referred to by process work practitioners in India. Custodians would likely demonstrate prudence combined with sagacity—'How has this been done before?', 'Lets step back before even thinking of changing this and ask ourselves if it is necessary to', 'Here's the price we might have to pay if we do this differently, so lets think' are some questions and statements you are likely to hear coming from the Custodians. They may, like in the last statement above, use anxiety or mobilize fear to garner allies or compliers. They may be resistant to change, and they are likely to hold on strongly and with pride to that part of their identity that is inherited.

When issues crop up and difficulties emerge, as they invariably do in the story of any life, the Custodians would be quick to scan their memory and point out when a similar incident had happened and how that had been dealt with. They are great at pattern awareness and pattern recognition, like that. Additionally, they would attempt to find solutions that preserve the reputation of the system.

An example is Johnson & Johnson's handling of the Tylenol crisis in 1986 which is a management education classic. The company's decision to recall Tylenol from every outlet (and not just from the state where it had happened) when the issue of tampering with the drug hit it is a good example of the Custodian's action in a crisis—that beyond the math and the metrics lies something called reputation and that protecting that is the dharma of the Custodian.

In the world around us, the Custodian is present in many forms. Typically, for instance, family business owners take this psychological position once the son/daughter becomes actively involved and takes charge of the business. They are the musicologists, musicians and dancers who take great pride in preserving or resurrecting old and forgotten works. All India Radio used to have a programme called '*Bhoole Bisre Geet*' conceived of to present contemporary listeners the melodies from the yesteryears of Hindi film music. They are the craftspersons, the artisans, the 'munim' from family businesses, the ethics directors in most MNCs, the ombudspersons of institutions, the elder in the family, some heads of religious mathas and more.

What Is Their Inner World Like?

What the Custodians hope for would be preservation and conti-
nuance. They hold the ethos and the accompanying values as
sacred in a way, and what is sacred needs to be protected and
guarded. They would also seek to value the pride of 'where one
comes from', in that part of one's identity getting valued and fostered. They tend to see the lives of individuals and institutions as
sagas and not as short stories. And sagas unfold epic narratives,
not brief curtain raisers. Ergo, their valuing of the pride! They
would also hope that the institutional arrangements they support
will nurture a sense of duty and responsibility in the members
of the system. The word 'duty' holds the seeds of the inner
aspirations of the Custodian. They feel that there is something
that is owed to the larger institution that they are part of. That, in
turn, generates a moral commitment and an obligation in them to
do something for the institution. Fulfilling one's duty is a hope
that the Custodians would nurture in their breasts for a long time
and keep working towards it. Besides these, they may also hope
that they will be supported for their often conservative position
and that there will be reciprocity. And last but never the least,
they would hope that 'heritage' will be valued and not relegated or
dismissed.

The Custodians have tenacity in them—whether natural or
acquired—no matter how much one may try to change their ways
and ideas, they would bounce back to make a case for that which
they are the guardian or trustee of. They are endowed with an
ability to value one's history and origins, with a sense of loyalty
and with the strength to be a voice of experience and sagacity.

The Custodians' great fear would perhaps be that all that they
have stood for and fostered will one day vanish or disappear or be
decimated. And as a consequence, the world will be impoverished
and will never savour what they stood for—except maybe as a
sentiment or a memory.

Often the Custodians quiver in apprehension of the sight of
the marauding Warlord gone rogue who may simply trample over

the sensibilities as well as the protected artefacts of the Custodians, in their attempt to not only acquire but to also wash off all traces of any traceable history. Sometimes it may not be the berserk Warlord but just some shifts in tastes and preferences that render the Custodian's obsessions obsolete or irrelevant. Like when after four generations of chartered accountants or lawyers in the family, the millennial son or daughter wants to be an RJ or start a gym or train to be a scuba diving instructor. This is a big fear AND very often, a sorrow of the Custodian. The fear is thus of institutional destruction, annihilation or degradation. As Frank Stokes says in the 2014 film *The Monuments Men*, 'If you destroy an entire generation of people's culture, it's as if they never existed. That's what Hitler wants and it's the one thing we can't allow'.

Another apprehension may be of being overrun by fads and diversity—that these may kill the ethos, the character and the quintessential spirit of the system (unless, of course, if the ethos of the institution itself is all about diversity, in which case all people who think non-diversely may be hated or vilified).

It is a well-known fact that Google last year fired the male engineer at the centre of an uproar in Silicon Valley after he authored an internal memo which seemed to suggest that there was a biological basis behind gender inequality in the tech industry. While the act was criticized by many as having proved that the company does not really respect diversity, the Custodian identity in the company had decisively acted.

The Custodian in the Extremes

'As the war at Infosys escalated earlier this year, then CEO Vishal Sikka famously announced, "I am a Kshatriya warrior, I am here to fight." What he did not bargain for, perhaps, was his opponent Narayana Murthy becoming a Parashuram, the Brahmin in the Hindu myth who went on a killing spree of Kshatriyas', writes Sandeep Goyal, on the now famous case of how Infosys sacked their CEO Vishal Sikka and the purported role of Infosys co-founder Narayana Murthy. The

myth of Parshurama can be deconstructed as the Brahmin Custodian (who inhabits the world of structure and order) who can go to the extremes to bring about balance (or, shall we say re-establish Brahmin supremacy?) when the forces of the World of Autonomy and Initiative (WAI) go beyond a threshold. So, the Parshurama avatar of the Custodian emerges and the normal guardrails of the Custodian end up becoming millstones, nooses or axes!

This form of Custodians would tend to have an uncompromisingly strong bias towards one way of being and thus be intolerant of any other way. 'This is how it has been and shall be' would be their refrain, reflecting certain righteousness coupled with some obduracy, perhaps. This may lead to a 'me versus others' or 'us against others' orientation, often polarizing groups and communities and forcing a taking of sides.

Paranoia and catastrophizing can also be seen, if you wait and watch. 'If we do not practice this tradition or observe this ritual, we will be doomed' will be their shrill cry. And if the inexorable forces of change sweep their beliefs aside, they are likely to be embittered, cynical and reactive (which is counter to their normal 'responsive' orientation). And in a location of not being open to change that happens around, they may even become anachronistic.

A rock in the midst of rolling stones—at one level—can be a positive symbol denoting a force that helps manage continuity, and the same can equally be seen as a symbol of 'clinging on' or 'stony rootedness'—when we look at it in the context of the overdone Custodian.

If the custodian is underdone, there may exist a certain undervaluing of 'where you come from', perhaps even a narcissistic overvaluing of oneself, as though one comes from nowhere and has no history.

There may also exist an absence of feeling rooted, of being somehow transient and ephemeral like a bubble, without an acknowledgement of belonging to something that is more enduring and perhaps larger than one's immediate context. Archetypes are ignored in the search for the latest accessories for living, but that does not make them go away though!

Angst	Hope	Gifts	Fear/ Vulnerability
That no matter what, there *will* be change and things of value will disappear and that I have to fight a lone battle standing for what I believe in	That the ethos of institutions can be preserved and traditions continued	The ability to value origins and history. The tenacity to stand up if what I stand for is repressed or threatened	What if all that I have stood for is lost, washed away? What if we are overrun by fads and undiscerned diversity

The Custodians as Leaders in Organizations

- Custodian–leaders would help maintain time-tested traditions and practices to manage continuity for the system.
- They would enlist other people to all be upholders of the essential order of the system.
- In this, they would strongly believe that certain 'core' practices/traditions are not available for change and will watch out to see whether any advocated change is prudent, even if inevitable.
- To aid and support system growth, this leader may meaningfully recontextualize traditions and conventions without destroying their character/essence.
- At times, they may appear dogmatic and potentially avoid dialogues around what they may consider as 'holy cows', thus keeping the system engaged in some ritualism and stasis.

14

The Guide–Mentor

I am not a teacher, but an awakener.

—Robert Frost

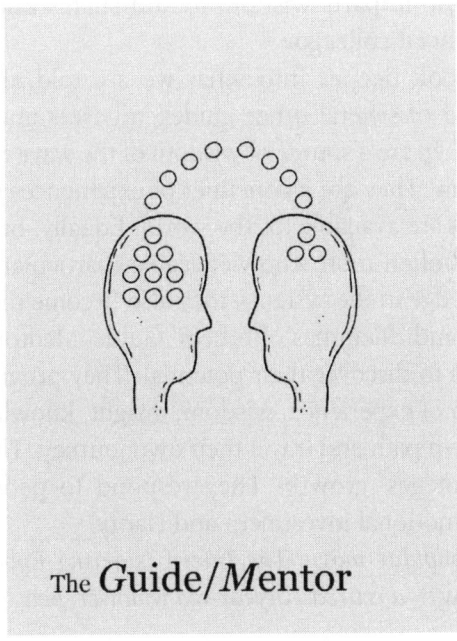

The *Guide/Mentor*

Who Is the Guide–Mentor?

Any thought of the Guide or the Mentor and one of the characters that comes to mind is Vidura, the Wise One, from the great epic Mahabharata. Vidura was a respected adviser of the Pandavas. *Vidura-niti*, or Vidura's Statecraft, narrated in the form of a dialogue between Vidura and King Dhritarashtra, is considered the precursor in some ways of *Chanakya Niti*, which is another collection of aphorisms for statecraft for rulers.

In Homer's *Odyssey*, Mentor was a friend of Odysseus who placed Mentor in charge of his son Telemachus when he left for the Trojan War. When Athena visited Telemachus, she took the disguise of Mentor to hide herself from the suitors of Telemachus' mother Penelope. As Mentor, the goddess encouraged Telemachus to stand up against the suitors and go abroad to find out what happened to his father. Because of Mentor's relationship with Telemachus, and the disguised Athena's encouragement and practical plans for dealing with personal dilemmas, the personal name *Mentor* has been adopted in English as a term meaning someone who imparts wisdom to and shares knowledge with a less experienced colleague.

If we look deeper into what we are told about Vidura or Mentor, and of several other guides, advisors and overseers, we know that they are a source of wisdom of the ways of the world and of the system. They are a container of experiences and assimilated insights that are available for the world. Equally, being more experienced and often more knowledgeable (particularly knowing the tacit knowledge in the system), they also become the containers for the doubts and dilemmas of others. Guide–Mentors guide people and systems to discover their potential. They provide illumination (in the form of experience, wisdom, insight, knowledge) as people find their own path and travel their own journey. They are invested in their protégés' growth. They respond to people's needs for guidance, emotional investment and clarity.

In the popular movie The Intern (starring Robert DeNiro and Anne Hathawy), a retired 70-year-old widower, Ben (played by Robert

De Niro), is bored with retired life. He applies to be a senior intern at an online fashion retailer and gets the position. The founder of the company is Jules Ostin (Anne Hathaway), a tireless, driven, demanding, dynamic workaholic. Ben is made her intern, but this is a nominal role—she does not intend to give him work and it is just window dressing. However, Ben proves to be quite useful and, more than that, a source of support and wisdom. From starting as an intern, he becomes her Guide–Mentor!

In the world, Guide–Mentors may not be so universal and for all. They may tend to be Guide–Mentors selectively, for people they believe they can invest in and would take their investment forward in life meaningfully and add to it.

What do they look and feel like? Let us look to some illustrative examples. Gandalf from the *Lord of the Rings*, Dumbledore from *Harry Potter*, Yoda from *Star Wars*, Master Shifu from *Kung Fu Panda*—all from recent cinema come to mind. In the Hero monomyth as popularized by Joseph Campbell (and on which basis several movies are unfailingly made), the Guide or the Mentor is a critical part of the journey of the Hero. 'The Buddha' is another powerful symbol of this identity. This may also be a point to distinguish the Sage and the Guru from the Guide–Mentor as we have introduced them. The Sage is often personally on a quest to seek the truth himself. He may not provide direction so much as to say 'Come join me, let's figure out together'. The Guru is more like a teacher. Not necessarily one who teaches in a class but one who has an agenda to help the seeker learn knowledge or skills or necessary attitudes.

Says Karan of his music guru—'I never learnt from him as much inside a class. But he would invite me to come for his concerts, to travel widely with him. And I did all that—for days on end I would travel with him; watching him play in concerts gave me learning of knowledge and skills and watching him conduct himself in the circles that he moved in gave me invaluable learning about the attitudes necessary for a musician. Conversations with him helped me acquire new perspectives and challenge my own'. And so, some Gurus and Sages might be Guide–Mentors but not necessarily all and vice versa of course.

The Guide–Mentor's effect on any system or on a person can be life changing. The first thing that they would generate is confidence and encouragement in the protégé for the task at hand. Guide–Mentors enhance the implicit and tacit knowledge in any system as much as they would the explicit and open knowledge. They know deep down that access to and use of tacit knowledge are what make a great 'hero' or a great system. And they choose where to share this. In doing this, they also provide a thread of temporal continuity in the system.

They also keep alive the culture of the system for the pro-tégés to make sense of and to adapt to. You might say that the Custodian identity also keeps culture alive, would not you? Well, the distinguishing thing with the Guide–Mentor is that they would offer learning about the culture in a more dynamic way than the Custodian. For example, they would not 'give' the culture on a platter, instead ask the protégé to 'figure it out' through mini-assignments and learning tasks of different kinds. Under good guide–mentors, protégés get a safe space, a sense of support and a forum to voice concerns. They can take their dilemmas to the Guide–Mentor and hope to receive perspectives they can then work with. They would feel invested in and important to the system. Net result—the invested protégé grows AND with them, the whole system becomes more capable. In fact, it is a truism that the presence of excellent Guide–Mentors is what makes some organizations and communities manage knowledge better than others.

Aubrey and Cohen have a good framework to illustrate the typical behaviours of a Guide–Mentor. According to them, Guide–Mentors 'accompany', 'sow', 'catalyse', 'show' and 'harvest'.

Guide–Mentors are quick to 'meet and greet' those they spot as talent and then accompany them to facilitate their understanding of the system—such accompanying can be physical or virtual (*Lalgudi Jayaraman, the violin maestro of yesteryears in Karnatik music, used to spot budding talent in young musicians and actually 'accompany' them by playing the violin support for them in concerts to show the world that new talent had arrived and had the stamp of Lalgudi's approval!*). They would then 'sow' seeds of the system's cultural traditions and practices or seeds of desired behaviour in these new protégés. Having done that, like a good gardener, they would 'catalyse' their growth by fostering them and giving them sparks of challenge, support, affirmation and exposure. They would 'show' their protégés to critical others in the system to get them noticed (*a la Lalgudi, described above*) and 'harvest' their talent for the system's benefit.

Guide–Mentors are typically good at asking provocative questions of their protégés—get them to think differently so they will learn to act in ways that are good for the system—that is their mantra. They let their protégés know that they are present and available for them, when they seek them. In many fairy tales, the Guide–Mentor could be summoned at the Hero's will by doing some symbolic action like rubbing a stone or making a special ritual wish! In these tales, the 'Use by' date of the Guide–Mentor is usually unmistakable—'You can summon me but thrice and no more' or 'Choose wisely, young Hero, for I will be available for you till the winter moon'—typical statements from such tales which point to an important feature of the Guide–Mentor—that their psychological agenda is to foster support but to not breed dependence!

They are the go-to person for counsel on a wide variety of issues—advice on how things were handled in the past—what worked and what did not. They may also provide invaluable 'connections' not discernible otherwise (not only people connections but perhaps also in the form of opportunities and tangible directions). They would nudge the protégé towards a path and, quite interestingly, would deploy three orientations—breadth, depth and height (either individually or in a combo). Let us look at some illustrative examples of each orientation from what a Guide–Mentor may be telling a protégé in, let us say, a corporate organization:

Breadth: 'Here are what you could do about this problem—have you spoken to anyone from Finance about this? What is HR's view? What does the MD think? When will you find out?'

Depth: 'Perhaps, if you dig a little deeper, you may unearth something interesting about this—what do you think? What could you do to research this more? Get to the bottom of it?'

Height: 'Ok, so you do this—exercise option 1, where will that take you? What will it achieve for you? For your team? For the organization? And how good is that? What new possibilities could emerge from this option?'

We must also bear in mind that the Guide–Mentors are not merely agents of dynamic worlds. Their agenda is not to move the protégé towards the world of autonomy and initiative (WAI) or world of flow and unfolding (WFU) only. If a protégé is over-engaged in WAI, it is quite conceivable that the Guide–Mentor may suggest interventions in the WCN for them, for example, and similarly, if a protégé is entrenched in WFU, a Guide–Mentor may invite them to experiment with some WSO immersion. Assimilative growth is perhaps what the Guide–Mentor would work towards for the protégé and not just linear growth—transcendence AND immanence, striving AND abiding—the operative being the experience of the AND.

Typical verbs and actions you could associate with Guide–Mentors are—asks questions, challenges, stretches and encourages; provides space for the mentee to voice dilemmas and confusions and enquires; promotes inquiry, coaches, offers wisdom/experience and perspectives; and expands boundaries of thought, action and spirit. Where do you find them and how do you spot them? Like we have said, they are the 'go-to's—who people gravitate to when in need of counsel or a 'talk-to'. They are also the ones that people in a system point to or direct one to ('Ah, have you spoken with Kshitij Desai about this? Go to him, and I can tell you that you won't have this dilemma any longer' is a kind of statement to illustrate this). From mythology, we learn that there are both the 'ever-present guide' (they are by your side and you do not have to search them out) and the 'guide-who-appears-when-needed' (this guide comes to you when you need them the most, when all seems bleak and hopeless—perhaps like Gandalf the White in the *Lord of the Rings*).

We believe that Guide–Mentors would tune their approach to the need and the level of intensity of search of the protégé. At one end, they may just provide *expertise* (not necessarily functional expertise but expertise of the organization and the system). Typical statements here may be of the nature of 'This is what this organization is about' or 'Meet X to get insights into this dilemma'. Another step and you see the Guide–Mentor who provided *exploration* help. They would ask challenging/provoking questions, often triggering insight generation for the protégé. Examples would be—'Why do you think this is occurring repeatedly in the organization', or 'How do YOU think this ought to be addressed?' The third possibility is the *experiencing* Guide–Mentor who would say, 'Hey, why don't you and I go together and dig around a bit to see what might be happening'—in this step, the Guide–Mentor actively works with the protégé as a companion. If we look at this another way, Guide–Mentors may, at the basic level, help their protégés work with their tasks and/or their goals. At another level, they may help the protégé work with their vision (vision clarification, mission sussing out and so on), and at yet another level, they might just help the protégé with their dreams. It may also be noted that often Guide–Mentors operate from 'first principles'— boiling things down to the most fundamental axioms/positions and helping the other reason from there. Thus, a Guide–Mentor can even be a teacher at one level.

In Parampara Creative Arts Foundation, Bangalore, Savitha is the quintessential Guide–Mentor for her more-than-forty students who learn Karnatik Music from her. She knows each of her students like the back of her hand. And while she conducts her lessons in batches, she also attends to each person's unique needs very carefully. She sees her role not only as a teacher of the art form but also as a psychopomp to guide her students to appreciate the aesthetic elements of beauty in the art. 'I study with my students' is very simply how she sums up her approach which reflects the 'experiencing' Guide–Mentor.

What Is Their Inner World Like?

Murali was the Asia-Pacific Head of the Global Software Operations of a telecommunications MNC. One of his erstwhile colleagues, Kevin, once approached him for some counsel. Kevin used to work with Murali, but had moved on to another company. And now Murali's HR team was trying to headhunt Kevin back into Murali's company.

Murali agreed to meet Kevin privately since Kevin wanted Murali's time as an informal guide and sounding board. In the conversation, Kevin shared his dilemma of not wanting to go back to an organization that he had left years ago yet feeling the pull of a good role there AND simultaneously feeling the pull of setting up his own freelance consulting entity. Murali ended up counselling Kevin to go off on his own and not join the company! Murali shared later, 'When he approached me as a guide, it was not about my company, it was all about what is right for Kevin and his life. So, I am totally convinced about what I did even though as a company we lost a talent opportunity...'. This about sums up the basic desire of the Guide–Mentor, *the desire to be in service of the protégé in their context.* The desire of the Guide–Mentor is to seed growth, to enable blossoming. And their pride is in seeing the protégé come into their own!

The Guide–Mentors come with a nuanced understanding of the inner workings of the system as well as of the protégé. Their understanding of the wiring of the system comes largely from insights they have personally obtained and assimilated over time, to be offered at the appropriate time to other deserving people. This also implies that they have a deeper gift for contemplation and self-reflection. The Guide–Mentor is also capable of working towards helping the protégés generate insights for themselves from their experiences. Their nuanced understanding of the protégé's mind helps them decide where to pitch their support—breadth, depth, height or a combination thereof. In addition to these, the other gifts they have are their ability to believe and invest in another, patience and being with someone on their path.

One of the apprehensions of the Guide–Mentors, especially if they are entrenched in this identity would be, is—will my protégé one day be better than me? There are numerous stories of great and wise godfathers who could not bear to see their wards coming of age. They would do many things to maintain their own significance and the status of their protégés as dependent children. Growth of the protégé would sometimes be punished (wings clipped or put in situations where they would be shamed somehow), sometimes ignored and very often these would lead to such capable and 'now grown-up' protégés departing from the Guide–Mentor and striking off on their own. Such Guide–Mentors perhaps seek eternal beholdenness (just gratitude will not do for them, if you please) and become bitter and wallow in hurt pride and sorrow when they do not get it.

One of the defensive ploys of such Guide–Mentors is to somehow co-opt their protégés into their work projects or into their life itself. Cope with their fear by neutralizing the protégé by giving them a certain status, centrality and significance. Fear of abandonment, betrayal and desertion by the protégé are related to this theme and the root of that would seem to be 'with the protégé growing up, my identity as a Guide–Mentor and the status associated with that would no longer exist and that, I cannot bear'. And if the protégé sees through the co-option efforts and evades it, the Guide–Mentor's fear might give way to anger—distancing, speaking ill of, retaliation, spreading canards about—the list can go on. This is perhaps the core psychodrama of the Guide–Mentor in the grip of fear.

A resonant identity on the other side for the Guide–Mentor is the student, the seeker and the apprentice. The student and the apprentice seek to learn, and the seeker searches for the truth. In addition, you also have the 'newbie' in the system who searches for direction. Now before you move away from this thread, let us also remind you—the warrior–crusader, another identity that you will encounter in this book, also often seeks a Guide–Mentor—for challenge and support on their quest, perhaps.

The Guide–Mentor in the Extremes

The know-it-all and the overbearing advisor and perhaps the unsought free-advice spinner would perhaps be the deeply entrenched Guide–Mentor. Such are also likely to be similar to blowhards or backseat drivers. Grima Wormtongue of *Lord of the Rings* comes to mind as an example.

Sometimes Guide–Mentors do not reveal themselves fully and underplay themselves if they apprehend an extractive process that is out to get what they have. Further, if a system does not have good Guide–Mentors or has underdone Guide–Mentors, it might end up suffering from 'temporal blindness' of the past—forever in the here and now and without possibilities of assimilating any wisdom from the past. In other words, when the Guide–Mentor is low in a person or system, we might get to see an inability or difficulty in asking the important questions that give direction, knowledge and wisdom. Mistakes and errors might get made over and over again, with the system progressively becoming more and more myopic.

Angst	Hope	Gifts	Fear/ Vulnerability
That people and systems never truly recognize and do justice to their potential. That systems fail in passing on worthwhile guidance and direction	That I may be of service to the other in their context	Nuanced understanding of the person and the context and willingness to invest in the other	Of losing credibility and relevance

The Guide–Mentor
as a Leader in Organizations

- The Guide–Mentor would operate from a dictum that their primary task is to help their team members grow and become 'better' and more capable, more agile, more resilient.
- They would help others (especially new members) to settle into their roles, learn how to execute their role responsibilities and be accountable to the system.
- They would spot potential and talent in people and guide them to realize the same.
- They would provide appropriate advice and caution (especially insights on likely obstacles/derailers), helping protégés in sculpting the change in the system/derailers.
- They would provide support, encouragement and advice particularly to the 'vital few' who are driving growth in the system; some Guides–Mentors place personal bets in selecting the vital few.
- At times, they may end up being seen as an 'advisor'— whose own vulnerabilities appear masked. Some may even see them as patronizing.

15

The Healer

Let your heart sing from those wounded places.
When you sing your song with everything you've got,
it will not only heal you, but it will heal all of us through you.

—Gemma B. Benton, Then She Sang a Willow Song:
Reclaiming Life and Power with the Ancestors

The *Healer*

Who Is the Healer?

The etymology of healing takes us to the idea of 'making something whole' and to 'restore to well-being'. It is perhaps harder to talk or write about Healers than to viscerally experience their touch and its impact. And we are not talking only about the physical realm here. The Healers are ones whose touch feels deeply nurturing and caring. They actively engage with toxicity in people and in systems and strive to restore them to health and well-being. At their hearts, Healers know that pain and sorrow may exist in the world but suffering does not have to—that it is really a choice. They are concerned about the deterioration in the quality of life of any person of system and their mission is to do something about it.

They are all around us, even though they may themselves feel rather lonely, as we describe for you below. Many therapists are good Healers, helping people enhance their quality of life, in an unbiased and supportive way—they bring in authenticity, empathy and non-judgemental guidance. They may help others find inner strength and the courage to confront issues that hurt or render them dysfunctional. We may have heard the term 'Good Samaritan'—from biblical origin, a term that refers to one who gratuitously offers their help to others in distress. Mother Teresa comes to mind as a Good Samaritan, as does Kailash Satyarthi and perhaps Albert Schweitzer—the first two of these won the Nobel Peace Prize for their unmatched humanitarian efforts. At another level, people deeply concerned with ecology (whether of the earth or of the ecology of human living) often tend to be Healers too. We offer here two examples with a caution that while they are Healers, we will see other identities like the Warrior–Crusader, or the Artiste, also coming alive in their stories.

An example of a dear friend of ours Seetha Ananthasivan, the Founder Trustee of Bhoomi College and Prakriya Green Wisdom School, Bangalore, is an eco-healer at heart. She has a deep interest in understanding how we can build and restore communities which are coherent with nature's principles. She is passionate about the development of ecopsychology as well as organic food and farming.

Another space is the institution of Sumedhas—Academy of Human Context. In stating their purpose, Sumedhas writes— 'The purpose, at a basic, granular level in all Sumedhas offerings is to provide an opportunity for people from different walks of life to take a pause and reflect upon themselves, their relationships, their roles in the different systems—family, organizations, institutions, communities, society and nation—to which they belong to. Yet, this focus on self-reflexivity and the primacy of dialogue is not just a tool for transforming our individual selves and our relationships. In becoming aware of the different parts of ourselves and discovering the possibility for integration of these parts at a personal level, we also become aware of how we participate in creating the world around us'.

Restorative work is another face of the Healer. Have you seen how conservation and restoration of archaeological sites happen? The diligence, the care, the focused attention and the concern to get the structure back to how it was (or at least as close) are all typical of the drive of the Healer. So too is the shaman, the much-misunderstood practitioners who practise reaching altered states of consciousness in order to perceive and interact with a 'spirit world' and channel those transcendental energies into this world, mostly for healing others, be they individuals or communities.

We must also note that Healers work simultaneously at several levels where hurt exists—it could be physical (as in an injury to the body that a doctor may work with), mental (imagine an argument that has led to bitter accusations and name-calling and so on and then sitting down to address what may have gone wrong), emotional (deep hurt that a counsellor or therapist may work with) or spiritual (where shamans typically help).

What is the impact of the Healer? Healers are, as we have read, likely to be generous and go out of their way to help others who may be in distress. They would be involved in others' lives, in a compassionate, caring and nurturing way; thus, in their watch, people and systems become wholesome and healthy and exude a sense of well-being. In turn, this could bolster their ability to expand and grow, and also make them more resilient. Thus, the Healer is in effect a capability builder as well. In the presence of the Healers, 'ease' in the system goes up because the Healers combat disease—they seek out things that corrode the system from within and bring things back to wholesome balance. We are reminded here of Ayurveda—as a system, it is about healing and not about treating/suppressing symptoms of ill health like allopathy. Thus, the Healer also has the impact of being a 'balance restorer'. Healers—in their cathartic function—address toxicity, strife and pain, and give space to the entity for dissolving blocks, and thus move towards enhanced quality of self-expression. Have you been in the presence of one who says gently, 'It is ok to cry, do let it all out' and thus helps you free yourself to find flow for your suppressed emotions? THAT is a Healer in action—the Healer who also courageously goes over and faces the pathologies of the world.

Healers are, first and foremost, great (not just good) listeners. They listen from a deep location of care and concern and thus go far beyond the words and palpable expressions (including tone of voice, body language and so on) of the other to be able to touch the subliminal messages that do not find reviewable expression. Through their deep listening, they provide support to the other, a shoulder to lean on. You would see them as being available to people during difficult times. They would allow and even encourage people to vent their frustrations and air their feelings. Sometimes they even absorb barbs hurled at others. 'Absorbing and softening the emotional pain', as a landmark article in the *Harvard Business Review* puts it. Healers suggest solutions, and they work behind the scenes to reduce pain or suffering. When a semiconductor giant decided to let go of a sizeable number of people in one of its businesses in its India site, the then HR director spent days on end individually meeting people who would be losing their jobs, meeting their colleagues who were likely to stay on and meeting their managers who were feeling impotent and helpless.

His act was like that of a man possessed, and he did not rest till every last person was individually spoken to by him, and his act did serve to lessen the inevitable agony of a painful business action. In fact, it led to a number of people continuing to repose faith in the organization and then be able to be hiring ambassadors for the organization when better days returned in their businesses.

You will see Healers wherever pain is experienced. Nurses in hospices, a friend who turns up or calls unerringly in your moment of need, a tree-hugger protesting tree felling, therapists, counsellors, reiki masters, life coaches and shamans—good Healers abound. You will also see them walking along with the disenfranchised and the oppressed. Unlike the Warrior–Crusader who may bring the plight of such oppressed to light and battle the oppressors, the Healers would be in the hamlets, the hovels, the houses where the victims lie with no hope and speak words in soothing tones to them and in this they are like the balm that reduces the pain before going deeper to make the person more resilient in facing continuing oppression.

The Healer may appear to be reflective and introspective in their persona. They would also be attentive persons, ever on the lookout for where 'illness' and dis-ease or un-ease exists. Compassion and empathy are their watchwords. They are usually rather adaptable and patient—they know that making things whole is not a quick fix, and that they need time on their side. They may have an aura of tranquillity about them, but deep within they are indeed a cauldron of passion and emotions.

Healers care deeply about causes that interest them, and they often pursue those causes with selfless devotion. What distinguishes them from Warrior–Crusaders, who we have alluded to earlier and who we will encounter later in this book, is (a) that the Healer approaches her cause from an essentially feminine orientation and (b) that most of their causes would have a humanistic angle and concern for sentience and ecology. Healers have the feminine quality of expression, reaching deep within, getting in touch with their passion and expressing it, especially where the cause is in danger. Gandhiji's role in soothing the communal tensions during the Noakhali riots in 1946 has been widely documented and is an example of this quality.

We mentioned empathy a little earlier, did we not? Well, the authentic Healer's empathy would have a quality of being non-collusive. What we mean by this is that in the name of empathy, Healers are not likely to dress and serve up dollops of sympathy, pity or lip service. Their love would also include tough love, calling out the other's contribution to what they describe to Healers as the cause out there that is causing them so much grief. 'What about the cause inside you?', they are likely to unflinchingly ask, while equally not dismissing the lament of the remedy seeker. They also have this knack for finding out almost presciently as to where issues are likely to arise, needing their intervention.

The Healer will be drawn to problems where they think there is some sort of suffering or incompleteness. Their approach will be to solve the problem gently without causing any real disturbance or threat to another. Healers will be clued in, or intuitively aware of where fissures may occur, where the fault lines are and will ensure they are watched and maintained so they do not crack and cause grief.

What Is Their Inner World Like?

One view of the inner working of the Healer, and maybe we can call this the 'expansive' view, is that of a passionate seeker of an intimate connection with something larger than themselves and larger than us, beyond our actions, thoughts and emotions. Some call it 'spirit', some call it the 'divine'—we can never be sure which but one thing we can be sure of—such Healers hold a deep desire for moving themselves and others towards that 'something beyond'.

A great example of this is the Timbaktu Collective, a registered not-for-profit organization that works for sustainable development in the drought-prone Anantapur district of Andhra Pradesh (AP), India.

The Collective works with those affected by chronic drought, unproductive land, unemployment and poor infrastructural facilities in the region—among them the landless, small and marginal farmers with special emphasis on women, children, youth and Dalits.

Bablu Ganguly, one of the founders of the Timbaktu Collective, is an 'expansive' healer who had a vision of helping rural communities take control of their own lives, govern themselves and live in social, gender and ecological harmony while maintaining a sustainable lifestyle. The Healer in the Collective's work is particularly evident in how they restored ecological wastelands of that district to sustainable farmlands. The forests around Timbaktu were not what they are today. There were barely any trees in Timbaktu or the hills that surround it. The soil in the area was highly degraded, calcified and compacted making it difficult for anything to grow. This combined with very low rainfall made it a challenge and an opportunity to demonstrate, to the people in the area, what concerted conservation efforts can do. The Collective adopted the approach of natural regeneration with minimal interference, a 'permaculture' philosophy. This involved protecting the area from too much human interference while allowing the ecosystem to repair itself. Glimpse the visionary healer here?

Our second hypothesis is that some Healers seek an internal healing for themselves. We may call these as 'self-restorative' Healers. 'By healing others, I heal myself' may be their theme. An example of this could be Lady Diana, once the Princess of Wales. Her story is well documented and the Healer in her includes her deep connection with support for HIV/AIDS patients, cancer treatment, leprosy treatment and care for the homeless. Equally well documented is her own pain of growing up, the disappointment of her marriage and the pathos of a parrot in a gilded cage.

A true Healer is a vessel, a container for the 'unbearables' of the other, which is no small task in itself. No matter what the orientation, whether expansive or self-restorative, the inner world of the Healer involves walking the path of pathos and being comfortable in its company. This may involve *actively choosing to* work with the intensely personal pathos of another, of a community's (or system's) pathos and of course, the universal pathos—the pathos of the whole humankind.

While on this, we would like to offer what we believe are two important points to note:

1. Just because one feels oppressed or is suffering, or sees the oppression or the suffering of others, does not make them a Healer automatically. Authentic Healers have an inner drive *to do something about* that oppression or suffering and often discover early in their lives that their very presence often helps those in pain.

2. This 'doing something about' can take myriad forms, not necessarily involving physical touch or body language resonance, or paraphrasing and so on. Abhay Phadnis, a process consultant, offers a healing experience just by reciting appropriate Urdu couplets that capture the essence of the experience that the other is going through, and very often these evocative couplets also contain a seed of action for an entire new future to emerge for the protagonist in suffering.

In walking this path, the Healer intuitively follows an inner compass—consisting of two gifts—the one of being able to sense where fragmentation and suffering exist and the other of being able to visualize patterns of health and wholeness. They are the holders of the power of touch. The ability to look within and around them for resources that may aid the healing effort is also perhaps innate to them. This quote from Albert Schweitzer may illustrate—'In everyone's life, at some time, our inner fire goes out. It is then burst into flame by an encounter with another human being. We should all be thankful for those people who rekindle the inner spirit'—these 're-kindlers' of the inner spirit are the Healers who know and use their gifts well.

What of the fears and sorrows of the Healer? In the 2017 release *Logan* of the *X-Men* series, we find Wolverine, the auto-healer who could heal himself back from any injury, with diminished powers and not being able to heal as well as he could earlier. The popular theory behind this development in the series is that Wolverine has inside his body the element Adamantium which gives him the amazing healing power but also poisons him from the inside. This may clue us to one of the likely fears of the Healer—'what if my ability to heal diminishes, what if I cannot heal anymore, what if all the suffering that I work with numbs and anaesthetizes me?' Feeling resourceless and helpless in the wake of relentless hurt and suffering is another worry that might plague them. 'No matter what I do, does it really matter? Will the world ever change?' goes this lament. In a way, if the Healer and Warrior–Crusader can go hand in hand in a person, this worry might abate, but that is not always the case. The other side of the fear is anger—that there are people, systems, structures and inevitabilities that are rapacious, plundering and hurtful (even if they do not mean it)—anger that their healing will not suffice, ever. And going beyond their fears, anger and worries, the inner cry of the Healer may be 'who is there for me, when I am so selflessly there for the other'. And when they do not find an echo or response, they often turn to stoicism.

For the resonant activation of the Healer identity, on the other side, we would need the victim, the needy, the wounded, the marginalized, the oppressed, the impoverished and the succour seekers. One of the downsides of the Healer's identity is that it often leads to what systems psychodynamics would call as 'basic assumption dependency'—where the Healers get set up as 'saviours' of sorts. They are idealized. And if they do not live up to expectations, they are denigrated with equal alacrity. Says Joyce Chinnamma, who runs a shelter for the aged and homeless, 'When I sometimes take people in my shelter, there is immense gratitude and I am blessed for my selflessness. But at times, if I request my inmates to share some belongings, or make space for a new person, or help me here and there, I am met with rebuke and malevolence'.

The Healer in the Extremes

A boundaryless Healer, looking to heal everyone all the time, can have a cloying effect. They perpetuate the basic assumption dependency stated above. Behind this version of the overdone, Healers may be of the view that essentially the other is *always* unwhole, unwell and a perpetual victim needing their touch. When they thus occupy the space of the others as much, they lose touch with what it may mean to be comfortable in their own space, in their own skin. All meaning and purpose come from the sorrow of others and thus a fantasyland is created and occupied.

The other, a perhaps macabre version, is the Healer as the captor. The miserable price extracted for providing a healing experience is that the other remains captive or beholden forever to this Healer. We need to go no further than Stephen King's much acclaimed book *Misery* to encounter Annie Wilkes. In the book, the protagonist Paul Sheldon is a best-selling author who just ended his popular series of romance/adventure novels by killing off the lead character, Misery Chastain. After finishing a new novel at a Colorado resort, Paul has a car accident and awakes to find that his legs have been shattered but that he has been saved by his self-proclaimed number one fan, Annie Wilkes. Unfortunately, Annie (who is a nurse, a Healer if you will) turns out to be more than just a little crazy, and when she learns that Paul killed Misery in the latest book, she demands that he write a new one that brings back her favourite character. Held captive by a madwoman, Paul is almost helpless to resist the physical and psychological tortures she uses to get her way while insisting that it is really for his own good.

Hurt, wounds and pain are essential parts of the human experience, whether it is physical, emotional or spiritual. When the Healer energy is absent, we will not know how to heal and restore. Sure, we may manage it, find a way around it, get stuck with it but never truly address it and work through it. People and systems will not find a space for catharsis and rebuilding or for rest and restoration. Wounds and hurts fester, they may even continue to grow and corrode the system.

Angst	Hope	Gifts	Fear/ Vulnerability
No matter what, there will always be strife, fragmentation, hurt, violence and suffering in the world	That there will be a space beyond, where we will find harmony, health and universal well-being	Of touching and ameliorating pain	Of feeling numb, anaesthetized and loss of healing touch

The Healer as a Leader in Organizations

- The Healer-leader is first and foremost a leader in the realm of people and relationships.
- When it comes to execution and task achievement, Healers would spot actual or potential toxicity or distress and would step in to help and thus enable delivery to happen.
- They would provide touch with compassion and empathy, spot conflicts and like to help resolve them. They are great leaders to have when teams are in the 'storming' stage of their existence.
- When it comes to leading change—when disruptive change brings collateral emotional damage in its wake, they would provide restorative touch and support and for people experiencing such change.
- At times, they may not hold the needed emotional/ 'affect' boundaries and thus may compromise their own well-being. They may also have a tendency to be distressed by what they may consider as divisiveness or fragmentation.

16

The Mother

Children are the anchors that hold a mother to life.

—Sophocles

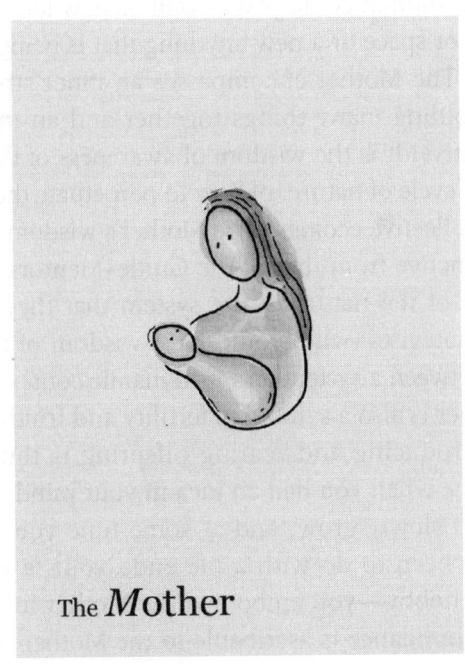

The *Mother*

Who Is the Mother?

If we look to popular films and scan the Mother identity and its characterization, we can get several interesting glimpses. Consider Sybil Stone in *The Family Stone*; she is the strong-willed bohemian matriarch and the glue that holds the family together; Mrs. Gump in *Forrest Gump*, who loves her son unconditionally; or Peg Boggs in *Edward Scissorhands*—a lovely and kind person who believes in everyone having a fair go at life, who tries her best to make her family happy and make situations seem not as bad as they originally were; Sarah Connor in *The Terminator*, who fights to protect her son even before he is born. The Mother is the glue, the love giver, the happiness provider and the fighter. Of course, there is more—so let us move into a character sketch of this identity.

The Mother is one who brings a being to life. She is the ground of being from which life emerges, the womb that contains, nurtures, supports, nourishes and allows a being to grow. And the children she gives birth to are not necessarily all human beings. The Mother's children could just as well be new ideas, a project, a new territory or space or a new anything that is being birthed and given life to. The Mother encompasses an inner strength that is capable of holding many things together and an inner wisdom that is distinctive. It is the wisdom of awareness of the inexorable and rhythmic cycle of nature, of how to perpetuate the species and survive as a collective ecology. The Mother's wisdom as portrayed above is distinctive from that of the Guide–Mentors (who would have wisdom of the nature of the system that they are part of) and of the Strategists (who would have wisdom of the nature of relatedness between a system and its dynamic context).

The Mother is also a symbol of fertility and fruitfulness. A gift of bearing, producing and rearing offspring is thus indicated. Think of a time when you had an idea in your mind, you allowed it to exist and slowly grow, and at some time you materialized it—may have been to do with a life endeavour, a work project or a personal hobby—you embodied the Mother in this process. A quality of abundance is ascribable to the Mother—a quality of being conducive to an abundant yield, of being prolific and fecund. Perhaps the Mother offers the uterus of the fertile ground in which the Artiste, the Curious Child, the Warlord, the Warrior–Crusader and the Strategist can come together to create. No wonder then that the Mother is often identified with the Earth—the visible and tangible 'ground' of creation!

Samkhya philosophy talks of the Mother archetype as 'Prakriti', which has three characteristics or gunas—sattva, rajas and tamas. According to Jung, 'These are three essential aspects of the Mother: her cherishing and nourishing goodness, her orgiastic emotionality, and her Stygian depths'. Sattva is that aspect of the 'Divine Mother' that is invoked as Goddess Saraswati. According to the Bhagavad Gita, sattva binds (the glue function referenced earlier) by attachment to 'happiness' and knowledge; it is luminous. Rajas is that aspect of the Divine Mother invoked as Goddess Lakshmi. The very nature of rajas is activity and passion. Tamas is the Divine Mother who is invoked as Goddess Kali. Tamas, according to the Gita, has qualities of imbalance, destruction, heedlessness and lack of discrimination, as some examples. There is a word often used in the parlance of Tamil Brahmin families in South India—a Sanskrit word called 'ajnyaanam', a tamasic quality born of ignorance and delusion—often used with the Mother who would forgive all that her errant son does because of her undiscerning attachment to the son.

In several cross-generational families in India, we find the Mother identity in the patriarch or matriarch who holds the thread of the family together—no function in the family is ever held without their benevolent presence, they are often visited by relatives and the neighbours—not necessarily for their advice or wisdom but just for the joy of their benign presence. Somewhat related—this identity may also be the moralistic matriarch and homemaker who takes care of the family and also of family's problems with good humour—à la Marge Simpson in *The Simpsons*.

The Mother is also to be found in the idea of 'commune living' like Auroville, the first and only internationally endorsed ongoing experiment in human unity and transformation of consciousness, also concerned with—and practically researching into—sustainable living and the future cultural, environmental, social and spiritual needs of mankind or in organizations like Pipal Tree and Bhoomi College, which strive to create 'a symbiosis of the personal, social and ecological'.

The Mother identity is also ascribed to the Earth in the form of Gaia, the ancestral Mother of all life, the primal Mother Earth goddess. In several Bollywood films, we come across the self-sacrificing and caregiver Mother (mostly played with aplomb by actor Nirupa Roy in the past). And, we may also see the wish-fulfilling Mother in the fairy godmother in *Cinderella*.

The identity of the Mother would impart life to things. There would be an experience of tenderness for the other in experiencing the Mother—the Mother would offer love and care, encouragement and emotional infrastructure. The Mother is often the first teacher, giver of safety and security, touch and a sense of belonging. Her teaching is different than that of the Guide–Mentor in that she teaches basic life skills—what to do to survive and learn to experience autonomy. (Have you seen a Mother Hen crossing a road with her chicks?) The Mother's engagement comes from a deep sense of ownership that can go deeper than the Guide–Mentor or any other teacher. Systems would experience touch and nourishment from her. Failure would be encouraged with the understanding that she would provide the learning that comes from the sting of such failure. Life lessons around intimacy, relationship and love are typically infused by the Mother. In the Mother's caretaking, life is created, and physical, mental and emotional sustenance is offered and is distinctly different from how a custodian would manifest the same. Without the Mother's fostering and care, things would be dry and lifeless—as you can see, the Mother infuses life.

You may have heard the term 'maternal solicitude'—to do with the great concern, thoughtful attentiveness and 'hovering around' that is received from the Mother. One clear example of how this plays out comes from one of our coachees, Raman.

Raman had accepted an offer and was to join the Q Mean Company as an HR Director in a month. He had quit his previous job

and was taking some time off before joining Q-Mean. In the meantime,
the leadership team of Q-Mean was having their annual leaders' offsite
to work on issues of trust and planning for 2018. While Raman had not
formally joined, his new boss-to-be, the MD of Q Mean, Amar, invited
Raman to the offsite. Throughout the offsite, Amar found every moment
that he could, to sit down with Raman and ask him how he was
experiencing the team, what he thought of the issues, how Raman
was feeling and what he as the boss could do to ease Raman's entry
even more. Right from the invitation to Raman to experience the
emotional container of the team, the vignette points to how Amar
displayed maternal solicitude to help Raman break in, ease in and
begin to feel familiar and settled.

If you were to quietly watch the Mother in life, what would
you see? What actions and behaviours might make themselves
evident? The Mother would 'endure the pain of birth', 'give birth
to' and 'nourish at the breast'. All these three are expressions of
a direct and unmediated bond between the Mother and their
progeny. Nothing can come in the way of the Mother's direct
expression of love. You would then see the Mother exhibiting
selfless devotion and love. The Mother would be present for the
child, attend to and care for the child.

Take a recent TV commercial for a skin lotion, Nivea. The
commercial begins with a mother applying Nivea crème on her
little daughter. The mother continues to fret about her daughter, as she
applies the cold cream on her arms. 'You must be wondering that your
mother must be saying something, but you have no idea how much
I worry about you. What if something happens to you?

My heartbeat stops, but you don't listen to me', the mother mutters
to herself. Her daughter, who is deaf and mute, gestures to her, wanting to
know what her mother is saying. The mother then uses the sign
language of the deaf to tell her daughter that she loves her. The child
replies that she loves her mother too. The child playfully puts a dab of
cream on her mother's cheek and her mother tells her in a gesture that
she could go out and play. The child hugs her mother and her mother
holds on to her tightly for a moment too. 'Yeh hai maa ka pyaar' (this is
a mother's love), narrates a voice in the background.

The Mother will nurture the body, mind and spirit of the child not as a luxury but as a necessity. The Mother will watch the child like a protective hawk, especially if and when the child is vulnerable. Mothers employ their sensibilities in order to engage in protective action. They stay tuned to threats to their young ones, and if the threat is identified, the Mother can and will attack. For this behaviour, they may even come under attack from their underlings themselves, but the Mother is not put off—not in the least. They take it upon themselves to teach, explain and guide around physical and social survival; they would take pride and delight in the emergence and flowering of the offspring—which can be very affirming.

Three stages can be gleaned in a Mother's engagement with their child—(a) complete and total protection, (b) gradual letting go as the child gains autonomy and (c) hands-off being available, watching from a distance and being there as infrastructure for the child should they need such. You can see these stages in many MNC technology companies that have offshored work to India.

Speaking to Kavi Rajan, who served as an HR Director of one of the big few semiconductor MNCs in India, here is what we heard. 'My company was one of the earliest to do set up shop in India starting with a center in Bangalore, way back in the eighties of last century, if you please. The 1980s and 1990s were the era of near total protection. Expat leaders would lead operations and key designs right here in India. Gradually, as we demonstrated ability to handle certain designs by ourselves, the parent company started letting go and gave us more autonomous work. You could say that the first fifteen years of this century were in this phase. In the last two or three years, however, we are now running global projects from right here in Bangalore. For most things, we rely on our own local expertise, and approach HQ in the rarest of instances. Such is the quality of letting go, and of course they are always there for us, when needed'.

A sense of 'dutifulness' would also be ascribable to the Mother. This sense of duty would arise not out of some contractual obligation but out of an authentic concern for the others' well-being. Could we call this the dharma of the Mother?

Awareness, observation and vigilance—in a Mother's distinctive way—are how we believe the Mother would meet and greet life's tests. Especially so, if these are to do with the well-being of their wards. And these would be founded on a bedrock of her intuition—typically holistic, affect-laced judgements that happen without necessarily conscious or deliberate weighing of facts. With the scaffolding of their intuition solidly by them, the Mother's awareness would be sharp and deep. We have earlier alluded to the hawk in this essay—the Mother would observe like a hawk, especially if she intuits threat to her offspring. You could call this their vigilance too—they observe with vigilance. Besides, they would also bring in a maternal relentlessness—quite different from the relentlessness of the Warrior–Crusader who would be so for the progression of 'the cause' while the Mother would be so for the well-being of her lot.

In the world around, the Mother is the 'feeling' led or affect-laden person who would worry about the physical and emotional nourishment of others that they have responsibility for. The manager that is very clued in to his reports' daily lives, the teacher who engages with their student at a personal level, as can be seen in the craft-learning systems in India, the fussy manager who will call in to check if his team member reached home after the party, the caregiver in a hospice and the son or daughter who take upon themselves the responsibility to take care of and provide for their aged and infirm parents—these are but a few examples of how we may see the Mother around us in our lives. We have also listed some common examples of the 'overdone Mother' identity in the section on 'The Mother in the Extremes'.

What Is Their Inner World Like?

The Mother's greatest desire may simply be to birth and nurture new life and aliveness that can be fostered in the world and through that to experience the fullness and bounty of the world of connectedness and nurturance. The Mother would hope to sow seeds of well-being and their nature is such that wherever they see hope, they will volitionally invest even if not specifically approached for such. Their other desire would be that others do well and succeed and are in good health—a wishing of well-being for the other. In holding hope for these, the Mother carries the gift of seeing the promise in the other—the promise that is yet a seed and needs the touch and care of the Mother that would allow it to sprout and grow. The Mother also has the stamina to give birth to and natural ability to nurture. Stamina is often associated with the world of autonomy and initiative (WAI) and particularly the long race that the Warrior–Crusader runs and the mighty growth projects that the warlord embarks on. Do we even know the stamina required for birthing and nurturing that the Mother has as a natural gift? And then, going beyond, the Mother would understand the natural cycles of nature and know when to hold and foster AND when to release/let go.

They are also endowed with immense resourcefulness. 'The Mother's prayer' is a distinctive gift—the free and unconditional ability to seek benediction for their lot. In prayer, there is a seeking from the limitlessness of the cosmos, simultaneous with owning up one's vulnerability and physical limitedness—that quality of seeking in itself is a gift, one that is all the more sweet, considering it comes from the one that also gave birth to the one that is being prayed for. The Mother clearly has the ability to put their chosen others ahead of themselves.

Walking alongside her desires and hopes are the Mother's fears and sorrows and their anger and angst. 'What if I lose my offspring' is perhaps the greatest fear of the Mother—the death or hurt of the child and of the Mother's inability to adequately protect the child. What of the sorrow and angst?

Says Kavitha, a homemaker, 'What I often feel sad about as a Mother is the lack of any visible affirmation or acknowledgment or reciprocity. Not that I seek it, but in the moments when I am fatigued, I would love to know that my efforts have been visible and when I don't receive that, I do feel hurt'.

Besides Kavitha's clearly expressed feelings, there may also be the anticipated sorrow of not being wanted or not being somehow relevant to the context with the passage of time. The Mother also feels a sense of 'damned if you do, damned if you don't'.

Listen to Radha, a consultant who has taken time to bear her child—'At one level, the world judges me as not "doing anything really worthwhile" since I am at home and caring for my child AND if I take time to go for work, there is the other voice from the family which suggests that I ought to be at home and tending to my child—what do I do with this!! There is no win anywhere, except in my own eyes'.

And then there is also the Mother's pathos of never really investing in oneself as much as one does in others. This coupled with the often inadequate or absent acknowledgment can be a double whammy for the Mother!

The Mother in the Extremes

When the Mother is not able to contain her natural tendency to care for and protect, she can end up in smothering or strangulating the other. When the Mother's hold tightens, there is no letting go and her hold can be one seriously claustrophobic hold. And when the Mother is so, they end up either infantilizing others or idealizing their children, as we can glimpse below.

There are many interesting variants of the extreme Mother identity in life around us. The **Helicopter Mother** (also called a cosseting Mother or simply a cosseter) is the Mother who pays extremely close attention to a child's or children's experiences and problems. You see them in workspaces—the manager who is constantly hovering around their team members to solicitously make sure their needs are taken care of and that their problems are promptly addressed. Then, there is the **Soccer Mom** which broadly refers to a woman who spends a significant amount of her time transporting her school-age children to their youth sporting events or other activities. The phrase has taken on a negative aspect. Soccer moms are sometimes accused of forcing their children to go to too many after-school activities; overparenting them in 'concerted cultivation' rather than letting them enjoy their childhood. You see the Soccer Mom in life other than its originally intended usage, in people who constantly push their dependents and wards to 'better themselves'. This is quite similar to the **Tiger Mom**, who is fiercely competitive for their wards and wants them to achieve greater heights and pursue excellence. The **Best Friend** Mom wants to be seen as a **Cool Mom** who does not wish to really be a mother. She never disciplines her child, preferring to gently remind them of their wrongdoings. She is sugar sweet to her kids; you will never hear her raise her voice. This mom is literally killing her kids with kindness. You see this version too in people all around us who somehow seem to believe that world of structure and order (WSO) in any form will be at the expense of WCN and thus refrain from setting even needed boundaries especially for those that they are responsible for. In all these, the extreme Mother fails to take care of her own well-being and often ends up feeling like the martyr.

If the Mother's energy is muted or absent, we can expect a certain dryness and lifelessness in the system, arising from a lack of adequate nurturance and care. The expectant recipient of care and nurturance can also experience being abandoned or orphaned.

At another level, there can be a non-acceptance of or inattention to the cycles of life, leading to the person or entity feeling relatively unprepared for changes in the context.

The Mother identity is best matched on the other side by the child's identity.

Angst	Hope	Gifts	Fear/ Vulnerability
Who will acknowledge me, affirm me and who will nurture and care for me?	Through me, new life will be born, and I will be able to bring about well-being in the world	I see the promise in the other, and I have the will and stamina to birth and nurture that	What if I lose my offspring or if they are grievously hurt? And also, will I be taken for granted?

The Mother as a Leader in Organizations

- In dealing with situations of high pressure and stress, the Mother would step in to allay anxieties and apprehensions, and help bring back focus on the tasks.
- People and relationships will be their priority and they would care for and protect (even defend) those who belong to the system.
- In a personalized way, the Mother would support and affirm change projects, new initiatives especially when they are shared with them by those they value.
- They would also freely share their own apprehensions and anxieties about the implications of the change, thus opening up the change protagonists to see their blind spots.
- The Mother would aid a system's growth by enabling and providing the emotional infrastructure (support in the form of companionship, empathy, container for catharsis and so on) for its members.
- At times, they may have a tendency to create dependencies, not encouraging people to freely grow/sprout wings.

17

The Muse

*Like a splendid mosaic of myriad colors, she in all her hues of
sensitivity would paint her feelings in your mind's gray skies. She
was the butterfly making you run after her. She was the Zahir, a
mirage that transcended borders and time-zones.*

—Avijeet Das

The Muse

Who Is the Muse?

What makes you feel vital and alive? What inspires or lifts you? What drives, enthuses and excites you? What provokes you or makes you mad enough to act? In responding to these questions, peek behind the veil of pat responses and you are likely to see— in the shadows and drifting in the mist—the Muse. The Muse is something or someone that has the ability to excite our creative passion and call forth our creative spirit to emerge.

The Muse derives from Greek mythology; the Muses were the goddesses who inspired music and poetry, drama and science. The myth of the Muse was any of the nine daughters of Mnemosyne (memory) and Zeus who presided over the arts and sciences. They included Calliope (eloquence and epic poetry), Clio (history), Erato (lyric and love poetry), Euterpe (lyric song and music), Melpomene (tragedy), Polyhymnia (sacred song), Terpsichore (dancing), Thalia (comedy and pastoral poetry) and Urania (astronomy). The more modern definition of the muse sees the muse as a spirit or power regarded as inspiring poets and artists. However, this concept of the muse, whether it be the Greek myth or some other definition, embodies the muse as a female providing inspiration in an artist's life or as a spirit or power regarded as inspiring poets and artists.

Artists and scientists have long noted that some of their greatest works or intellectual insights seemed to mysteriously appear fully formed in their minds. The Muse is an identity that holds intense 'dynamic energy' but in a container and gifts this energy to deserving others.

Beatle Paul Mc Cartney reports that he first heard the melody for 'Yesterday', one of their most popular songs of all time, in a dream. The famous Tamil poet Subramania Bharathi had an imaginary muse that he called 'Kannamma'. Bharathi has used this as his goddess, child and also beloved as the context of his literary work demanded.

The Muse is an interesting identity in its offering an intense archetypal attraction. The attraction of the Muse is not led by thought, feeling and action alone (though these do play a part).

Can we call it soul led or spirit led? That might be problematic as the ideas of soul and spirit have religious or metaphysical and thus often political connotations. Suffice it to say that the Muse pulls one to flow and unfolding at a level and intensity that may not be normally comprehensible. It is said that solitude is the muse of the writer and death or truth the muse of the philosopher. The Muse thus offers neither love nor lust, but a numinous and intense inarticulable attraction. The Muse inspires by its very presence and not necessarily by an active engagement or by what it says or does.

In fact, the word we might use for the Muse is 'evocation'. Let us understand evocation and distinguish this from words in the neighbourhood like 'inspiration' and 'motivation'. When a person is motivated by another, a desire is created in them to do something. Inspiration would have the added element of having the desire to do something creative. Evocation on the other hand is an act of calling forth or bringing up. The 'action' or 'creation' is not in the foreground when one is evoked. A Muse would evoke a deep feeling, an inner state of being, a memory—and leave it at that. What happens after that is not the care-about of the Muse, but often a new being emerges.

Impact-wise, the Muse would spark generativity and creative expression in others that are ready to receive the energy of the Muse. It would provoke and challenge thought boundaries by creating a churn and a turbulence *in the unconscious* realms of the other, and this ability to churn the other comes from an ease of access the Muse seems to have to the unconscious.

Think here of J. Krishnamurthi and how his intense and pro-vocative questions would make the others think and revisit their construction of their values, helping them discover layers beneath layers of thought. The Muse would disturb one's equilibrium—but would do this in a muted way—not necessarily by crusading or by acting but by its very presence. The energy of the Muse would move one to contemplate (to muse upon, if you will) and that would in turn lead to action. Perhaps, the Muse leads one to 'contemplaCtion'—to contemplate AND to act. Suffice it to say that when people are motivated to seek and find the Muses in the world out there, they are but mirroring an internal unconscious process of seeking and finding the fount of creative spirit within them. The Muse allows one to find bliss and joy while living one's natural life, unlike certain spiritual practices that demand a certain quality of asceticism to find bliss and joy.

The actions of the Muse are mostly inactions—the Muse functions in a passive or inert way yet is a ground of enormous creativity.

As K. Ferlic puts it, 'by focusing our attention and awareness on it, whether the muse is in our life or not, we keep before our mind a focus which is reflective of what is symbolized by our heart desires to create— our heart's desire. Hence whenever they think of the muse or have them in their life, our focus is on what the heart desires to create. On this note, sometimes we will never get the muse for if we did get it, we would not complete the creation process carrying it out to the end because we have what you seek. It is only in tension of "not having" that then energy flows'.

Our view is that the Muse is an intensely dynamic energy field that cloaks its dynamicity. This ephemeral cloak is the lure— you see the Muse yet you do not. You can feel it but not touch it. The Muse creates a yearning and a longing yet one never really knows where one stands with the Muse. It calls one's desires forth, yet it does not let one grasp it and this energy between the 'perceivable and desirable' yet 'unattainable' generates the libido that sparks creative expression. The Muse does not appear bothered by others' evaluations. Muses do not actively seek to be leaders. What they do is to quietly live their conviction. They are the embers and not the fire—they are not activists, they may be more of 'passivists'—but with equal impact/influence. One more thing—the Muse is a fickle entity, not 'norm' able, and so anyone seeking consistency from a Muse is best warned to drop such expectations and go naked.

Indian Actor Rekha is perhaps the quintessential muse. She epitomizes enigma, charisma and mesmerizing, magnetic attraction in almost any role that she takes up. Whether it be her smouldering looks as Vasantasena the courtesan in Shashi Kapoor's Utsav, or the sensuality and sequins in her dance item in Jaanbaaz, or her exquisite grace and portrayal of femininity in Silsila, or the sheer radiance and romance in her eyes in 'Umrao Jaan' or the 'vintage' vibe in her special appearance in Parineeta, the list can go on, but there you have it—that is Rekha, muse to many a heart that yearns and soul that longs! There are and have been male muses in artistic history, too. The Barbara Hepworth exhibition at London's Tate Britain reveals how the sculptresses' husband, Ben Nicholson, became an all-encompassing source of inspiration for her, while painter Frida Kahlo was inspired by her artist husband Diego Rivera.

We also believe that each person finds their muse—the Muse does not have a specific location. Mythology and History provide us rich sources of stories and chronicles where some character might become a Muse for one. As an illustration, the Goddess Saraswati is a muse of learning and creative endeavour, and she is celebrated annually on the auspicious days of 'Vijayadashami'; in the Hindu lunar calendar—new learning is ritually begun on this day. Characters in fiction and great films offer us nooks to find the Muse in—perhaps Eowyn from the *Lord of the Rings* or Belle from *The Beauty and the Beast* come to mind? You might also find them in the vast corridors around the ecosystem of expressive art, music and dance. Often, they are the art aesthete who appreciates creative work. They are not critics and not artistes themselves, but they channel the aesthetics of the art form, like 'shrota-biradari', a popular listening community in Indore that contemplates what the aesthetics of the music and poetry it immerses in is all about— and in doing so, channels the form for the practitioner. The 'aesthete' in any ecosystem also holds tacit knowledge of the 'form of practice'—they would freely discuss this, mostly in informal chats laced with anecdotes and, in this process, create a longing for the practitioner to access such knowledge—you can find such aesthetes in diverse locations, be they corporates, or guilds, or crafts, or art forms, or in schools and learning communities of various kinds. *The legendary musician T. Brinda of the Karnatik music system was such a renowned practitioner-aesthete that several musicians would long to even be at the receiving end of her usually brutally direct critique as even that would mean that somehow they had partaken of some of her wisdom and received her touch, however backhanded.*

When it comes to life's situations and challenges, the person holding the Muse identity would typically be seen having a focused and pivotal approach that might be unconventional and offbeat—a signature approach that may be difficult to replicate. For many, Malala Yousafzai is the Warrior–Crusader, but to many others, she is also simultaneously the Muse—and one who would take problems head on by being outspoken and 'taking on' her perpetrators. In day-to-day situations, the Muse is perhaps the grandmother whose culinary craft is the channel of precious memories, or the rare stand-apart female Uber driver in Mumbai, India, or maybe it is you and us—living our lives and perhaps in that, setting some example somewhere for another to love a bit of THEIR life!

What Is Their Inner World Like?

Given the rather elusive quality of the Muse in general, we find ourselves using a 'telescope' of sorts to try and access the inner world of the Muse.

We believe that this inner world is all about honouring and fostering awareness through change (one's truth is not about the container or the person who is attracted to the Muse—in fact one may have a quality of indifference to the so-attracted persons—but to the phenomenon of awareness). It may well be that the desire of the Muse is to 'awaken spirit' and to expand awareness. The Muse may be the agent bridging the unconscious with the expansion and deepening of consciousness.

The Muse perhaps hopes that those that are attracted to it are able to touch that part of their spirit which is knowable yet unfamiliar. The hope may be to reveal the 'unthought knowns' as contrasted with the 'unknown thoughts'.

The other desire of the Muse (and this may be in service of the expansion of awareness that we have referred to) could be to dismantle and deconstruct all barriers to whatever energy they are channelling. Norms, people, habits, traditions, social mores, tastes and enshrined practices are all no exception. Thus, it is little wonder that people in the 'grip' of the Muse appear at times like they are antisocial, radical, maverick and all that. But if change and expansion of awareness are the deeper desires of the Muse, what are these but minor potholes?

The Muse is gifted with the ability to channel and be a medium for the unconscious and alongside, the ability to excite a creative trigger in the receiving entity or person receiving that energy. This does take us to consider the Muse and its connection with sexuality. The Muse triggers off creative passion, desire and longing—there is no doubt about this assertion. These forces in turn often trigger off a concomitant experience of awakened sexuality. This awakened sexuality at times tends to get turned and directed towards the force that has made that awakening possible. It may even get trapped there, and thus it is that the Muse is often turned into the seductress or seducer—and the entrapment is complete. The Muse by itself is an energy that cannot be trapped. This phenomenon is located in the protagonist, experiencing its awakening touch and not knowing how to channel that touch beyond experiencing it sexually in the Muse. Perhaps the Guide–Mentor is a useful identity for the protagonist to encounter, especially when they are in sight of the Muse? Sigh … if only psychic events could be thus ordered! Another version of this gift is somewhat like the ability of spiritual gurus to give 'Shaktipat', a spiritually awakening one-time touch (often physical), that awakens in the shishya (the disciple), a longing to be one with that touch, except that once having awakened, the Guru does not keep providing it—the determined shishya then sets out on their OWN path to realize their own gift to be one with that touch.

Justin Faerman talks of various levels of the development of consciousness in which we find the stage that he refers to as

'Life happens through me' stage that approximates the Muse in some ways. A stage of surrender, letting go, non-resistance and flow, 'and realizing that every moment is perfect and there is great wisdom, intelligence and order in the unfolding of life, although due to its immense complexity, to the unaware eye it is perceived as chaos'. To the 'unaware', the Muse's gifts may be experienced as chaos, while the Muse is just being themselves, looking for a container that can receive their energy and manifest it in creative expression.

The inner fears, apprehensions and sorrow of the Muse can perhaps be depicted through this imaginary monologue of a muse—'Will I end up being a mere crutch and a medium for others? I should not be the anchor for the other but be that which helps the other find their anchor in themselves; Or would it be that in place of touching me, the other ends up going after the seductress, chasing an illusion instead of discovering their substantiveness? Also, what do I become of myself.... Am I but a still-born artiste?' The pathos of the Muse may be that people may attach to them or love them for the 'idea' that is them and not them truly. Thus, they might well end up being but a screen carrying multiple projections of others, feeling unreal and not substantive.

The identity that is best suited to receive the Muse energy is that of the Artiste. There is great complementarity in this combination. So too, we can think of the Hero who has heeded the call and descends into the psychic underworld to undertake the Hero's journey. The Hero needs to encounter the Muse and answer her riddles to move forward on his journey.

The Muse in the Extremes

Ratchet up the Muse energy to the extremes and you may find them 'possessing' the protagonist. Muses being who they are reside in the unconscious—that is their abode. The seeker of the Muse lives in this world where you and we are—at times the Muses in their utter detachment and unawareness of the seeker's context and limitations draw them too far, too deep into a state where separation from the numinous symbol of the Muse becomes impossible. Thus, almost psychotically, the other may find themselves obsessing for the Muse, and not being able to touch the Muse in reality, they might settle for proxies such as alcohol and drugs or vacuous and extractive or hurtful relationships. Or, even worse, actually end up psychotic in the extreme where no distinction between worlds is possible. Second, in their demand that the other not be limited by and to constraints (whether personal or social or cultural), they may expect the other to constantly unleash themselves, even untether themselves sometimes from basic safety and security and thus imperil themselves. And if the seeker does not, woe betide, for the 'spurned' Muse can turn vindictive and push them to doom.

The weak Muse energy comes across as and insipid or feeble presence. A sense of stagnation and staleness persists around this person or entity, almost as though some vitality has been drained.

Angst	Hope	Gifts	Fear/ Vulnerability
The world has lost the ability to evoke; at best, it can only motivate. The world is afraid of its sensuousness	That I may be able to awaken the spirit of the other and expand their awareness	I am a channel and medium of the unconscious and can thus access her great and infinite treasures	Will I end up being a crutch for others to get by?

The Muses as Leaders in Organizations

- The Muse as a leader might encourage and be a role model for others in the organization, supporting unconventional approaches, offering multiple perspectives for exploration and pushing the others to ask themselves deep, penetrative and insight-generating questions.
- By accessing and enabling access to a vast and deep space of human consciousness, they would enable deep and transformative change in relationships, particularly in 1:1 relationships.
- They would have a distinctive approach and presence, often being an exemplar and role model to others to enable deep change.
- They would blend a sense of 'unconventionality' and their own substantiveness, thereby offering the system new qualitative directions for growth.
- At times, they may take their explorations to a limit that may inspire awe but also leave others at times with a sense of distance.

18

The Provider of Resources

That is the thankless position of the father in the family—the provider for all, and the enemy of all.

—August Strindberg

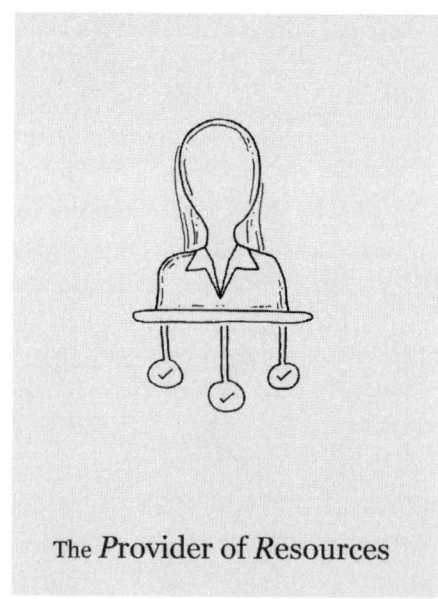

The *Provider of Resources*

Who Is the Provider of Resources?

When Arun Jaitley, the Finance Minister of India at the time this book was written, rose to present the budget for the nation for the fiscal year 2018–19, he did so in the role of the Provider of Resources. When the head of a state commissions new metro lines in key cities to bolster public transport, they are acting as this identity. When the staffing team of an organization goes out and hires talent and skills needed for the organization, there again is our Provider of Resources. When a parent takes an insurance policy to cover for his children's education needs, there we spot the identity again.

These are some quick vignettes to introduce us to the Provider of Resources—we see them as an identity that is on the containing side of the 'expressive-containing' continuum, preferring to work for continuity and stability (refer Appendix 1).

The Providers, as we will call them in this chapter, are ones who provide resources and help maintain a stable, predictable and orderly environment. They offer resources that will keep the system going, playing a supportive role. They are conscientiously occupied with the infrastructural needs of the system and often take pride in giving and providing. They are the go-to persons, who know where things are and have the keys to the store room.

Being in the location of Providers also generates a 'dharma' (the 'contextually right' action)—of providing what is needed to help the system be stable and on its task and to not let the system down when it comes to resources required for its survival, existence and growth. They need to keep the system operational knowing that not having a resource at the precise moment can disrupt the system. And, equally, they are often also the resource estimators, resource generators, resource negotiators, resource distributors and allocators and resource controllers.

They have 'one foot in the system and the other outside', constantly interfacing with 'the outside' for the needs of the system. They may do this within the system as well—resources abundant within one location in a system may be diverted to be used at another place where there is need and shortage. In situations of natural disasters, for instance, we know of the practice of the army moving from peacekeeping and defence roles to providing help, rescue and rebuilding efforts in the disaster areas.

Let us now look to a few other examples to get more deeply acquainted with the Provider.

Banks and credit agencies who provide financial resources to keep the wheels of commerce moving are good examples of how resource providers work in a large system. Another example is the operational side of foundations and trusts of philanthropy like Azim Premji Foundation, Bill Gates Foundation and the Ratan Tata Trust. If you visit the Gates Foundation website, you will notice that their stated belief is 'That by giving people the tools to lead healthy, productive lives, we can help them lift themselves out of poverty'. A closer look indicates their four approaches— (a) provide the poor with access to financial tools, (b) teach farmers how to increase production sustainably, (c) help women make informed family-planning decisions and (d) ensure that all students who seek the opportunity are able to complete a high-quality, affordable postsecondary education that leads to a sustaining career.

The Azim Premji Foundation works directly in changing the education landscape of the country in a systemic manner through setting up resources called 'District Institutes' (which work directly with teachers to equip them with new tools and methodologies), as well as a world-class university. The Tata Trusts provide grants to individuals as well as to organizations that wish to impact healthcare as well as education in the country.

Consider the nurses looking after the needs of the elderly and old age homes (no, they are NOT all healers, they mostly provide resources in the form of care to keep their clients' needs provided for).

The government is perhaps the largest resource provider—you can see this in public distribution and in provision of urban transport networks as examples. Perhaps the most ambitious Provider role has been now taken up by the just-announced National Health Protection Scheme—'We are now launching a flagship national health protection scheme to cover 10 crore poor and vulnerable families. This is approximately 50 crore beneficiaries, by providing them up to Rs 5 lakh per family per year for secondary and tertiary care hospitalisation', India's Finance Minister Jaitley said, presenting the 2018–19 Union Budget on 31 January.

Many men in Indian households are brought up to be Providers primarily, a socialized and deeply internalized responsibility they cannot easily shake off. A lament that is sadly heard in families that have tragically lost a son is 'Who is there to take care of us now!', a sad note that points to the deep-seated presence of this identity in the cultural fabric of families.

At a basic level, the survival of a system depends on having resources for survival, and then growth of the system further requires growth resources. This is the function of the Provider. Providers bring a sense of safety and security and comfort to the system—the needs of people and systems will be met, so that they may go on functioning or pursue their goals. The effect of the Provider is that the resources required for the efficient throughput of a system are made available—they keep a system healthy and well functioning—the machinery in the system is well greased. Spare parts are available and do not run out.

Employees in Intel often use a phrase 'KTBR' which is an acronym for 'Keep the Business Running'. The Provider creates a KTBR impact for systems. The Provider also gives a system a competitive edge where required. For example, the World Bank Sports Reference lists ten countries that have won the most medals at the summer Olympics (from the inaugural 1896 games in Athens to the London Olympics of 2012). These countries—the USA, the erstwhile Soviet Union, Germany, Great Britain, France, Italy, Sweden, Russia, China and erstwhile East Germany—are mostly wealthy nations that have seen *sustained state investment in nurturing talent*. Another likely effect of the Provider's presence is not just that resources are provided for the system's functioning but that over time the system's resourcefulness goes up. The system may become more creative or self-reliant. When parents provide for their children in the form of resources for education, the impact over time is that they create capacity in the children to become independent.

What actions might we see the Provider engage in? The word 'provide', in our framework, has a large canvas, encompassing resource estimation (what resources are needed), resource allocation and control (which part of the system gets how much) and resource issue (the actual giving of the resources). The Providers are often proactive about future needs of the system and anticipate what is required for its smooth operation and throughput. They bring in the supplies, often being responsible for storing them and making them available to the system as and when required. They ration, allocate and ensure that resources reach the right place at the right time. They discern and make resource provision decisions—they are the resources orchestrators, in that sense. To that end, 'measurement' would be an important part of their portfolio of actions. They would also be well networked in the sense that they would know where to find which resource. In that sense, they are the go-to persons—look at it another way, they may signal that they are the 'come to me' persons in a system, signalling their presence and availability for the resource needs. They are not limited to the provision of tangible resources, and even intangible resources are part of their remit.

Resource providers are likely to spend time anticipating and mitigating problems (particularly ones related to resource constraints, possible resource deficiencies). You might even say that they worry about much, but rather than worry and not act, they would worry and do something about it.

You could say that a good part of the life insurance market in India thrives on the worry of the resource providers of the middle-class family. When faced with a problem (typically a shortage/inadequacy), they will look at questions like 'what resources are required', 'who needs what resource support to solve this problem' or 'what other resources can I get, who has it, and how can I procure it?' (Refer box below, which illustrates this through the concept of positive deviance [PD].)

Some Providers practise PD. PD, from sociology, is an approach to behavioural and social change based on the observation that in any community, there are people whose uncommon but successful behaviours or strategies enable them to find better solutions to a problem than their peers, despite facing similar challenges and having no extra resources or knowledge than their peers. These individuals are referred to as positive deviants. The concept first appeared in nutrition research in the 1970s. Researchers observed that despite the poverty in a community, some poor families had well-nourished children. It is reported that at the start of the pilot experiment, 64 per cent of children weighed in the pilot villages were malnourished. Through an inquiry, the villagers found poor peers in the community that through their uncommon but successful 'resource provider' strategies had well-nourished children. These families collected foods typically considered inappropriate for children (sweet potato greens, shrimp and crabs), washed their children's hands before meals and actively fed them three to four times a day instead of the typical two meals a day provided to children. Without knowing it, these Positive Deviant Providers had incorporated foods already found in their community that provided important nutrients: protein, iron and calcium AND had changed the resource consumption pattern. A nutrition programme based on these insights was created for the whole community.

At the end of the 2-year pilot, malnutrition fell by 85 per cent.

Providers are also good at negotiating for resources and making them available at the right time and right quantity and appropriate quality for the system they are part of. Many learning and development functions inside organizations go for 'at pace' learning for their staff, wherein they tie up with (mostly) digital learning modules from world-class providers (Harvard, McKinsey and so on). These tie-ups involve the Provider L&D Manager scouting for the right resources, negotiating their availability and price and channelling them to the right recipients.

Oftentimes systems do not assess risks related to resources, as much as they do with process, technology or unforeseen circumstances. The Providers would typically have an eye on 'resource risks', such as—are the right resources estimated, is the quantity right, do we have the specifications, are the sources identified and reliable and so on. They would diligently check to see whether the use of resources is optimized in the system or if there is over-/underutilization. Usually, they would tend to have a holistic view of the whole system and that helps them head off gaps before they arise—and coming from the strong containing and grounding side of world of structure and order (WSO), they would eschew acting on whims and fancies. There would indeed be a strong rational component to their decision-making.

What Is Their Inner World Like?

The hope of the Provider is that the system must survive, run and thrive. That it must be constantly replenished. And their hope, therefore, is that they have control of access (be it to tangible resources or even intangible ones like time/tenure) that will enable this. Think of the mothers in the PD examples we have quoted above. Think also of many Providers in several Indian families who worry about their falling ill or dying, lest their provided-for system collapses or otherwise comes to harm. You might hear them often articulating a wish that the system becomes self-sustaining. Yet, that is often just the 'stated' or 'espoused' wish—you might even find them just as reluctant to let go as they appear burdened by providing. Perhaps, then, one of their unarticulated desires is also for receiving the dependence of others?

Providers are gifted with the ability to figure out AND to provide the resources that the system may need. You could call it the gift of proactive anticipation, even. They would understand the gaps in the system, they would have the eyes to foresee and understand resource requirements. They would then match their knowledge of sources of availability, and their ability to control the flow to the right place at the right time. And if you have a pair of the Provider-Administrator, you have a story worth sharing, like that of the 'Akshaya Patra' scheme of the International Society of Krishna Consciousness (ISKCON, Bangalore, India), a well-documented 'Provider' story.

Akshaya Patra is an initiative of ISKCON Bangalore to provide midday meals in the rural schools for the underprivileged children and thus support their education. On the outskirts of Bangalore, one of the most modern and hygienic kitchens supplies midday meals to 94,000 school children every day. Work begins as early as 1 in the morning for the preprocessing and processing of nutritious food at the Doddakallasandra kitchen of ISKCON.

'Cleaning of raw materials, grounding of masalas and cutting of vegetables are a continuous process that is mechanised as well as manual, while cooking of the meal itself takes four hours. A total of 2,000 kg pulses, 5,000 kg vegetables and 7,000 kg rice are used for cooking meals for 94,000', says Sundeep Talwar, Chief Marketing Officer of The Akshaya Patra Foundation. This is EVERY single day.

If most of the work is done by Akshaya Patra staff, on some days, they have corporate volunteers from various firms helping in the preparation of meals. However, the volunteers are allowed to work only in cleaning of grains, pulses or cutting of vegetables and that too by maintaining proper hygiene.

A supervisor informs, 'It is race against time as the first vehicle with large containers of food leaves the kitchen at 8 am, while the milk is sent by 4 in the morning. Volunteers are always at the kitchen to see how the midday meals are prepared and help simultaneously'.

And this is a testimony to the Provider—who estimates the scale of the need and accesses a ready and steady supply of the material, time and effort and resources needed to provide for the needy. A great tribute indeed to the WSO, in which the Provider resides!

'Who do I go to, when I need' laments the Provider in their moment of sorrow, when they realize that for long they have been unidirectionally offering, never seeking. 'I am needed, but I am not need-less, needless to say', they moan. 'And why don't people want to know me as a person', further goes the cry, as they realize their sorrow that in many ways the world has truly valued them—but for what they provided and not always for who they were. Some Providers also wonder, 'Who will I allow, to take care of my needs', and perhaps a corollary to this—'what will the world think of me, if I am seen as needy!'. And last but never the least, 'Very soon, they will not need me'—the resource seekers will become self-sufficient and move on. We call this the 'pathos of the retiree'—as long as they were in service and earning, and providing for the home, they felt valued. But what after? We often come across the 'post-retirement provider' identity in India, where the retiree parents then become babysitting and guardianship providers to grandchildren, especially when the parents of the grandchildren go out for their dual-income careers. And, finally—apart from the sorrow that there is nobody to take care of THEIR needs, Providers also fear for what if their tap runs dry. Would they then have a raison d'etre?

The Provider in the Extremes

You may see the entrenched Provider in the overgenerous providers who may not acknowledge or articulate their own reciprocal expectations or even their resource-lessness at times. They then become the silent sufferers. And when this symbolic identity is fused with the social/family role, a 'silent killer' cocktail emerges. People in India may be familiar with the vignette of the head of the family who is eking out a living for a dependent family, ploughs on in a lonely furrow and head ever to the yoke and back-loaded with burdens, worries and anxieties—till one day the ever-waiting-in-the-wings heart attack or stroke (where the body finally speaks what the mind never does) does them in.

The other entrenchment is 'provide to control'—especially where one denies their world of autonomy and initiative and seeks to surreptitiously live this world out through proxies.

The overbearing, intrusive and inundating Provider is next in queue, and this may well come from the denied Mother or Collaborator identity—so in place of reaching out to understand what is needed and to help, there is a download of excess. In place of a pitcher of water, a fire hose is deployed.

Next, we also come across the patronizing Provider—the prideful, privileged elite and resource-controlling Provider, who makes the receiver feel beholden and ingratiating to them. Sometimes, the excessive Provider is also constellated in cases where the Provider does not believe that the system is ultimately responsible for itself or that the system cannot take care of itself. You may have heard this story of the boy scout who helped a lady cross the street—that was his 'good deed' for the day. Except that the old lady was just standing at the corner of the road as a bystander—she never wanted to cross the street! A combination of Warlord and Extreme Providers also manipulate the other to be dependent on them.

This same combo of high Warlord and Extreme Provider can also lead to visible waste and unaccountable excess, so much so that waste is never seen as waste or as depletion—just as inconvenient excess. We see this many a time in developed nations—there is typically excess of infrastructure, excess of fuel, of water, of money, of land and so on—that little things that might make a huge difference to people's lives in poor nations are typically wasted or consumed without an ecological care about.

Sometimes, they lack the realization that people need to have 'enough hunger' in order to grow—if that hunger is never allowed to surface, or it is artfully covered up and camouflaged with make-believe consumption, it results in an overfed, utopian system that will move slowly but surely towards a fall. The movie 'The Big Short' brought this aspect out clearly in highlighting how the extreme Providers (and Warlords) of Wall Street manipulated consumption in the subprime real estate market in the USA, eventually leading to one of the worst financial disasters in the US history.

Without the presence of the Provider, or if the Provider energy is depleted in the system, starvation and depletion (or even eventual death) is likely to be a consequence. The system huffs and puffs and hobbles along. You see this all the time in dilapidated government buildings, offices and government-provided facilities. Things simply do not exist, or they do in ridiculously low quantities or of pathetic quality. Government guest houses, railway coaches, the state of roads, government hospitals and you can feel free to add to this somewhat cynical list, but you will get the picture, we are sure. Sometimes as a politico-economic strategy, the Provider is deliberately diluted to get certain desired behaviours in the other or even as a punitive measure—think economic sanctions, for example.

The Provider might like to encounter the needy. Their companions could be the Warlord, the Ruler, the Strategist and the Collaborator.

Angst	Hope	Gifts	Fear/ Vulnerability
No matter what, my own needs will not matter to anyone	That the system must survive, run and thrive	The ability to figure out and provide what the other (the system) needs or seeks	That eventually I will not be needed

The Provider as Leaders in Organizations

- They would help stabilize a growing system by providing the needed resources at the right time.
- They would establish processes through which the systems resource needs are met consistently.
- They would proactively anticipate the resources and support for system-approved 'legitimate' changes.
- They would consistently try and keep people secure and reassured by providing them the necessary resources, help and support.
- They may, however, also, end up creating a dependent and extractive system that does not own up its responsibility and take care of itself.

19

The Ruler

A powerful process automatically takes care of progress, productivity and profits.

—Amit Kalantri, Wealth of Words

The *Ruler*

Who Is the Ruler?

To understand the Ruler, it is important that we understand the concepts of 'niti' and 'nyaya', from classical Sanskrit. Niti stands for organizational propriety and behavioural correctness within and for the system. Nyaya stands for a more broad concept of 'realized justice'—it is about justice in the world as it emerges, with the context and circumstances in which niti is applied.

The Rulers stand at the confluence of both—they are the establishers of niti in the system and of ensuring nyaya. It is a truism that all effective systems require 'shoulds and musts' that need to be adhered to by the whole system, for things to function towards their primary task. The Ruler knows that establishment of, interpretation of and compliance to rules are key in this regard. When the Ruler energy is absent, systems are likely to end up in chaos and anarchy. This archetype sees itself as a role model for others to emulate and seeks to help others secure stability, prosperity and security. As the name implies, Rulers tend to not only follow the rules and behave 'properly' but also expect the same of others.

You are likely to espy the Ruler energy in ample evidence in at least two types of organizations. One—in traditional organizations which have consciously or otherwise used patriarchy as a model of their functioning. Here, you are likely to see a great valuing of hierarchy, rules, concerns and elaborate detailing around eligibilities and authority.

Says Karun, of the company he first joined in 1987, a family-run auto components company in Chennai, India, 'When the Chairman walked into the office, conversations would cease, a hush would descend, when he walked in our direction, we would stand up; his word was law, his wisdom was unquestionable, you could even say that he was worshipped by some'.

Such organizations take the energy from symbol of the 'Chairman' into other lower levels also—at their individual levels, each leader would behave 'like' the big man. Cabin sizes, parking lots, canteen privileges, company cars and the list of perquisites associated with level were clear and unambiguous.

The second model of the Ruler comes up in organizations where there is very low tolerance for error. The Ruler energy is critical in such places. (The Airline industry, NASA, ICUs in hospitals, as examples.) Let us look at this side of the Ruler.

A study of the cause of aircraft crashes suggests that the proportion of crashes caused by pilot error has increased and now stands at around 50 per cent. Aircrafts are complex machines that require a lot of management—and the Ruler has to be evidenced in setting the imperatives for pilots. Of course, it also requires the Administrator energy in pilots to scrupulously follow the Ruler's *diktats*. Another system where the Ruler is crucial is critical surgery; the World Health Organization (the Ruler) has published a 'surgical safety checklist' to reduce morbidity and mortality in the global population arising out of postoperative surgical complications.

To look to the impact of the Ruler, we need to consider another concept from the ancient philosophical traditions of the Indian subcontinent, that is, Dharma—etymologically arising from 'dhri', which is to sustain, to carry and to hold. The idea of dharma is the idea of righteousness. Dharma looks to the underlying order in nature and human life and asks how that might be sustained and restored, if dislocated. The Rulers believe that they know what is the 'right path' for the system and they show that path and prescribe actions that will sustain that path. They would also unequivocally specify what is to be done if there is any form of straying from that path. Thus, the Ruler's advocacy would lead to 'proper functioning of the system', ultimately leading to both dependability ('I can count on this system to be such and such') and safety ('I know the boundaries of this system and as long as those are maintained, I know I will not come to harm').

The idea of 'Ramrajya' (the reign of Rama) comes to mind here—spoken of very fondly by Mahatma Gandhi as an idea for rulership. In his vision of Ramrajya, Gandhi says, 'By Ramrajya, I do not mean Hindu Raj.... Whether Rama of my imagination ever lived or not on this earth, the ancient ideal of Ramrajya is undoubtedly one of true democracy in which all citizens would be governed by rules that are fair and just and the meanest citizen could be sure of swift justice without an elaborate and costly procedure'.

What do Rulers do, did you ask? Oh there's a lot. To start with, they don the 'governance' hat—they would discern what is right and not right for the system. In that sense, they are like the 'superego'[1] function—they spell out the 'oughts' for the system and its members. This is in the world of principles. From there they also spell out the 'shoulds and musts'—the imperatives for the system. In this role, they would create rules, standards, norms and processes. They would affirm others that uphold the principles through their actions, and equally they would disaffirm those that do the contrary. And all of this does not have to be through their words alone—their silence and their deeds are equally articulate.

You can see various examples where violent acts are sometimes committed in the name of religion, race and faith. At such times, the common man looks to the Rulers in the political establishment to condemn wanton aggression and provide perspective and healing. If Rulers remain silent, it can be then perceived as affirmation of such actions. On the other hand, if the Rulers condemn such acts, another 'ought' is brought in—it clearly spells out the Ruler's mindset and principles and this can curb/limit downstream action of further violence and also ready the state machinery (the Administrators) to carry out action in accordance with the principles advocated by the Ruler.

The identity of the Ruler establishes how power will be distributed through the system but does not necessarily always

---

[1]Superego—the one of the three divisions of the psyche in psychoanalytic theory that is only partly conscious, represents internalization of parental conscience and the rules of society, and functions to reward and punish through a system of moral attitudes, conscience, and a sense of guilt (from Merriam-Webster dictionary, https://www.merriam-webster.com/dictionary/superego).

hold power. As an example, a committee set up in a corporate to decide how to conduct meetings would lay down the rules/ guidelines and sanctions for non-adherence, but it does not automatically become an adjudicating authority. In fact, after framing such rules, such a committee may even be disbanded. Rulers would be spotted framing laws, legislation and policies. You see them in legislative assemblies, in the senate, in the courts of justice, in board meetings of companies, even in playgrounds where children get together to decide how they will play a particular game that day and so on. Inside corporate organizations you might see them in functions such as process quality, production planning and control, personnel management and accounting. The world would view them as those that will provide safety, clarity, predictability and dependability on the one hand and as 'sticks-in-the-mud', imposing and focused rule-bound conformists on the other.

In any situation, Rulers would enter by being the specifiers of the boundaries—typically boundaries of time (when should something happen), task (what should happen), space (where will it happen) and experience (how it ought to happen). They may also redefine/refine/replace such existing boundaries if they deem them inappropriate or inadequate—thus they provide a container for events to take place in the system. They would also look to precedents to see how something was done earlier. That said, they would not necessarily be bound by the past. They would be more contextual creators of boundaries as described above. Our constitution framed for an independent India is a good example of this.

What Is Their Inner World Like?

The Ruler staunchly believes that it is better to be at the table than be on the menu. 'To be at the table' means that the Ruler would like to be in control of how the system ought to exist and inform the actions that would do so. To be so in control would mean that the Ruler is aware of the whole system, the context around it and provide both physical and psychological safety for those in the system so that it may function effectively. Their raison d'etre would be to enable the system to create bounty that the system can then partake of.

Says Ajay Srinivasan, the MD of a large financial house in India, 'My desire is for a controlled environment that is efficient and working predictably. I would like for everything to work like clockwork and to be able to create this world for me and for others. No surprises, no upsets'.

Though the Ruler may present a flattish, monochrome exterior to the world, they have an inner garden that hybridizes many other identities and then some more. The Ruler is gifted with reasonable and rational patterning, an ability to sense the norms needed. They have also the ability to spot the structural dynamics behind flaws so things can be ordered at a deeper level. An example of this—we live in a world of 'collaboration overload' and 'collaboration tool overload'. It is now becoming apparent that the costs associated with emails, IM and other forms of structured workplace collaboration are greater than the perceived and often suspect benefits. Attempts to liberate unproductive time by employing new tools or imposing new guidelines and meeting disciplines will prove fruitless unless steps are taken to deal with the underlying organizational dynamics, which is often 'organization complexity' and a culture of 'collaboration for collaboration's sake'. A Ruler would look to the underlying dynamics and direct what needs to be done for THOSE rather than to order the next new fad or tool, which the undiscerning resource-provider identity *might* just do. Rulers have the ability to stabilize chaos and to norm behaviour. Besides, they have the ability to see things with an accommodative yet firm eye, the ability to discern and decide what boundaries need to be set and what oughts need to be advocated, simply because they 'see' the whole picture.

The other big gift is their courage to take stands on what is best for the system. Now, no matter how this may sound to you, we offer that one of the biggest gifts of Rulers is that they are the 'anal retentive' kind, per Freud's classification of personality types in psychoanalysis. Their gift is perhaps their commitment to be in control of all aspects of their surroundings, holding on, not letting go. This helps them in articulating two important voices for the health of the system—the voice of sanity (that stabilizes chaos and norms behaviour and identifies the right oughts to adopt) and the voice of 'due process' (that identifies the shoulds and musts that will actualize the oughts).

The Ruler fears ambiguity, chaos and disorder in the system. What if the system breaks down? All control melts and things go haywire?

When the Indian self-proclaimed 'godman' Ram Rahim was recently convicted and a verdict pronounced against him, the law and order machinery in the state of Haryana virtually collapsed, leading to much embarrassment for the state government. Our expectation of the government is often of being the ruler and when things spin out of control, it can cause as much worry for the Ruler as the constituents in the system.

The other apprehension of the Ruler might be 'if things don't go MY way, they may turn out badly'. In knowledge-driven organizations, for example, this might take the shape of the 'Not Invented Here Syndrome', also referred to as NIHS—a classic example is how Nokia lost out in the smartphone market with their 'ruler within' obstinately staying locked into their ageing Symbian OS and refusing to make the switch needed to drive new consumer demand.

A third cause for some dismay in the Ruler is in their being seen as the punitive one, the imposing and obdurate object-entity. This dismay may also be part of their angst and sorrow. The other sorrow being their observation that most people do not see and appreciate the link between their 'rules' and the overall health of the system and that compliance to their diktat comes from a grudging sense of choicelessness.

The best 'matching identity' to face the Ruler would be that of 'the subject' and 'the law abider' or 'the complier'. A certain amount and quality of dependence is what the Ruler might look for. Perhaps linked to the first fear of the Ruler that we have described above, the presence of gadflies would irk them. Counter-dependent and ever under the skin, the Ruler is 'ill-met' by the gadfly and might do whatever they can (mostly unsuccessfully) to shake them off. What the Ruler does not perhaps realize is that gadflies can be stirred but not shaken (off). Examples of the Ruler's bête noire abound—Activist-investors in corporates, public-interest litigants, Change.org or Subramaniam Swamy—take your pick!

The Ruler in the Extremes

'Draconian' is an interesting word. Originating from the ancient Athenian statesman Draco who was known for his severe code of laws (remember Draco Malfoy from *Harry Potter* if you do not wish to go all the way to ancient Athens); this word points us to the overdone Ruler. Let us call them Draco for now. Rules and norms are overdone by Draco leading, often ironically, to the creation of counter-dependents and gadflies.

An example might be the antiterror law enacted in India after the Mumbai terror attacks in 2011. There is a belief that this law has ended up becoming a tool for human rights violations and denial of justice, mostly imposed on minorities and the marginalized classes as a political tool to silence them.

The grandiose Draco suffocates the subjects, compliers and law abiders, leaving no space or wiggle-room. Oppression is a natural consequence.

Interestingly, Draco is also sensitive to criticism and comes down with all their might on the uprisers if any.

There is no prize for guessing the effects of the enfeebled Ruler. The system moves to a stage of 'free for all' with neither distinction nor discernment. The lack of controls can make the system unsafe and vulnerable.

Remember King Theoden of the kingdom Rohan, from the Lord of the Rings trilogy? In his effete state, Rohan became open to attack by the advancing Orc Army and had to be saved rather heroically by members of the Fellowship of the Ring. The weak Ruler is also susceptible to paranoia. Idi Amin, Saddam Hussein, Gaddafi and Robert Mugabe come to mind—externally strong appearing but internally perhaps wondering what REALLY made them strong.

Angst	Hope	Gifts	Fear/ Vulnerability
That no matter what, I am seen as tyrannical and the one who imposes	That everything would work like clockwork and can be meaningfully controlled	Of clarity and the ability to provide structure	Of losing power to establish rules and control. Of the system spinning out of control

The Ruler as Leaders in Organizations

- The Ruler-as-Leader is at home where the context needs the establishing of structure, defining of order and deployment of control.
- Ruler-as-leader would set rules/guidelines/norms/ standards, they would take control of execution.
- Their relatedness with people would be guided by their systemic role; the Ruler would tend to provide safety and security to the system and the members of the system.
- When it comes to leading change and innovation, the Ruler's approach would be to provide a 'sandbox' within which transformations can occur and manage the boundaries of the sandbox as needed.
- They would provide the necessary structural support and rigour to enable growth—like role clarification, review systems and programme management.
- They may end up being over definitive and obdurate and thus create an over-regulated and rigidly hierarchical system.

20

The Strategist

The victorious strategist only seeks battle after the victory has been won, whereas he who is destined to defeat first fights and afterwards looks for victory.

—Sun Tzu, the Art of War

The Strategist

Who Is the Strategist?

We invite you meet one of the most prominent political figures of our times—Amit Shah. Mr Shah, the current President of the Bharatiya Janata Party (BJP), India's largest political party, started his political career in 1983. He joined BJP in 1986 and gradually rose in the hierarchy, holding various posts from time to time. In 1995, BJP formed its first government in the state of Gujarat, with Keshubhai Patel as the Chief Minister. At that time, BJP's main rival, the Indian National Congress, was highly influential in rural Gujarat. It is said that Shah worked together with Narendra Modi (the current Prime Minister of India) to decimate the Congress in the rural areas. Their strategy was to find the second most influential leader in every village and get him or her to join BJP. They thus created a network of 8,000 influential rural leaders who had lost elections to the pradhan (village chief) post in various villages but were hungry and raring to go. The cadre and leadership they built through this approach helped BJP win the state elections and the party has held power in that state for 19 years now!

The illustration, although by no means comprehensive, may clue us into the mind of the Strategists and understand this change supporting, yet strangely containing, masculine identity. They are those that would build an orientation for the future, creating a bridge between current reality and resources and future possibilities and opportunities; you could call them a combo of idealists and pragmatists—head in the clouds yet feet on the ground.

Opportunity spotters, they are adept at looking for possibilities, with ideas and resources that are both normal and beyond. In fact, it might look as if they take reality, construct an algorithm with it and proceed to play scenarios with every conceivable variable in the algorithm. They would have an idea of where the system needs to go, and will find a way to get there, like Amit Shah did with Gujarat politics. The time straddlers, with access to the past, present and future, and people with breadth of knowledge (assimilators of many fields) and those with an understanding of constraints and resources—internal and external—the Strategist emerges as the person who can 'see' the way to get to another place.

The Strategists are on the side of system movement and change. In many ways, they are the closest allies of Warlords who want to get somewhere—the Strategist would help them plot the how, the when, the who and even the where. A great example of how the Strategist complements the dynamic penetrative masculine Warlord is Mukesh Ambani, arguably the most successful businessman ever from India.

When Mukesh Ambani launched Reliance Jio in India, he sent the existing telecom service companies scurrying for cover under his price onslaught. Mukesh is the combo deal of the quintessential Warlord, backed by the quintessential Strategist. What drove his strategy essentially? Simple—it was Ambani the Strategist's astute decision to price the consumer while all his competitors were pricing their products/services. Ambani, the Strategist, knew that data is the new oil, and played his cards very well, and the new history is being made as you read this. Ambani, the Warlord, wanted to achieve, win, play big and get farther and higher and recruited the astuteness of the Strategist in himself to get the right path charted out for him to launch his 'shock and awe' move.

Even though they have a masculine orientation, they are simultaneously 'containing' and to know this side of the Strategist, we may benefit from understanding what ailerons and rudders in aircraft engineering are all about. In an aircraft, the combination of ailerons and the rudder allows the pilot to control the horizontal direction in which the nose is pointing. The ailerons and rudder are not like the engine which provides power and thrust; rather, they help the power and thrust be used in the desired direction in which the system needs to move. And they help the pilot control the direction of the craft. And THAT is the role of the Strategist— help 'contain and channel' the system in the desired direction, provide the desired roll, provide coordinated turns for the systems movement and proactively help the system avoid slips and skids.

We have already pointed out some examples of the Strategist energy in examples like Amit Shah and Mukesh Ambani; we can also look to more and variegated examples such as Sun Tzu, the great military strategist, Le Corbusier, the design strategist, Unilever LLC, one of the all-time great marketing strategists, portfolio managers of funds as investment strategists, and not to forget Chanakya aka Kautilya, the master political and economic strategist of ancient times in India. They are the students of futurism, just as they are the executive chef in a star restaurant, deciding the menu plan for the coming quarter. You find them in business, the military, in politics, in environmental activism and, well, in organized crime.

As Stephen Covey says—the leader is the one who climbs the tallest tree, surveys the entire situation and yells, 'Wrong jungle!', while busy, efficient producers and managers often respond, 'Shut up! We're making progress!'—that leader who gets out of the treadmill and climbs the tree is the Strategist—their joy coming not from just the goal but in designing how to get there and in designing the blueprint.[1]

From an impact perspective, the Strategists would help enable broad as well as deep thinking for a system. They would provide a way of helping the system understand the dynamism of the context and the environment. In the watch of the Strategist, capabilities would be built and thus needed development, focused competency growth and relevant learning would be core features of their presence in the system. Through this, they would enable a system to be future ready. Strengths would be identified and built and constraints ring-fenced.

As business complexity grows, companies are increasingly looking at building cutting-edge human resources (HR) strengths. The impact of the Strategist wave watching over the HR function has ushered in a new focus—HR analytics. It is now clear that the use of analytics in HR is growing, with organizations aggressively building people analytics teams, buying analytics offerings and developing analytics solutions. Strategically oriented companies are

---

[1]Covey, *The 7 Habits of Highly Effective People.*

hiring people analytics staff, cleaning up their data and developing models that help transform their businesses. People analytics today brings together HR and business data from different parts of the business and is now addressing a wide range of challenges: analysing flight risk, selecting high-performing job applicants, identifying characteristics of high-performing sales and service teams, predicting compliance risks, analysing engagement and culture and identifying high-value career paths and leadership candidates. That is the impact of the Strategist, for you!

Let us now zoom in—The Strategists seem to operate simult-aneously in three dimensions. One, the time dimension—they are the time travellers who can visit the past, be in the present and scan the future—all at once. Two, in terms of knowledge, they are able to bring in breadth—what else do we need to know to do this well. Three, they are masters of the context—what is important in the current context. They are the masterminds of what can be done to move something forward. The box below gives us an idea of this aspect of the Strategist (rolled in with another identity, the Collaborator) and what it can do for helping nudge a system towards success/growth.

As they go about living out their raison d'être, the Strategists would have conversations with wide-ranging sets of others. You would see them often challenging the status quo. They would search for new capabilities to be built. They would forecast trends and build analytical tools. They are masters at the art of asking searching questions, scrutinizing critical assumptions. One eye would be focused on outside trends and examples. They would readily use data, generate per-spectives, what-ifs and a variety of scenarios. They are likely to spot potential disruptions and offer advice. They would ask 'how can we stretch this to a new level' or 'what more can be done'. They would make trade-offs. The Strategists would typically know which pawns to move on the board. They would be able to go after understand and simplify complexities. They would generate plan Bs and Cs. In service of the goal, they would attempt to integrate all the perspectives that 'The Balanced Scorecard' speaks of. They would combine incisive analysis and intuitive leaps.

A good example is the 'Oracle of Omaha', the very wealthy Warren Buffet! An insightful look at his approach in Nic Liberman's book reveals a few things about this master strategist—for him, making money is like 'collecting money'—a hobby; he firmly believes in deferring gratification to counter anxiety and impulsiveness; he often refers to a notion of a circle of competence and how important it is to operate within it and to know its boundaries, and, not to forget his much talked about approach of operating counter to the market sentiment—sell when the market is buying and buy when it is selling!

Strategists tend to be oriented towards goals and the direction. When tests and challenges come up, they would tend to treat them as another part of the dynamic strategic puzzle. Rather than get in to the tactical space and the thick of things, they would step back and do what they do best—make an assessment of the current context and capabilities, use data and intuition to review the goal as well as the direction and look at the long-term impact and consequence of the 'problem and solution'. They are good at providing a space for divergence—allowing diverse and varied data points to emerge. They are thus likely to create an expanded view of the emerging reality which may solve the issue at hand for now and the future. Cindy Diamond is an innovation strategy consultant and the below extract from her blog lets us know how she describes her approach in facilitating for divergence, which she calls the 'expansion space'.

Expansion phase:

Step 1: Clearly identify the issue that is to be addressed with the innovation process.

Step 2: Immersion: Explore information relevant to the problem. This could be trends, current operating environment, market research, competitive data and so on—specific information that helps to shed light on the issue being explored.

Step 3: Identify opportunity areas: The team identifies buckets called 'opportunity areas' where a solution may be found. For an innovation session focusing on introducing a new snack product the opportunity areas might be 'healthy snacking', 'kid-focused snacks', 'snacking for energy' and 'indulgent snacks'.

Besides these, the Strategists would invariably consider options and weigh consequences. They would use a judicious combination of logic, intuition, imaginative reasoning, systemic reasoning and more, but the core thing for them would be the preferred future—'Am I addressing this in a way that creates the future we wish to create' would be their care about.

This vignette of Rashmi presents us a picture of how individuals energize the Strategist identity outside of the world of work. Rashmi was keen on going to Germany to study. Even a few years before the application process, she proactively enrolled herself into Max Mueller Bhavan and learnt German. She had no assurance that she would be going to Germany when she enrolled but she wanted to be prepared. This capability building made it easier for her to get an admission in a university of her choice. Her need was not to learn languages per se but a focused capability building effort in order to make it possible for her to get where she wanted to. Besides Rashmi, there are several known cases of students in India who systematically strategize and work towards career options—be it engineering, medicine, law, management or any else. Capability building begins years before the testing happens. The intent is carefully fostered. Choices of courses, universities, cities and the like are vetted. Data is carefully collected and collated, sifted through and analysed. Others' past experience sought, future prospectuses studied and employment opportunities predicted in a way that would put Paul the Octopus to some shame. In short, all that a Strategist would do would be done by the student ecosystem in India.

What Is Their Inner World Like?

If we put an inner voice to the Strategist, it might be 'I hope I can visualize and create a path towards the destination that we are going towards. I long to shape the future and to help the world. My desire is that by my actions and approach, clarity of purpose will emerge as well as the actions that support it. I also hope that in the real world, my "strategy" will blend well with the "tactics" that would inevitably come into play. I wish that I am always prepared, and that I will always find a way, manoeuvring the system around obstacles and uncertainties'.

The biggest gift of the Strategist is clearly their ability to anticipate what might emerge, to see ahead. *Ask Gorur Gopinath, the man who conceived of the ultra-low cost Deccan Airlines, and the man most identified with the compelling tagline 'SimpliFly'—till his enterprise was acquired (and killed, unfortunately) by the predatory Kingfisher Airlines. Gopinath had clearly visualized and anticipated the aspirations of the rising middle class and strategized to provide for it. (It is a different matter that he was never able to run it consistently well, perhaps because of the underdone Administrator and Ruler identity in him.)*

On the side is their ability to channelize the pragmatic and intuitive part of oneself. They have the gift of the rational and enquiring objective mind, often associated with INTJ in the MBTI scheme.[2] Seeing the moving parts AND how they are all interconnected is part of what the Strategists are endowed with. They also have the ability to 'deeply familiarize' themselves with the context—not in a gesture of tokenism but with integrity.

But then, what if the emergent situation demands action without thought and demands improvisation? Will tactics trump strategy? Will the big picture be sacrificed at the altar of the day's crying need? These would be some of the thoughts that might

---

[2]INTJ (Introverted, iNtuitive, Thinking, Judging type) is an abbreviation used in the publications of the Myers-Briggs Type Indicator (MBTI) to refer to one of the 16 psychological types.

haunt our Strategists. They may also worry if they would ultimately be able to see all the twists and turns in the increasingly
complex and approaching-chaos context. And talking of chaos,
they may quite fear it—knowing that in that cauldron, there is no
such thing as strategy. This sorrow may well be that that the
world wants a 'yes man' in the garb of the Strategist and that
the world may not really want to take their 'nos'. And perhaps as
a corollary—that the world does not see what the Strategist sees
and may not even wish to see it. *An interesting example of this is
what happened to Tata Steels' botched acquisition of Corus, and the
subsequent 'wash-hands-off' sale. The Strategist's nightmare. Could the
Strategist in Tata Steel have seen all the twists and turns like the global
recession (that was like almost waiting for this event of 2007 in the steel
company, to emerge from the wings!), demand contraction and worse—
Chinese steel being dumped in the global markets? And even if an astute
Strategist had seen these (in fact, the Strategist in the markets saw it
clearly and pummelled the Tata Steel prices down when they got wind
of this acquisition possibility), was anyone listening? As our resident
punster quipped, 'the acquisition was steel-born!'*

The Strategist in the Extremes

Firm conviction gives way to unyielding, dogmatic stances in the
case of the overextended Strategist, where the strategy itself
becomes a straitjacket. Here, there would be typically an over-
crystallized, congealed understanding of a situation, permitting
no flexibility whatsoever.

There would be way too much planning and looking ahead,
without looking at the 'now'. They may get so abstract and
theoretical that the system may not be able to execute anything.
There are also cases of companies where the so-called annual
Strategy cycle or exercise takes about 4–5 months, leaving one
wondering what they may be able to execute, if at all.

If the Strategist energy is not activated in one, we might
encounter stasis, or movement without coherent direction. There

may also be an inability to see one's capabilities in relation to the context, or even to examine the capabilities required or asking how those may be acquired or grown. A driftwood-like situation may ensue, with the inability to articulate or shape future events.

The Strategists may find resonant allies in a number of other identities—the Trickster, the Ruler, the Warlord, the Warrior–Crusader and the Artiste—largely because of their grounding complementary presence to contain and channel these vibrant penetrative and expressive identities.

Angst	Hope	Gifts	Fear/Vulnerability
No matter what, the world will not wish to see all that I can see, my gifts may not matter	That I can see, anticipate and shape the future	The ability to anticipate and see ahead and to blend idealism with pragmatism	That there will be twists and turns that I cannot hope to see and that in the real world, tactics will trump strategy

The Strategists as Leaders in Organizations

- By bringing in a big-picture orientation, they would enable alignment of tasks for efficient execution—people in the system will clearly see where their efforts will lead towards.
- By providing a clear sense of direction and strategy, they would galvanize people.
- They would assess and determine the need for changes and innovation and make a compelling case for making required shifts.
- They would enable the creation of the system's vision and the strategy for achieving the vision.
- They may end up having unrealistic projections about future scenarios and an obdurate way of not looking at ground realities and shifting micro-patterns.

21

The Troubleshooter

We can not solve our problems with the same level of thinking that created them.

—Albert Einstein

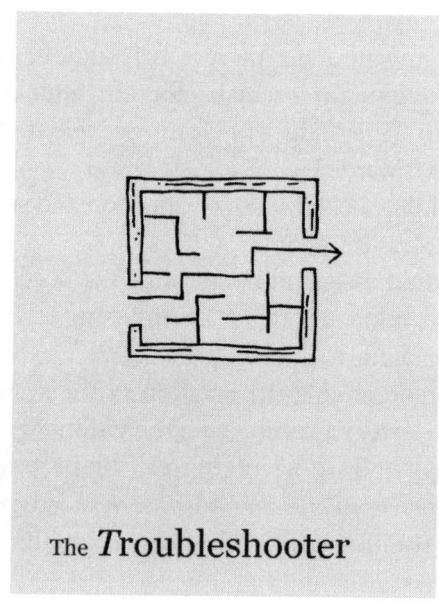

The *Troubleshooter*

Who Is the Troubleshooter?

On 15 January 2009. Captain 'Sully' Sullenberger and his co-pilot Jeff Skiles took off on US Airways Flight 1549, but roughly 2 minutes into the flight, a large flock of geese flew head-on into the engines, causing both of them to falter. Sully maintained contact with the people at the control centre, but the flight was lost from the radar. Sully decided in that moment that if he had to minimize the loss of lives of the passengers or on the ground, he had no option but to make a dramatic decision. He warned everyone on board to brace for the impact. The flight attendants mind the passengers and repeated instructions for them to be careful. Sully and Skiles then made their descent onto the Hudson River where they made a safe landing and all 155 human beings aboard the aircraft were saved.

In the investigation post the incident, the investigating officials ran simulations to indicate that if Sully had chosen any of the two airports nearby he would have made it. However, Sully convincingly proved that it was not physics and aeronautical engineering but his and his crew's presence—the human factor—that made the difference between life and certain death.

That is the Troubleshooter for you!

The Troubleshooter is the identity that intervenes, bringing in its judgement, discernment, knowledge and skills in situations of challenges, problems, trouble or crises and resolves them in a way that keeps the system intact or with minimal damage. The Troubleshooter is one who works to solve problems, resolving stalemates and impasses, and dissolving system stuckness, and thus helps the system grow and be revitalized.

In fact, *Global Edmonton*, one of the premier TV channels in Canada, has a show called the Troubleshooter, where consumer complaints are taken up in full public view for resolution. In the show, the anchor works with the complaining consumer and the sellers, identifying issues, finding out where a matter is stuck and attempting immediate closure. Many local panchayats in Indian villages also perform a Troubleshooter function, closing open issues right then and there.

Straddling the past (what has happened before), the present (what is happening now) and the near future (what is likely to emerge imminently), they are also ones that would foresee, intuit and pre-empt trouble. They have a sense of what a well-functioning system ought to be, what the current state is and how to bridge the gap (or how to prevent the gap from arising). They could be skilled negotiators, or mediators, sometimes they are 'in the moment discerners' estimating payoffs and making trade-offs before you could blink an eye. They could be arm-twisters, or authorized representatives usually with plenipotentiary power, and these are but a few illustrations of the avatars of Troubleshooters.

They could also be autonomous—see a problem or challenge and jump in to solve it (*Spiderman*, *Superman*)—or they could be specifically called upon to do so (those that negotiate with hijackers or hostage keepers). Their methods may be direct or blunt, and sometimes they may involve craft and sophistication.

Troubleshooters impact the system deeply and are of great value to it. The system runs productively and efficiently and that is of import not only to maintaining the status quo but also to be able to grow the system—after all, any system bogged down by problems and disease can hardly grow. The Troubleshooter's actions ensure functionality and ease, which become the foundation for growth and vitality. Very often, you find consultants as troubleshooters playing this role.

Several years ago, Edgar Schein wrote about organization consultants and their possible approaches to consulting. He identified these approaches as expert, pair of hands or collaborators. And in a broad frame, all these have troubleshooting embedded in them. In an 'expert' role, the consultants provide solutions based on their knowledge, experience and proficiency in a given area. The solutions prescribed by the expert, and the process, include very few other people. An easy example is the medical doctor. The 'pair-of-hands' approach is often that of a technician, where the consultant can literally roll up his sleeves and go to work alongside the client as a member of the client team. You often see this type of Troubleshooter as members of outsourced software coding or testing teams or IT systems maintenance folks in organizations. The 'collaborator' approach takes on problem-solving jointly with the client and assumes that the issues presented can most effectively be dealt with by joining their specialized knowledge with the client team members, in an equal status. The goal is not to solve problems for the client but to co-create solutions *with* the client that the client then applies to solve the problems. This leaves the clients with their own problem-solving resources for longer-lasting impact. Examples are often process consultants or consultant-facilitators or systems psychodynamics consultants who work on organization development, or leadership team dynamics or strategy and so on.

They also ensure that the system does not get mortgaged to conflicts. Unresolved conflicts could possibly turn toxic and corrupt the system. Troubleshooters would help douse fires, sort out conflicts and free up flow. They thus bring new energy into the system. Along with such energy come agility and resilience. Over time, systems that have good troubleshooters in them find their agility improving—their ability to move quickly and decisively across and beyond challenges and to do so with some ease and comfort ensues. Agility also translates to an ability to remain calm and productive during changing times, to seek out information where it is available and to act on opportunities even when you do not have all the data to mitigate all risks. So also is the Troubleshooter's ability to gift resilience to systems. Resilience is a system's ability to quickly and effectively recover from a challenging situation. While the mechanics of resilience may include everything from developing an optimistic orientation to managing personal energy of various people in the system, the essential key to resilience is to find the growth opportunity that comes out of the challenge that is being faced. So, the effect of resilience is twofold—it helps quick recovery AND it aids growth. Besides, even big and insurmountable-looking problems seem insignificant once the Troubleshooter goes to work on them.

We are reminded here, of big trouble in the form of 'boggarts' in the Harry Potter story series and how the Boggart-Banishing Spell is one called 'Riddikulus' which simply shows how ridiculous the trouble really is for the Troubleshooter who knows the spell. It causes the creature to assume a form that is humorous to the caster, along with a whip-crack noise, thereby counteracting the Boggart's ability to terrorise. Boggarts are defeated by laughter, so forcing them to assume an amusing form is the first step to defeating them. The spell is nothing but an ability to face up to the trouble and to show that often it is our fears, anxieties and apprehensions around the issue at hand that causes it to assume monstrous proportions.

That ability lies with the Troubleshooter—the ability to see the challenge for what it is—rather objectively. We shall add this in to the gifts of the Troubleshooter later in this chapter, of course, but the point here is to see the impact—that challenges and 'trouble' are seen for what they *are* rather than for how they *appear*. With this identity around in a system, the system can go about its business as usual because issues are taken care of. This is the 'hatchet-man' version of the Troubleshooter. And then there is also the 'capability-builder' version of the identity where over time, the system develops capability to work through challenges that earlier used to be addressed by the Troubleshooter.

How and where does this identity operate and what do they really do? This identity operates in the 'Urgent and Important' quadrant of the 'Eisenhower Matrix' popularized by Stephen Covey. Unlike the Strategist, they are not essentially thinking long term (though some of their actions do have long-term consequences, e.g., capability building, as we have seen earlier). They are here to remove obstacles in the path of a system's growth.

Here is an example—The Minister of Parliamentary Affairs is one of the key roles in the Union Government of India. This minister's major function is to efficiently handle the day-to-day diverse and enormous parliamentary work in lieu of the government in the parliament. It also serves as an important link between the two houses of the parliament. While these functions remind us of the Administrator identity, this minister is also the 'floor manager', often conversing with multiple interest groups inside the House of Parliament, and negotiating ticklish issues, identifying and resolving issues which are at an impasse or stalemate and in general to get the House to function smoothly and make legislative decisions. They also operate often at the interface between systems. In their book on *Boundary Spanning Leadership*, Chris Ernst and Donna Chrobot-Mason talk about six boundary-spanning leadership vectors—vertical (across levels), horizontal (across functions), stakeholders (across interest groups and between one stakeholder system and another), demographic (across diverse groups) and geographic (across markets and distance). We believe that Troubleshooters typically operate in the horizontal or stakeholder vectors (though you can find them in the other four too). They are good interface managers, protecting the needs of one system, locating friction between systems (either existent or imminent), reducing the friction proactively or 'ASAP' and in general enabling unhindered action and movement.

The Troubleshooters typically see patterns and connect the dots, not in the 'reading the tea leaves' or 'watching the cloud formations' sense, but more in the practical day-to-day sense, and through this, they anticipate and forecast issues and challenges that are likely to arise in the near term. Then, they would put in the effort to break big problems into manageable chunks and then put them back together again, banking on their strong rational and analytical side. They would 'formulate' the problem—then solving it becomes a matter of skill and practice. In their presence, it is not uncommon to hear the question 'What is the problem-statement out here?' You are likely to see them as calm, self-assured and composed and not flustered and anxious. You could consider Mahendra Singh Dhoni, Indian cricketer and ex-captain of the Indian team, who was famously known as Mr Cool. Troubleshooters would plan for near-term contingencies, and they are likely to be aware of how the cookie will crumble and what the consequences are going to be. And typically, they would have plans to mitigate crises and the capability to address them when they come.

Sometimes, you also see them display an air of arrogance that the whole world will come to them when a problem cannot be solved.

Harvey Specter in the popular TV show 'Suits' is a good example of what we have stated—a charming, confident and sometimes arrogant man who does not apologize for who he is. In an early scene in the serial, Harvey asks Mike, his apprentice, 'What are your choices when someone puts a gun to your head?' Mike replies with 'You do what they say or they shoot you'. Harvey then replies with this unforgettable line: 'Wrong! You take the gun, or you pull out a bigger one. Or, you call their bluff. Or, you do any one of the hundred and forty-six other things'. Harvey chooses to focus on solutions. Many of them.

In the world, you typically find them in most organization teams—a hatchet person to whom you could give an intractable problem and get traction on it, if not resolution. The character of Ryan Bingham in the film *'Up in the Air'* typifies this, who does what others are loathe to do—lay off people from the organization.

They could be ombudspersons who investigate complaints and issues and attempt to resolve them. You would find them in the world of politics, in service call centres, they could be the hackers in the software world or they could be skilled negotiators and mediators.

Problems and trouble are to Troubleshooters like water is to a duck. So, when we ask how they may approach problems, the phrase 'Duh!' escapes our lips almost involuntarily.

Let us linger a bit longer with this question and treat ourselves to a story. This story is about a certain ship, its engine and an old man with a hammer. The engines in the ship had failed and the crew tried to get in many experts to repair the engines but none could. Then, they heard about an old man who had apparently been fixing ship engines since he was a young fellow. This old man came, lugging his tools with him. He inspected the engines carefully, reached into his bag and pulled out a hammer. He tapped a part of the ship and the engines jumped back to life. He had fixed the problem! A week later, the captain of the ship received an invoice from the old man for a thousand dollars. The incredulous captain wrote back, asking him for an itemized bill. And the old man sent them one with the following items:

| Tapping with a hammer | $2 |
| Knowing where to tap | $998 |

If you are smiling, you *get* the Troubleshooters. They know that effort makes a difference, but all the more that knowing where to make an effort makes an even greater one.

Often, the identity of the Troubleshooter is understood in a limited sense as 'give them a problem and they'll work to solve it'. Peter Belohlavek paints a wider picture of this identity. They may use the approach of 'Repair' to find a symptom-reducing solution. This is what a plumber might do. Or they may use 'Palliatives' to mitigate the consequences of problems. The practice of 'golden parachutes' where considerable payouts are made to ask employees to voluntarily quit an organization is an example of palliatives. If the efficiency of processes is the issue, the Troubleshooter may be called upon to come up with 'systemic solutions'. Most six-sigma projects and total productive maintenance (TPM) approaches are systemic solutions. And finally, they may generate 'adapative solutions' where they go deeper than root cause analysis (which is a linear process) to reshape the whole context which not only solves a problem but also revitalizes the whole context (and therefore the particular system within that context).

Nobel laureate Mohammed Yunus's pioneering work on microfinance and microcredit is an example of an adaptive solution. It must be borne in mind, though, that at the level of adaptive solutions, you may find other identities prominently sharing space with the Troubleshooter (such as the Warrior–Crusader or the Strategist), just as at the 'Repair' end, you are also likely to see the Administrator's presence. We have elucidated this a little more while sketching the inner world of this identity, below.

What Is Their Inner World Like?

'Self is for the system', in the inner world of this identity. They value action for the system and get restless if the system gets stuck or mired. Their desire is for challenges that would test their dynamism and mettle. And it would appear that their own self-esteem and pride is tied in to their ability to unclog systems and solve challenges.

This identity's gift is its love of solving problems. They possess the ability to cut through obscurity and find clarity—a clear understanding of what stands in the way of achievement or movement and the ability to put that out of the way. They can be logical, analytical and at times can be intuitive and take leaps of faith as well—think Hercule Poirot at the one end and Miss Marple at the other!

Their role often needs patience. And they can adapt to this possibility as well. A 'no' is never a no, but more of a 'not this time', so they circle back to try a different way. That they are also gifted with a sense of *sangfroid* even as they do what they do is a precious one for them.

And then, they are also observant—their eyes and ears are constantly scouring the moment for any and all information and they process it real time.

'Will there be that ONE unsolvable, intractable challenge that I will not be able to crack?', the Troubleshooter might worry. They would know that the toughest problems to solve are the ones that are hard to detect and require humans to change their behaviour—perhaps requiring systemic or adaptive solutions. And since their pride is usually attached to their identity, unsolvable matters hit them personally. It is perhaps because of this that we often find the Troubleshooter functioning in 'combo deals' as we have suggested earlier in this chapter—the strong complementary presence of the combining identity would give them additional agility and resilience to go after the elusive solutions. If we take conservation efforts, for instance, we see the Troubleshooter and the Warrior–Crusader coming together. If we see issues around geopolitical boundaries, we may see the Troubleshooter and the Strategist coming together—as in the vexatious boundary issues between India and China or the Kashmir issue between India and Pakistan.

Their sorrow may be that they are generally the unsung heroes of the growth story. Often relegated to mentions in the 'vote of thanks', their regret may be that they put themselves often at high risk and stress and yet remain invisible.

Partly, through their own collusive stance of being 'for the system', they seem to keep themselves alive in a zone where their actions are instrumental and value utilitarian. Could it be that one of their laments is 'I am not worthy of being loved'? Though it must also be said that many Troubleshooters also seem to prefer being in the wings. One of the unintended consequences of the Troubleshooter is collateral damage. When chemotherapy attacks cancerous cells, it also attacks healthy cells and damages them. There is no moral discernment, and there is just needed action. And for that, sometimes the Troubleshooter is also avoided by the system!

The Troubleshooter in the Extremes

'My way or the highway', cries out the extreme Troubleshooter. Being a product of the system and existing in service of it, we can expect the Troubleshooter to, in any case, be beset by the pressures and inexorable turbulence of such. As these pressures grow, we can expect to see some of these people taking a grandiose stance and declaring that *their* way out of the morass is *the* best and no other voice needs be heard. Perhaps a paranoid delusionary stance, we wonder. Closely related to this is the obsessed trouble-shooter who will neither let up nor let anyone else enter the problem-solving space. And then there is the brusque trouble-shooter whose eye is ONLY for the problem and not the context—and this stance can result in SNAFUs (or OSPD—operation successful but the patient is dead). We also have the 'one-tool' troubleshooters who are like the hammer wielders for whom every problem is like a nail. Next on the list is the 'create-the-fire-to-put-it-out' firefighter, again a paranoid position—an 'out there' problem has to be crated and vanquished so the Troubleshooter can be the hero. Some Troubleshooters may also try to fix what may not be broken.

Push down the Troubleshooter energy, and what do you get? Unresolved issues become unresolvable issues. Productivity of a system can easily be hampered by the low Troubleshooter, for the same reasons. In low Troubleshooter configurations in a person or a system, the victim identity may also get constellated. The victim who plays the 'Yes, but' game. The 'Low Troubleshooter—High Victim' will definitely complain and even whine to others about how hard life is. But if there is any attempt to trigger troubleshooting, this identity classically comes back with a long list of 'Yes, but's'.

Angst	Hope	Gifts	Fear/Vulnerability
No matter what, I will always be the unsung hero	That I can keep things from spinning out of control. That I can minimize damage	The ability to solve problems, challenges and resolve stuckness	That there will be that *one* unsolvable problem that I will not be able to solve

The Troubleshooters as Leaders in Organizations

- They would diligently work towards dissolving blocks that come in the way of smooth throughput.
- They would enable breaking of staid/old patterns of relationships and help reconfigure relationships and forge new links between people.
- They would strive to find solutions and workarounds to get for change initiatives that get stuck.
- They may come across as 'mercenary', leading to high anxiety in the system, perhaps leaving people with wounds and bruises in the system.

22

The Trickster

Many native traditions held clowns and tricksters as essential to any contact with the sacred. People could not pray until they had laughed, because laughter opens and frees from rigid preconception. Humans had to have tricksters within the most sacred ceremonies for fear that they forget the sacred comes through upset, reversal, surprise. The trickster in most native traditions is essential to creation, to birth.

—Byrd Gibbens

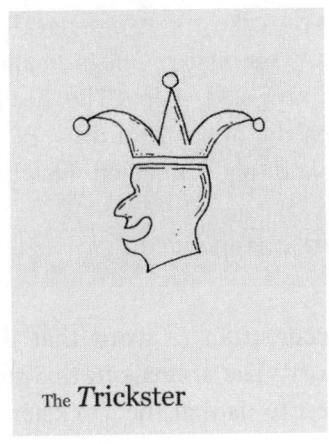

The Trickster

Who Is the Trickster?

Allow us to narrate a story to you, to introduce the Trickster. A story that many of you would be familiar with, perhaps. We present it here to indulge the trickster in you...

Two cats were prowling together. One of the cats saw a big cake on the path and jumped to get it, and missed. The other cat jumped up and picked it.

The first cat said, 'Give me the cake. It is I who saw it first'.

The other cat said, 'Keep away from it. It is I who picked it up'.

They fought and they fought, and they fought some more. But there was no solution. Just then, a monkey passed by. He thought 'What foolish cats they must be! Let me make use of this chance'.

He came to the cats and said in a loud voice, 'Don't fight. Let me help you share the cake'. The cats handed over the cake to the monkey.

The monkey split the cake into two parts. He shook his head and said, 'Oops! One is bigger. One is smaller'. He had a bit of the bigger and now said, 'Eeps! This has become smaller now'. He ate from the other. And thus, he went on eating from part to part and finally finished the whole cake.

The poor cats were disappointed.

Now, let us deconstruct (a word that the Trickster likes very much!) this story. The animals in this story—the cats and the monkey—suggest to us that the Trickster's arena is close to the animalic level of consciousness—partly instinctual and therefore unconditioned, no mores, no norms.

Then, we come across the cake—the lure that is sought to be appropriated and the 'frailty of the desire for absolute possession' that accompanies it. The Tricksters have an olfactory sense that picks up these frailties and the vanity that lies behind them, or maybe it is the other way around—maybe they pick the scent of vanity and the frailties that lie beneath! The Trickster always makes use of opportunities and chances, as did our monkey in the tale. Then comes the trick—on the face of it, it is all sleight of hand—the monkey breaks pieces off that are never equal halves, and what's more, he gobbles them up—the dice are always loaded by the Tricksters in their favour. But the underlying payoff is that the round goes to the Trickster and the vain-frail other is left disappointed. In human situations where reflexivity is possible, such an experience could catalyse new awareness in the system, something that we will shortly see as being characteristic of this identity.

And, now, let us move forward and meet the trickster in their lair.

The Trickster *knows* that they are the Trickster. They are fully aware of the context, the dynamics operating in the 'here-and-now'. Who is doing what, who is saying what and who is NOT doing or saying something—these and many more are the signals that their ever-present antennae are picking up and using all the time. And to top all of this off, they remember—oh yes, they do! All of the whats and whos and whens and wheres that we talked about—they remember them all and bring them in where they deem necessary.

The Tricksters are psychopomps, who bridge the conscious and the unconscious. As the psychopomps, they provide passage for any person or system to access the 'underworld', often without the conscious knowledge of that person or system. If we look at it that way, all dreams are Tricksters and working with dreams and symbolic work of any sort (as often happens in individual, group therapy and process work or group relations work) is an encounter with the Trickster. And as psychopomps, their task is never to judge—they would take you to the edge of the cliff, get you to see that there really is no way but to jump into the chasm and the clincher is this—they would jump with you, to see where it all leads. The Trickster who leads you to the precipice, exhorts you to jump and stays behind is probably a charlatan. Joseph Campbell, the celebrated world mythologist, says that the Trickster is at once the Devil, the Fool and the Creator.[1] All at once, they can bedevil you with their unpredictable nature, they can fool around and thus fool you, and in all that they can help you create an alternate to the existing. Campbell goes on to suggest that this identity can upset your very notion of a deity—the Trickster can be that deity that behaves in the way you do not expect deities to behave. Think of Lord Krishna from the Indic mythology.

Sigmund Freud famously used a term 'polymorphous pervert' to denote a person who obtained sexual gratification through the means outside of social norms. Pulin Garg of the erstwhile Indian Society for Individual and Social Development used the term more broadly to denote persons that could assume many forms and derive gratification from their ability to bedazzle and befuddle others simultaneously. We tend to take the latter view—to us, the Trickster is an identity that is constantly shape-shifting—it is a *behrupiya*—you cannot tie it down. In so doing, it confounds you and leads you to the edge of new discovery. In many ways, we believe that facilitators of human processes and systems work need to have a bit of the polymorphous Trickster identity in them and our lament is that such folk seem to have chosen to get stuck to a 'Healer' identity or 'Custodian' identity or in recent times the 'Warrior–Crusader' identity—without adequately inviting in the Trickster. If we ever were to meet the Trickster and ask it to talk about itself, you might hear this, 'I am this and I am that…. You can find me here and there…. I have many faces…. I am

---

[1]Campbell, *Hero with a Thousand Faces*.

many things, in the true sense.... I shift my shape, my colour ... I shift my space and I shift with time.... And ergo, no one will ever know who I am—I hide and I slip away...'. The Trickster would catalyse change and raise new awareness by challenging normal rules and conventional behaviour. They are the ones that playfully challenge the seriousness, the idealism, the romanticism, this -ism, that -ism and the many such stances we take in life. And if you challenge the Trickster on grounds that they contradict themselves, you are likely to be rebuffed by a disarming smile and a quoting of Walt Whitman's lines 'Do I contradict myself? Very well, then I contradict myself, I am large, I contain multitudes'.

Shrewd attorneys and lawyers are usually good Tricksters. And they tend to have such an uncanny knack of seeing through the opposing parties' arguments that political parties often tend to nurture them as official spokespersons. Ergo, you see them often on national TV news channels, arguing down the show host or the other panellists. Sambit Patra, Shaina and Kapil Sibal are personalities that might be familiar to Indian audiences, so too a gadfly like Subramaniam Swamy. Many cartoon and comic strip characters were fashioned out of the Trickster identity, as this is one identity that allows the cartoonist or commentator to bring in a tongue-in-cheek look at the goings-on in the context and express it creatively. Wile E. Coyote, *Bugs Bunny*, Jerry in *Tom & Jerry* and Brer Rabbit, all from some decades ago, are such characters. Frank Abagnale Jr, in *Catch Me If You Can*, brings us face to face with the Trickster as the con artist. Several talk show hosts and stand-up comedians—like Trevor Noah, Jerry Seinfeld, Jerry Springer and the neophyte Ramki Muthukrishnan (this guy even gets us to believe that he is a respectable Wall Street executive when he is not doing stand-ups!)—fit the Trickster bill. Edward Snowden and Julian Assange are worthy members of the Trickster club, as are the many Yakshis, the mythical beings of Indic mythology.

Now that we are somewhat well acquainted with the Trickster, let us gauge their impact on us and the world. Let us start with what might seem like an unlikely impact, their wisdom! Huh, we hear you say, and we exhort you to read on. The typical zen koan is an example of the wise Trickster. Sample these koans—'What was your original face before you were born?', 'When you can do nothing, what can you do?' and 'If you meet the Buddha on the road, kill him'. Koans are self-paradoxical riddles that open up the mind, by catching intelligence unawares and making it irrelevant, thus by pushing your mind to go beyond its known limits. Very much the Trickster. In a similar vein are people like Osho and Sadhguru Jaggi Vasudev. Their pithy spiritual commentary often pulls the rug from under one's feet—you land with a thud and wake up a little bit more. We have come to believe that with the wise Trickster, it is no longer just about a twist in the tale but rather more about the tale in the twist! Figure *that* one out!

The Tricksters' actions tend to disturb the flow and influence changes—not symptomatic ones but deep changes in the structure of one's thought. So new action is always around the corner when they are at play. Since they subvert power structures and the normal 'givens', traditional or positional or structural power is usually on shaky ground when this identity is in action.

Another impact of the Tricksters is that beyond their appetite for games, they are often known for bringing the balance for the well-being of communities: they make people laugh in times of sadness, and they moderate the most optimistic ones. Remember Robin Williams in *Patch Adams*, who in a distinctive Trickster-Healer avatar uses humour to treat patients (and of course compassion)—a stark Tricksterian contrast from the stodgy and stiff approach of the medical school hospital which is trapped in the underbelly of the world of structure and order (WSO).

Igniting the groundswell is another impact of the Trickster's presence. Several groundswell movements are apparent in today's digitized world. *The bay area company, Yelp, and Zomato in India, let the patrons of restaurants rate restaurant food, service and overall experience. People frequently use this before trying new restaurants or looking for new types of cuisine. Some savvy restaurants even have signs on their door asking to be rated, and this is a new shift that puts formal restaurant reviewers in a slightly less relevant position. 'Rate*

My Teacher' is an app that has been around for some time—to find out which teachers are good, which are not and which are easy. Students rate teachers and provide real-time feedback. Rasikas.org is a website where listeners and audiences share their opinions and feedback about music concerts by Indian music artistes and, in many ways, have put the traditional music critic out of relevance.

We will stop with one more impact—the Trickster as change shaper and context shaper. There are some of us that adapt to change that has already happened. Then, there are some of us who are in the 'eye of the storm' of the change process and know they have to change along with the moment. There are some of us who see change coming and proactively prepare or adapt. The Trickster decides what they would like to see as the context or the change and then create the conditions to make that happen. Gandhiji was successful in pushing the independence narrative for India largely on the account of the fabulous Trickster identity in him—be it the civil disobedience movement, ahimsa as a strategy to fight, his fasts that forced the hand of the powerful or his ashrams that simultaneously worked for a new social order—we doff our hats to this magnificent embodiment of the Trickster and need we say, much much more!

Let us now examine the Tricksters' actions, behaviours and stances. They can be seen questioning the given knowledge, social systems and power structures by pointing out some of the absurdities, ironies and paradoxes in them. Through playfulness and shrewdness, they would question orthodoxy, traditions and conventions. Through wit and cunningness, sometimes even scurrilous, they may overcome physically stronger others.

Many activists petitioning for change in media like change.org are warrior–crusader tricksters. Karnatik musician T. M. Krishna's famous 'Poramboke' song is one such example, where he uses music as a medium to question the establishment and to help us question our complicity in social ills.

They would confront authority—not eyeballing them down but in a skilfully adroit way, with adequate wriggle room for themselves—they would always have an escape hatch that would confound those that attempt to chase or hunt them down. Their confrontation would not threaten the other (who is being confronted) physically but in a way where the other's reputation, pet stances and the hollowness of the other's so-called philosophical position stands exposed. It may be appropriate to say that there is a disarming and an outflanking in their style of confronting. Never in your face, they are likely to be more like Charlie Chaplin— you are helplessly giggling while simultaneously receiving a jolt! They would make a situation and perhaps life—a little lighter, playful, would help us to laugh at ourselves, move outside of defined boundaries and get the system to do so as well. The Trickster often brings forth the point of view of the devil's advocate. There is playfulness that hides their subversion. They can also be political, ignite and incite trouble and prey on human 'emotional weaknesses'. Perhaps their only conviction is that play does not have morals, so anything works and is alright. They are also able to work in the moment and change direction spontaneously, and that is why they are also called the shape-shifter.

Trickster spotting is fun. They are not always people. Like we have said before, zen koans and dreams count. The great 'Unconscious' part of our psyche is a great Trickster. Besides unfailingly producing, directing and script-writing dreams, it gives us the Trickster effect through gaffes, 'Freudian' slips, goofs and faux-pas. 'Eeps, did I just say that' or 'Damn autocorrect', or 'That mail went before I intended it to' or 'Officer, I can explain'— typical statements that follow the Trickster's visit, however brief. Another view we hold is that you spot the Trickster when you cannot spot them. Sounds like a koan? Precisely our point! And of course, you see them in politics, and they are speech writers, snake-oil salesmen and more. You can freely add to this list.

When it comes to challenges and 'problems', the Trickster relishes winning. They play to win. Not that they never lose, but losing is part of a longer game to them and they will stay in the game to emerge out triumphant another day. And they are very likely to seek out, spot and go after the flaws, chinks and the fault lines of the challenge—not for them the muscle flexing, teeth baring and chest thumping.

Here is an example of this—If you have watched the Raiders of the Lost Ark, you might remember the scene where in the marketplace, a fierce sword-wielding Arab comes at Indiana Jones doing some fearsome moves with his sword, with a lot of drama and action, and in return Indiana Jones simply and swiftly shoots the man down without getting into an equal fight.

Besides, using a postmodern lens—the Tricksters would wonder whose power needs are being surreptitiously met in any arrangement and question it—by this, they would go to the deeper underlying problem. They would wonder (usually openly) as to which 'subterranean flows' give rise to the problem in the first place. They would also problematize the 'givens' and question them. As an example, a 'generally accepted given' like 'Coaching is good for leadership development' would be problematized as 'a problem is in the assumption that coaching is good for leadership development', thus opening up such axioms and truisms for critical examination. They would deal with challenges as a chess player would—each move they make, they reckon, would need to present the other or the situation with a limited number of options to respond with, and for each such possible response, they would try and map their responses in advance.

What Is Their Inner World Like?

When thinking of the desires and hopes of the Trickster, one is immediately reminded of the great actor Raj Kapoor as the clown in the great movie *Mera Naam Joker*—the show MUST go on, no matter what. And while it is, one must play, have fun and win. Another desire may be that 'power must not creep in on my watch'— given that the world of masculine power is usually the bete noire of this identity. Their hope may be to keep a debate going on, that the fire must burn on and on. Often, the Trickster arises from a source of deep pathos of being an outsider—of a difficulty of belonging to a norm either because circumstances have excluded or belittled them, or they have ended up as victims of some power that somehow did that to them, provoking a defence or defiance. Thus, maybe their deep desire is to belong to someone or something but now on their (the Tricksters') terms! And their game then becomes an elaborate one of showing that there really is no system that is worthy of them, or one that can meet their terms, and so they roll on, from one 'unbelonging' to another.

This identity is endowed with the ability to unearth the irony in most situations and to question any given knowledge/institution. They have a sense of humour and ability to spot the ridiculous, multiplied by a critical faculty called 'no fear of expression'. They take life 'not so seriously' and enjoy trusting themselves. They are gifted with an innate restlessness, one that triggers them to poke and nudge anything static or congealed and to try and get it to flow and never to forget—the ability to disrupt without seeming to but certainly meaning to!

The Tricksters' fear may be of encountering deep stagnation and staticity that does not respond to their overtures and that grows in proportion, overwhelming them. They may still do their bit in the face of the engulfing juggernaut of the WSO, but then what is a few seconds of avalanche in the face of the inexorable and timeless flow of a glacier. So, R. K. Laxman would continue his cartoons, people would laugh for the day every day, but the indefatigable political establishment would continue slowly but ever so surely. And the angst of the Tricksters may be that in the final analysis, the system always gets to win—perhaps too many people get put off or threatened by the Tricksters, too few people get awakened by the Tricksters to be able to ensure lasting change and no one truly 'gets' them—that they are condemned to plough a lone furrow. For us to truly 'get' the Trickster, the others have to morph into the Trickster themselves or be indulgent fans. All others feel victimized and mostly end up displaying brute power or join the glacier of structure and order or slink away into the shadows—thereby reinforcing the Trickster's starting stance of having to defrock the world of its pomposity and starchedness.

The Trickster in the Extremes

Several years ago, Carl Jung wrote about the *puer aeternus*, the eternal child, who covets independence and freedom, opposes boundaries and limits and tends to find any restriction intolerable—in a pathological way. They tend to fear getting caught in a situation from which it may be impossible to escape and so all of their life is led provisionally. There is a persistent refusal to grow and face life's challenges, and instead all of life is treated as a game. Michael Jackson and his Neverland Ranch jump to mind immediately. Part of this phenomenon is also that of lying, cheating, infidelity and so on—aspects that the context might view as unethical. Perhaps communities that have failed to value and affirm the creative endeavour and playfulness of its people end up unintentionally deifying the *puer aeternus* who finds expression in scams, frauds, ponzis and the like.

India is perhaps a prime example—the 2G scam, the cricket T20 imbroglios, Vijay Mallya and the Kingfisher story, Nirav Modi and the Punjab National Bank story and the many scams that politicians regularly and almost predictably get into—the list can go as long as you wish. Equally perhaps this is ironically true of communities that may have overvalued the creative endeavour and ambition of its people—think no further than the subprime collapse of the USA and the shockwave it sent across several financial markets across the globe.

In contrast, structures would continue unquestioned and unchallenged when the Trickster energy is dull. Holy cows would roam the streets untethered. Systems would be dull monochrome spaces with no levity or low joie de vivre. Perhaps a community that is low in levity and cannot laugh at itself may be fertile ground for authoritarianism or fascism!

Angst	Hope	Gifts	Fear/Vulnerability
No matter what I do, the system will always win	That the show will go on and that nothing will stop it	The ability to see beyond what others can see and to express what I see	That structure and order will overwhelm me, swallow me, consume me and spit me out

The Trickster as Leaders in Organizations

- They would be open to jettisoning/modifying an existing plan of execution and may tend to look for shortcuts and 'jugaad' to get the task done. They would lead by catalysing change.
- They would trust the intelligence and the resilience of the system and the people in it. They would prefer dynamism and change and encourage people to question and challenge.
- If the Trickster leaders sit at the top of the iceberg, they would challenge the existing, set new rules and norms or at least break the old ones. If at the bottom, they would know which levers make the most impact and would interrupt, disrupt, incite, excite but kick the system into play.
- They may end up stirring up/amplifying 'political dynamics' in the system and/or generate an impression that it is ok to take rules and norms lightly.

23

The Warlord

*It is not those who can inflict the most but those who can endure
the most who will conquer.*

—Terence MacSwiney, Principles of Freedom

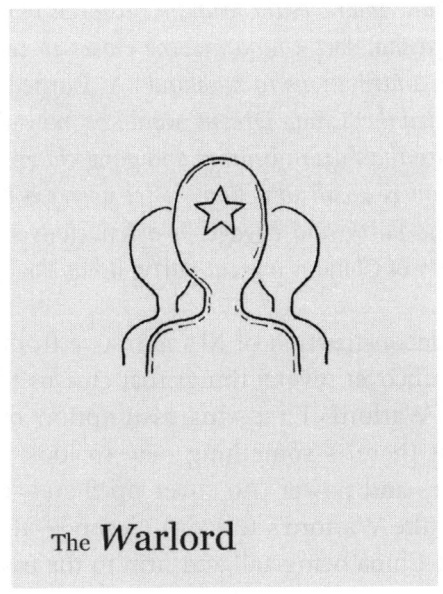

The *Warlord*

Who Is the Warlord?

The Warlord is not a bashful identity. Not in the least. They are the ones who would be quite unashamed about their desire for power and exercise of strength to acquire and retain power. They would expand the frontiers of any system and pursue new opportunities for growth. They would exercise power, be ready to compete and mobilize forces and resources for growth and expansion and achievement.

Xi Jinping, the 64-year-old President of the People's Republic of China, heralded the dawn of a new era of Chinese politics and power at the start of a historic Communist party congress celebrating the end of his first term in office earlier in 2017. Speaking in the Great Hall of the People in Beijing, Xi told delegates—'thanks to decades of tireless struggle, China stood "tall and firm in the east"'. Xi indicated that it was time for China to transform itself into 'a mighty force' that could lead the world on political, economic, military and environmental issues. 'This is a new historic juncture in China's development', Xi declared in his bold address outlining the party's priorities for the next 5 years. 'The Chinese nation ... has stood up, grown rich, and become strong—and it now embraces the brilliant prospects of rejuvenation.... It will be an era that sees China moving closer to centre stage and making greater contributions to mankind'. Xi warned that achieving what he has hailed the 'China Dream' would be 'no walk in the park': 'It will take more than drum beating and gong clanging to get there. [But] our mission is a call to action ... let us get behind the strong leadership of the party and engage in a tenacious struggle.... The Communist party of China is a great party; it has the fight and mettle to win'.

A simple deconstruction of Xi's narrative from just this one extract would uncover several things that clue us to the essential nature of the Warlord. First—his assumption of a 'new era', indicating that there is something new to look forward to in Chinese politics and power (no cover up there—the words are straight out of the Warlord's lexicon). Second—the letter of his words is about China being 'tall and firm in the east'—the spirit, however, is connotative of a towering monolith which is unshakeable. Third—he uses the term 'transform itself into a mighty force'—the words are inherently static but the meaning he creates in the listeners' and readers' minds is of unquestionable dynamicity and penetrative and assertive masculinity (a clear characteristic of the Warlord). Fourth, the individual elements of his words—all the verbs, adjectives and nouns ('new era', 'tireless struggle', 'tall and firm', how he envelops the whole of 'the east' before you could blink, 'mighty force' and so on) clearly convey strength and desire and power. That is the Warlord—they are about power, dynamicity, masculinity, potency, domination and prowess.

The Warlords pursue growth, and inorganic growth is par for their course. Conquests are valued—not necessarily for bloodlust but perhaps for the joy of competing and winning. Their focus is on expansion and expansive growth. Expand, acquire, conquer and scale-up, are their mantras. These are people who know how to propagate ideas, grow businesses, expand empires, reach the masses to galvanize the groundswell and find opportunities in all kind of places.

Now, you do not have to go trudging through a desert or a thick jungle to locate the warlords in a well-guarded hideout. No, dear reader, they are all around us. They may well be you and us, too! They do not have to be occupying physical territories or growing or expanding those, though that is also good for the Warlord.

Allow us to illustrate this with some examples. Google started out as a search engine way back in the 1990s. Today, it has expanded into (and this is a partial list, by the way) leisure (Chromebook, YouTube, Play), work (Gmail, Drive), retail (Android Pay, Assistant) and travel (Google Maps, Pixel). Apple started as a maker of 'the alternate computer' the Macintosh, and no prizes for guessing what this Warlord now dominates. We can add Samsung, Microsoft, Facebook and more to this, but we are sure we now have a picture in front of us. In the corporate space, increasingly, the Warlord dominates a territory called 'your attention'. And at the more physical or visible/tangible level, we have already given you the example of Xi Jenping. Consider adding Vladimir Putin to this (annexation of Crimea), Narendra Modi (to quote him from earlier in December 2017—'Congress under Indira Gandhi ruled in 18 states but the BJP and its allies have gained power in 19 states in the past three-and-a-half years. Soon, we shall win other state polls too') and Mukesh Ambani at the time of his launching Reliance's Jio service who said—'India's digital mother tongue will be Jio's IP'. You can also check out the territory where spirituality and yoga meet economics. Yoga Guru Baba Ramdev runs a highly successful fast-moving consumer goods (FMCG) enterprise, and the Art of Living (Guru Sri Sri Ravishankar) runs a successful Ayurveda-inspired business (candy, ghee, toothpaste, beverages, tea, hair oil, shampoo, gel, cream, soap and spices).

In terms of impact, the Warlord would change the very framework and deeper structure of the system (or even the ecosystem). Clearly, the arrival of Reliance's Jio in the 4G services space in India has done that—the landscape is not the same anymore. The Warlords would be dominant, demonstrate prowess and create growth, often having a galvanizing effect on people. Through them, the whole system gets in touch with its potency, desire and arousal. The system gets ready to not just meet challenges but also actively looks out for new challenges. They would embrace ambition and always look at 'what next' and 'what more'.

It is fascinating to watch the behaviours and actions of Warlords. They are naturally good negotiators and will typically show up as 'hard-ball' negotiators—no compromises, no ceding and no accommodating and may appear quite unreasonable, at times. More often than not, they are willing to take high risks and would set what Collins and Porras refer to as big, hairy, audacious goals (B-HAGs) and readily compete to achieve those. The consequences of failure do not seem to act as a deterrent to their ambitions. *Jack Welch, the once-iconic CEO of General Electric, is quoted as saying 'Number one, cash is king … number two, communicate … number three, buy or bury the competition'.*

When it comes to the systems they operate with, they may bend frameworks and systems to their advantage—not for them the compulsion to operate within prevailing institutional frameworks. You will find them creating and nurturing sound networks—not necessarily for collaboration but networks that would help them grow, like coalitions and alliances. This often results in their having a coterie around them—people who would form the power centre of the system with the Warlord often as the nucleus. This coterie would make all decisions, and resources would come to them and be distributed by them. And this coterie may be different from their administrators and professionals that run ongoing tasks in the system. The coterie would be the kin and the kindred who would offer their loyalty to the Warlord. Through the coterie, the Warlord would operate their power base and also grow it.

The Warlords are likely to surround themselves with people who remind them of the future, not the past. They are not great fans of history, at least not as much as they are of emergent futures (and we are not talking only of futures of the Wall Street kind).

As leaders, they will also spot talent internally—and invest in people who can enable their dreams of growth and expansion. To such individuals, they would offer protection especially to those that accept their status. They are defined by their urgency to act and are never easily satisfied. They are not embarrassed about their desire or prowess either.

Microsoft wants to put a computer in every home, Heinz wants to put sauce on every table—and they advertise their intent, in as many words, if you please!

They are capable of taking on a lot of pressure without feeling stressed out or cracking. 'Pressure can bust pipes, but it also can make diamonds' is likely to be their staunch belief. And they make others compete with THEM (*as an example, Apple which keeps rewiring the landscape of the markets it operates in and gets its competitors to emulate their products*).

And last in our limited list but never the least, they 'take the shot everytime', never miss an opportunity.

We have already mentioned that you do not have to go searching for the Warlords, for you are likely to be on their path (or in their way, if you do not step aside!) one way or another. You will spot them in the blazing headlines of newspapers.

Warlords do make for good cover stories. At the time we are writing this, an analysis of the last 30 days' headlines of world news throws up an interesting cocktail of (among other things) the bitcoin price surge, an ISIS suicide bombing, North Korea calling UN sanctions an act of war, Brexit talks (an interesting twist to 'exit' as a form of unhindered growth for the warlord), Trump's Jerusalem move and so on. Did you spot the warlord yet?

They are also likely to be 'tough talkers' who might talk against the prevalent discourse, without mincing words—*an example is India's cricket captain Virat Kohli who now seems to be in a mood to take on the Goliath-like Board of Control for Cricket in India (BCCI), at a time when the all-powerful cricket board looks to be on the back foot, especially after the Supreme Court appointing the Committee of Administrators to run BCCI affairs with an aim to reform the cricket body.*

Kohli has pushed the Board to look at the cramped schedules for Indian cricketers, then about demanding a greater share of India' growing cricket wealth for the players and has chosen to place himself in a position where he has publicly stated that he would voice his opinions with no fear—a position that players do not take for fear of incurring the Board's wrath.

Typically, the world seems to view the Warlords as those that would cash in on opportunities, as ambitious, worldly and aware of the emerging context—if not actually shaping it!

We believe that the Warlords would have an opportunistic orientation when it comes to dealing with challenges and life's circumstances. And we are not using the word 'opportunistic' in a pejorative sense here. Warlords seem to have a strong olfactory sense—they would approach challenges with the questions of 'what is the opportunity in this?' and therefore 'should I jump into action OR adopt a near-future orientation OR act like a strategic warlord?'

For instance, there are commentaries that indicate that Donald Trump never really thought that he would win. He had been talking of running for the office of the President for several years, but this time around, his keen olfactory sense kicked in (and how!) and the result is there for all to see. Warlords also tend to have a good strategist as part of their coterie—Trump and Bannon and Narendra Modi and Amit Shah being good examples. Either that, or they would assiduously cultivate their own internal strategist identity to complement the Warlord in them.

If the Warlords choose an immediate action ploy, they would bring in a laser-like focus on getting the challenge or problem out of the way and making it irrelevant. They would, for instance, raise the game to a different level altogether. Here, they would tend to jump into action and go for simple quick fixes that move the system towards closure rather than long drawn-out systemic/structural approaches; they would marshall (or maybe corral is the right word, do you think?) the best resources that can address the issue—leverage contacts and the 'network' as needed. If they choose a long-term orientation, they would apply a broad contextual understanding to define the problem itself, look at solutions from many points of view and deploy resources in their command to solve the problem, rather that roll up their own sleeves. If they choose a near-term orientation, they are likely to use current structural levers to get their way—they would use the loop holes to their advantage and 'dominate' the situation to get things done.

What Is Their Inner World Like?

The Warlords' greatest desire would be 'desire' itself and specifically the desire to acquire and consolidate power, significance, ambition and dominance. Their search for power would be both power as influence and power as autonomy but more of the former. In seeking power as influence, the Warlords would like to have control over other things, other people and the world outside.

And their way of getting this power is to simply acquire that territory (including non-physical territory like the Internet or social media for instance). Once they have that territory, they would bring in suitable Rulers and Administrators who would do what they do to stabilize and 'run' it. The Warlord's desire for power as autonomy is their wish to resist others' influence on them and to be able to shape their own destiny: if warlords do not have their autonomy, they may believe that they cannot have the influence that they seek.

Research suggests that when people seeking power as autonomy get their autonomy, their thirst for power seems quenched; they tend to stop seeking power, whereas power as influence works the other way—getting more influence fuels a need for more influence—over more people, over a larger territory, over more complex structures. THIS is where the Warlord resides and rules.

The Warlords carry with them the gift of penetrative-assertive dynamic masculine power that allows them to get to places where others cannot, have their way in things and not have to compromise.

Sanjay Subramanian, the reigning monarch of the Karnatik music field in India, got to the pinnacle at a young age (he was just 47 when he received the Sangita Kalanidhi, one of the most coveted titles in Karnatik music!), and he led a charge founded on talent but fuelled by ambition, relentlessness and restless dynamic energy. He converted his hoarse voice into a lifelong opportunity—no one can quite sing like him today—full-throated and with raw power.

We like the world 'chutzpah' (used in a non-indignant way), a gift of the Warlords, which allows them to imagine greater ends. What others may call atrocious, the Warlord may simply term as audacious and therefore achievable with a stretch. They are endowed with natural aggressiveness that arouses them, motivates them and spurs them on. They also seem to have this ability to never feel defensive in life, often living life 'on their terms'. Their belief may be that any and every mountain can be climbed.

In all their achievements, and living life in a 'spread out' and expansive way, the Warlord's sorrow is in not having plumbed depths. If they say 'I can't quite fathom that', you may know that they are not just punning. People have become numbers, relationships transactional and concepts sound 'abstract'. The bypassing of depth in their pull towards breadth leaves them with a sense of regret. *Says Sushil Saran, the CEO of an airline, 'All these past twenty years, there's not much that I have not achieved, and winning comes easy to me. But I really wish I had invested more time and energy in theatre, something that interested me in my college days. I daresay that that would brought out new dimensions in me even at the workplace and in my career'.* The other sorrow is that in their ventures and adventures, they leave things behind in earlier occupied territories—memories, relationships, unassimilated experiences and so on.

When they keep encountering parts of themselves, they rarely befriend them. Encounters become conquests, with one flat sense of self sought to be established as the dominant identity and the other parts of the self being relegated to the 'unimportant' or 'the subservient'. The diversity of the Self is not seen as a resource, and emergent identities are treated like vassals.

As one Warlord that we know put it, 'Over time, parts of me get to belong to so many things—things I have accomplished, things I have done, battles I have won, etc., that I wonder if I belong to any ONE thing, I wonder if I even belong to myself'. A classic case of 'In all that I am, what AM I really?'

The macho Warlords are also beset by many fears, which they tend to keep well hidden. One of the fears is—somewhat paradoxically—that they are not really grounded! That in their constantly seeking entry into and the occupation of new spaces, there is no 'familiarity' that they can take along with them. The second is their paranoia. That there is invasive malevolence around that is likely to 'get them' if they are not vigilant (and therefore the heightened vigilance that we often see in the Warlords). This leads them to often pre-emptively grow and expand so that the power that is waiting to swallow them up will have a tougher job to do.

The Warlord in the Extremes

When the Warlord energy peaks to high levels, you may encounter a force that is desensitized to the consequences of its being, with an inability or unwillingness to see beyond one's ambition to the impact of one's actions. Pain is often caused but not acknowledged. Growth may be mindless and accompanied by a delusional sense of grandiosity and disdain for consequences, even if this is unconscious (think of the growth of oil companies with scant regard for the adverse consequences of their growth, or of POSCO's botched project plan in Odisha, India, leading to nothing but thousands of felled trees and perhaps several lost livelihoods). The other side of this is plain tyranny and oppression—recent world history has several of them documented—in the form of phenomena such as the colonialization of several countries by the British, slave trade in the USA, forced occupation and the bloodbath in Indian settlements in the USA, or personalities such as Adolf Hitler, Idi Amin, Robert Mugabe, Saddam Hussein and so on.

And what of unwholesome Warlord energy? This would be where we see underplayed ambition, often presented as 'contentment with one's lot' or in the form of 'Oh, there's more to life than...'. Networks, alliances and coalitions may be avoided. So too, investment in learning and developing one's or the system's competencies may be low or limited to 'keeping the business running'. New capabilities are not developed and risks avoided. It is also possible that such individuals or systems may have stigmatized failure and thus attempt to ward off any probability of such!

Angst	Hope	Gifts	Fear/ Vulnerability
That my achievements are limited to an area and perimeter and not considerable in volume and depth	Nothing is unsurmountable; all can be conquered	I have vision and the matching ambition; I have ambition and the matching vision	What if I lose territory or lose in conquest?

The Warlords as Leaders in Organizations

- The Warlord leader would bring in dynamic masculine energy in a penetrative way and infuse a growth mindset in the organization.
- They would assign resources and make them accountable for efficient delivery so that their energy is channelled towards new opportunities.
- They may push people to their limits—at times even by being 'unreasonable' in their demands—and help them unexpectedly discover new sources of strength.
- They may create and sustain 'networks of similar others' to spot and pursue new opportunities.
- They would seek to enlarge the scope of change initiatives and consistently seek to maximize impact for the system.
- They would scan the environment for new opportunities and threats and take big bets for expanding the system.
- They may stretch the system when it is not ready, leaving the system vulnerable and at risk of implosion.

24

The Warrior–Crusader

The warrior's approach is to say 'yes' to life, 'yea' to it all.

—Joseph Campbell

The **Warrior-Crusader**

Who Is the Warrior–Crusader?

Much of the world's population, especially in poor countries, is made up of children and young people. To achieve a peaceful world, it is crucial that the rights of children and young people be respected. Following the tradition of Mahatma Gandhi, Indian activist Kailash Satyarthi has waged a peaceful struggle to stop children being exploited as labor instead of attending school. He has also contributed to the development of international conventions on the rights of children.

—Citation from the official website of the Nobel Peace
Prize Foundation for Kailash Satyarthi,
one of the winners of the 2014 Peace Prize

Satyarthi is a prime example of who we might call a Warrior–Crusader.

An extract from *The Guardian* in December 2013 shows up another well-known Warrior–Crusader.

Nelson Mandela's passing and the torrent of grief and tributes that has followed it show something quite extraordinary: the power of example, the power of legend, a power that still lives. In a sense, the world knows Mandela's story too well to be astounded by it afresh. It knows how, in his youth, he embraced the fight against apartheid and reached for the bullet and the bomb. It remembers his 27 years of incarceration and the defiant, unquenchable spirit he showed from behind bars when he greeted Soweto's uprising 'We who are confined within the grey walls of the Pretoria regime's prisons reach out to our people. With you, we count those who have perished by means of the gun and the hangman's noose. We salute all of you—the living, the injured and the dead. For you have dared to rise up against the tyrant's might.... Fight on! Between the anvil of united mass action and the hammer of the armed struggle, we shall crush apartheid and white minority racist rule'. Mandela was neither some passive, word-spinning proponent of eventual liberation, nor a plaster saint. He was a warrior.[1]

---

[1]Mandela, *Rebel, Warrior, Leader.*

And lastly for now, let us consider a lesser known but no less impactful Warrior–Crusader, Pragya.[2] Started by two graduates—Gargi Banerji and Sunil Pillai—of XLRI, Jamshedpur, in 1995, Pragya works for the appropriate development of vulnerable communities and sensitive ecosystems of the world. It strives ceaselessly to reach the benefits of development to the most remote and least developed regions, delivering an array of development services to isolated and underserved communities and building their capacity to help themselves. It also researches and supports reform of programmes and policies and advises and trains development actors, in order to spur development action in these regions. The organization was set up with a concern for last-mile communities neglected and marginalized in the development process and unique ecosystems (frequently the two converge) that suffer the destruction brought about by overuse of resources and inappropriate development. Its initial grassroots work was focused on the high-altitude belt of the Himalayan region across India and Nepal. Today, it has reached out to remote regions and isolated communities in other continents in its drive to address the development needs of all such areas and people in the world.

Let us now look more closely at the three examples we have chosen and try and elicit the essential characteristics of this identity. The Warrior–Crusader is the 'activist', the 'fighter for a cause' and the quintessential 'champion'. They are the ones who would bring in focused energy while pursuing causes—the words *waged a (peaceful) struggle*', *'the power of example'* and *'strive ceaselessly'*, in the examples given, give us a clue to this. They 'go after' and do not easily give up. The world may try to shackle them with various fetters—tradition, anecdotes of impossibility and lost causes, brutal power, whatever—but they can bounce right back with immense resilience. The Warrior–Crusaders' impact is felt most when the world realizes and recognizes that there is a person who is willing to stand up for something, often swimming upstream, and that their path can indeed be followed.

---

[2]www.pragya.org

The Warrior–Crusader is an interesting 'combo' identity, combining in itself the elements of:

1. The Warrior who would resolutely overcome adversities and challenges in pursuit of a cause or a cherished goal and
2. The Crusader who take up causes that he believes important to fight for and actually pursues them single mindedly.

The basic stance of Warrior–Crusaders is to go for deeply cherished goals and dreams. And 'go' here really means active, relentless pursuit. They would also take up and if necessary fight for causes that they passionately believe in. They are ones who have a purpose, something they feel connected to—and they live that conviction despite adversities. The Warrior–Crusader also knows that they create legacies—not necessarily ones for personal glory but legacies that would inspire people and stand as a beacon to guide others on similar searches or quests for time to come. Google's Pichai or Microsoft's Nadella or Pepsico's Nooyi may well know, deep in their hearts, that who they have become are icons for several others in this and in future generations to follow. In this, THEY are the legacies and not necessarily their products.

When the Warrior–Crusader energy is active, follower-ship ensues. Other people that are attracted to the cause come forward to volunteer their might. The system thus moves forward with increased momentum. We see this all the time in today's hyperconnected world.

Change.org is an example. Anybody can take up a cause and put forward their 'pitch' for change that they would like to see happening in the world around them. The 'pitch' instantly reaches tens of thousands of others connected to Change.org. Change petitions that appeal to people generate followership, signature volunteers and the Warrior–Crusader's ecology gets set up. Some of these crusades see light of day and go all the way through to legislative changes, while some others languish. Either ways, the Warrior–Crusader is constellated.

This identity further tries to ensure that whatever is taken up by them is taken forward in an uncompromising manner—no half-way measures, no cutting corners. They fully understand the gravity of what it takes to be Warrior–Crusaders. Another thing about their impact on the world is that they usually usher in a revolution in the world they occupy. This could be a dramatic one accompanied by sound and light, or a quiet almost invisible one, but they would change something in the world.

Like the example of Pragya earlier, consider Bablu Ganguly and Timbaktu Collective—a wonderful combination of the Healer and the Warrior–Crusader.[3]

'Back in 1989, the area near Chennakothapalli village of Anantapur (the second driest area in India) in Andhra Pradesh was a wasteland. Till C. K. Ganguly (Bablu) and Mary Vattamattam chanced upon it in 1991 and saw its immense potential to blossom into a green paradise. The couple, along with friend John D'Souza, then bought 32 acres of this barren land. Inspired by Japanese author Masanobu Fukuoka's seminal book on natural farming "The One-Straw Revolution", they began to plant trees regularly and help the land regenerate itself. Along with like-minded friends, they began to nurture a dream of transforming it into a green agro forest. The couple named the land Timbaktu. In Telugu it means Sarihaddu Rekha—the last horizon where the earth meets the sky'. This extract from an article in the Indian Express introduces us to Bablu and Mary's quiet crusade. They formed Timbaktu Collective, and NGO, and worked tirelessly for natural regeneration of the land. Under their watchful eyes and striving, what initially started with 32 acres of barren land has now spread to over 2,800 hectares (covering seven villages) of wasteland that has been regenerated into a forest.

Confronting odds, setbacks, adversities and hostility—check all these boxes to understand what a Warrior–Crusader would need to be ready to do in order to give shape to their dream. Oftentimes, they also put up with consequences at a personal level—giving up something or putting up in order to have the cause move forward. Some Warrior–Crusaders see obstacles as opportunities to charge forward. You typically spot this identity in the development sector and in politics, and in recent times, you see them in two other popular locations:

---

[3]www.timbaktu.org

1. In start-ups, where the team setting up the organization is doing so not necessarily with an eye on eventual sellout and exit, but because their start-up is the manifestation of their passion. Anand Anandkumar of Bugworks Research, Dr Devi Shetty of Narayana Hrudayalaya and V. S. Sudhakar of BigBasket are names that pop up when you think of such.

2. Micro-level Warrior–Crusaders espousing causes that they are passionate about, largely leveraging social media to share their work, attracting both interest and intrigue.

While confronting odds and working through and beyond those are what Warrior–Crusaders do, we must note that they typically have a 'long-haul' orientation when it comes to dealing with these. They are not the quick-fix seekers. They plough on relentlessly, carving out what they want. *Dashrath Manjhi, better known as the 'Mountain Man of India', is one example. Over 20 years, he single handedly carved a path across a mountain using only a hammer and chisel, to connect two villages so that the residents of one could have access to medical attention!* Accepting the status quo especially when they are convinced of a better alternative is not something this identity would rest easy with.

What Is Their Inner World Like?

The Warrior–Crusaders are born in the cradle of angst—of having to be the only one (or one of the very few) responsible for a cause that is for the good of the whole system. They have a vision for something—whether arising out of a dream or from roots in excruciating personal pathos and pain. They also believe that this vision has to be actively given shape to. Passively hoping that it would flower by itself and come alive is akin to giving up—not something that they are likely to even think of.

Alongside the angst, the *hope* of Warrior–Crusaders lies in their willingness to dream and to give shape to their dream. They believe that their relentlessness will yield a better tomorrow. In this, the greatest gifts that they are endowed with are, quite simply, the qualities of grit, courage and resilience.

A word of caution along with the gifts? The Warrior–Crusader perhaps needs to be aware of 'undiscerning obsession' with their cause. When the Warrior–Crusader starts (even unconsciously) seeing every process, every phenomenon, every system as a dragon that they are born to slay, you can bet that they are 'in the grip'. Miguel de Cervantes certainly had a better phrase for what we are trying to say here—'tilting at windmills'. The other caution here is perhaps the need for a cause to keep them going—a challenge, a dragon, an 'other'—in the absence of who or which, the Warrior–Crusader is caricatured into being but an armoured guard.

The lurking fear of the Warrior–Crusader would perhaps be that of having to face up to one's vulnerabilities and limitations, like Achilles heel. That there is invariably one 'soft spot' that is likely to cause all their strength to melt, and blunt their abilities, is what the Warrior–Crusader dreads. It could be the awareness of their mortality, it could be the irreversibility of ageing or a recurrent derailer—perhaps that ONE fatal flaw that could do them in? If we shift our focus to the 'Crusader' part of this identity, we see that their fear could be in facing the realpolitik of the system—perhaps in the realization that in the wheelings and dealings of the system, the Crusader ends up being the pawn rather than the one experiencing triumph in pursuit of his cause. As an example of this—Vishal Sikka held aloft a flag for the 'digital transformation' of Infosys to USD20 billion by 2020, till the system ejected him! And the sorrow of the Warrior–Crusader is seen when they, in rare moments of rest after another long day, remove the armour and sees the scars and wounds of battle. That a price has been paid and more would perhaps need to be paid is evident!

The Warrior–Crusaders enjoy the company of people that they would consider their 'equal or more' or people who authentic- ally see and respect their power. The other side of this coin is the shadow of the Warrior–Crusaders, often manifesting as hubris. For example, they are likely to get rather impatient when they either encounter what they see as lack of substantiveness in others and/or the inability of others to equalize with them. Examples of these could be 'passive aggressive' behaviour from others which include

- fawning ingratiation or sycophantic behaviour from others towards the Warrior–Crusader or
- seeming apathy or indifference to their cause

The Warrior–Crusader in the Extremes

What happens when this identity is 'overdone'? Taken to the extreme? This is where we encounter the burnt-out frame of the spent warriors, who sit and wonder if their cause has ultimately been a futile one. They are now staring into the abyss of their own utter insubstantiveness within, with perhaps a realization that all that they stood for was a chimera. For somewhere along the way, their cause defined them and then defiled them—that in place of pride came arrogance; in place of penetrative courage came violence; and in place of relentlessness came ruthlessness, and all this happened even when they thought they were being vigilant!

The denied or disowned Warrior–Crusader may hold a wish that has not yet become a cause. And it remains so, perhaps because this person has really not yet learnt what it means to receive hurt and continue to live. Receiving hurt is perhaps seen as death. Thus, the sword is there but it is sheathed still. Agency has not yet been discovered and is held in doubt and fear. One is reminded here of the Hero's Journey monomyth, with the Hero refusing to heed the call.

Angst	Hope	Gifts	Fear/Vulnerability
That I must fight for what I value. The world is a hostile place, and if I don't fight, what matters to me might never stand or it might just not last	Willingness to dream and to manifest the dream on behalf of the system	Grit, determination, courage	Encountering one's limitations

The Warrior–Crusaders as Leaders in Organizations

- The Warrior–Crusader comes alive in an organizational context that seeks focused goal achievement and sustainable excellence.
- Where this identity is at hand, there would be considerable focus on building the competencies, skills and capabilities of the system. After all, who knows the intersection between aspirations and capabilities better than the Warrior–Crusader?
- Warrior–Crusader leaders sense and tap into the aspirations of people and connect that to the larger cause of the system. People in their teams and organizations feel the galvanizing power of the pride that such leaders generate in them.
- They bring in laser-like focus on achieving tangible goals, while mobilizing resources and confronting obstacles. Similarly, when it comes to driving change, such leaders would aggressively drive it, mostly brooking no interference. They would be quick and agile to notice dissipation and confront it head on.
- On the flip side, the Warrior–Crusaders as leaders may drive things so aggressively that they may leave the organization and the people short of breath and resentful.
- Every once in a while, they are also called 'compulsive heroes'—who have to take everything and convert it into a quest that has to be tackled only by supreme heroic action.
- Their actions may lead to exhaustion, fatigue and burnout—for them and maybe for others in the system as well.

25

The TAM Playbook

Welcome to the playbook section! Here is an opportunity for you to encounter the Transformative Alignment Map (TAM) worlds and identities in a playful yet substantive way.

The exercises will help you experience and assimilate the identities towards wholeness and integration. You can either follow the Lewis Carroll route of 'Begin at the beginning and go on till you come to the end, then stop' or you could read through and engage with the exercises that beckon you and then come back to the others.

So this is a space for work and play. Sounds like an oxymoron? We hope so—here is to the promise of engaging paradoxes that they bring with them!

So, dear Reader, play on ....

Exercise 1—Mirror, Mirror on the Wall

Intended outcomes of this activity:

- Understand your Self at a deeper level and also get a glimpse of how you are viewed by others

Note—For a fuller and comprehensive understanding of yourself, please visit www.taminsights.com, take a TAM-Self assessment and schedule time with a TAM coach

Follow the instructions below:

1. The sixteen identities of TAM are listed below in ascending alphabetical order. In the column 'Self-image', place a ☑ mark against the three identities that you feel you most resonate with.
2. Then in the same column, place a ☒ mark against the three identities that you feel the greatest distance from.
3. Invite three more people who know you well for an informal feed-forward session. Share with them your top and bottom three identities and use the following questions to initiate the dialogue.
4. Fill out your reflections and actions in the space provided.

Questions:

1. How do you see this identity manifest in my life and context?
2. What do you see as the implications of these identities? (for myself and others)
3. What are the one or two things I can do differently?

Symbolic Identity	Your Self-image
The Administrator	
The Artiste	
The Collaborator	
The Curious Child	

Symbolic Identity	Your Self-image
The Custodian	
The Guide/Mentor	
The Healer	
The Mother	
The Muse	
The Provider of Resources	
The Ruler	
The Strategist	
The Trickster	
The Troubleshooter	
The Warlord	
The Warrior–Crusader	

1. What are the key insights and reflections from the dialogue?

    _____

    _____

    _____

2. What will I do differently going forward?

    _____

    _____

    _____

Please note that you could do this exercise with many other people as well—for example, you could ask people reporting into you, your reporting manager and so on, for inputs and then see the patterns emerge. Just feel free to add in additional columns to the Mirror's Reflection page!

Exercise 2—Embodying the Underdone

Intended outcomes of this activity:

* Understand the implications of my underdone identities and apply simple practices to bring these identities to life.

Steps:

1. Refer to the previous chart where you have a ☒ mark against the three identities that you feel the greatest distance from.
2. In the coming week, pick two specific contexts (e.g., your monthly review meeting, parenting) where you can deploy these identities.
3. Embody (not playact but be the identity) these identities in those contexts and come back and fill out the reflections.

Questions:

1. Describe the feelings that arose when you actually embodied these identities.

   _____

   _____

   _____

2. What are your reflections on where you can deploy these identities in your life?

   _____

   _____

   _____

3. What are some of the actions that you can take to grace and bring alive these identities in your life?

   _____

   _____

   _____

Exercise 3—TAM on the Go

Intended outcomes of this activity:

- Being able to spot TAM energies in the worlds around us
- Being able to spot where your own energy tends to get pulled to against your ideal

Steps:

1. In the rough-scale graph below, plot what percentage of time you would like to allot to each world on a day-to-day basis. Use horizontal bars/lines and do not worry about exactitude—a rough sketch would work fine!

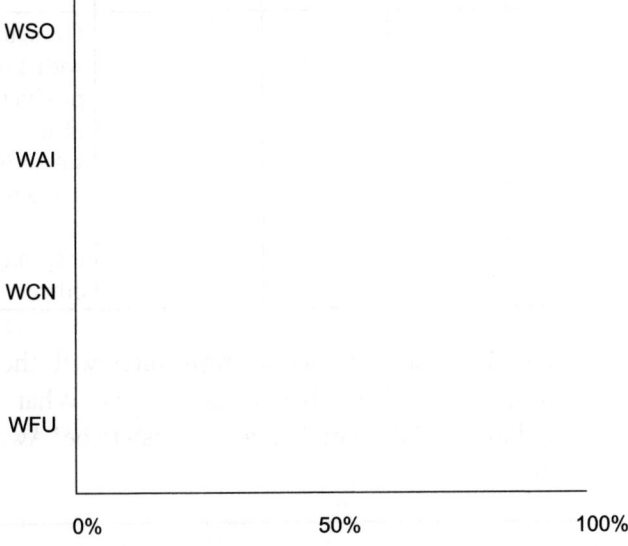

2. Now use the table below (*we have constructed a table to last you 4 days, you can always do this offline in a separate sheet of paper and add in as many days as you like!*). Each event you can recall that involved you during a day, make a brief note in the cell you think is appropriate. Try and do this as many times during the day as you can, and you will see that

TAM-World-Spotting is both easy AND fun! We have populated a few inserts just to give you an idea.

TAM World	Day 1	Day 2	Day 3	Day 4
World of structure and order (WSO)	Woke up to the alarm as always			
World of autonomy and initiative (WAI)		Our team got the best-team award!		
World of connectedness and nurturance (WCN)			Sat with my daughter and listened to her struggles	
World of flow and unfolding (WFU)				Came up with a new product idea—am sure it is going to be fun and inspiring to others!

3. After 5 days, compare your actual engagement with the TAM worlds with the ideal graph you had drawn. What is the picture looking like? Are you where you wish to be? Away? By how much?

_____

_____

_____

4. If there is a considerable gap, what could you possibly do to recalibrate your life? Even small tweaks can help a lot!

_____

_____

_____

Exercise 4—Light Up the World(s)!

Intended outcomes of this activity:

- Understand the psychological world that seems to pull you to it and the one that seems to block you
- Use this enhanced awareness to decide how and where you would like to deploy your energy

Steps:

1. Rank order the worlds, 1 being the world that you feel pulled towards and 4 being the world you feel most distance from.

The World	Your Rank
The WSO	
The WCN	
The WAI	
The WFU	

2. Then proceed to respond to the following questions. Look at the world you have ranked 1.

- What about this world seems to pull you?

  _____

  _____

  _____

- If this world is your primary pull, what key strengths are you likely to bring in to any challenge/situation?

  _____

  _____

  _____

- Ask someone who knows you well to describe a key strength that they see in you—how does that tie in with what you have yourself identified and to your preferred world?

  _____

  _____

  _____

3. Now identify ONE world that you seem to least prefer (ranked 4)—maybe a world whose descriptions make you feel an inhibition or a block. Maybe with this world you get a sense of 'Nah, that's not me ...'. Now proceed to respond to the following questions:

4. Watch the following clips based on the world that is most distant from you:

   a. If WSO was the lowest, watch the clip _The Toyota Production System_
   b. If WFU was the lowest, watch the movie _Shall We Dance_
   c. If WCN was the lowest, watch the movie _Hacksaw Ridge_
   d. If WAI was the lowest, watch the movie _The Pursuit of Happyness_

5. Having watched the movie, answer the questions below.

   - What about this world seems to inhibit you?

     _____

     _____

     _____

   - If this world is your inhibition/block, what opportunities are you likely to miss engaging with, in your life and career?

     _____

     _____

     _____

- What are some of the actions you would like to take to bring this world alive for you?

_____

_____

_____

Exercise 5—The Life Events Map

Intended outcomes of this activity:

- Understand the patterns of your stability and change orientation
- Use this awareness to create a working plan and refine your approach

Steps:

1. Sit back and give yourself time to go over your life events. Reflect on your early childhood, adolescence, your early adulthood and to where you are currently.
2. Pick out two events/a period/incidents in each time frame and plot them on the graph below. These incidents/events must be related to an experience of stability or change. For example, from years 5 to 10, we moved three houses, from years 10 to 15, I studied in the same college, had the same set of friends and so on.
3. Plot the graph.
4. Now answer the questions below:
   a. What patterns do you see for yourself as your life has unfolded?
   b. What have been some of the consequences of this pattern?
   c. What refinements would you like to bring to your life in this context?

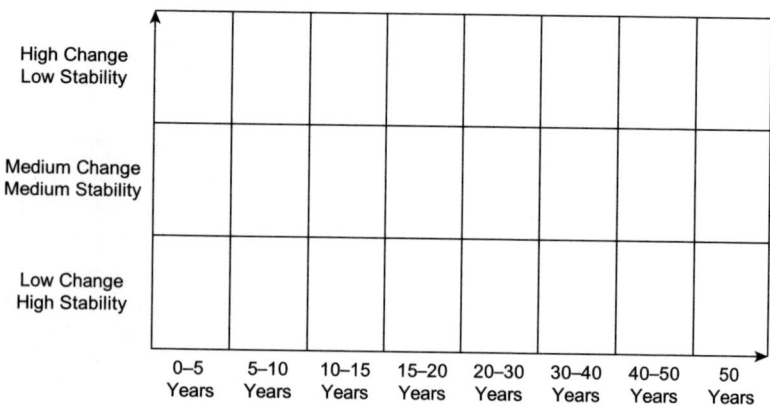

Exercise 6—What Would Your Role-model Do (WWRD)

Intended outcomes of this activity:

- Understand the way you deploy the masculine and feminine energies into the world
- Use the process of identifying role models to experience and deploy these energies in the world

Instructions:

- Read Appendix 1, particularly the part on the masculine and the feminine energy.
- Identify role models who deploy these energies.

Energy	My Role Model
• Penetrative—Assertive Masculine Energy	
• Containing—Grounding Masculine Energy	
• Receptive—Nurturing Feminine Energy	
• Expressive—Creative Feminine Energy	

- Sit back and think about what energies you would like to bring to which context of your life.

Contexts	Energy (Penetrative—Assertive Masculine/Containing Grounding Masculine/Expressive—Creative Feminine/Receptive—Nurturing Feminine)
Family	
Parenting	
Workplace	
Friends and Social Circle	
Community	

- Ask yourself what your role model will do? WWRD?
- What are some of the actions you would like to experiment with?

26

The Way Forward

Only he who keeps his eyes on the far horizon will find the right road.

—Dag Hammarskjold

As T. S. Eliott wrote, 'We must not cease from exploration and the end of all our exploring will be to arrive where we began and to know the place for the first time'. We feel immensely gratified to have been on this journey with you and hope you have gained precious insights and perspectives into yourself and the nature of human phenomena.

Like all journeys, the end just signifies the beginning of a new one. And for us, there is a long way to go yet. Having explored the different facets and identities of the self, our research now veers off into three different directions.

The first one, which is a natural pathway to the next phase of our project, is to explore the identity of 'systems', be it organizations, collectives, teams or communities. Our focus in this area will be to engage with the nature of 'system identities', explore its manifestations and the ways and means to intervene in the system to move towards wholeness and integration, which stands at the centre of our effort. While we have touched upon the Transformative Alignment Map (TAM) role and the TAM organization ideas, there is much to be said about exploring the nature of dissonances, alignment and misalignment among self-systems, role systems and organizational systems.

The second involves the application of our work in human beings and human systems. There has been a great deal of work that we and the TAM practitioner cohorts have done in coaching and organizational work using the TAM framework. Our intent will be to bring to the world the various ways of applying the TAM framework to work with human beings and systems at various stages. We are in the process of developing ways to work with organizations in different phases such as start-ups or mature service organizations. We expect to do action research that will provide the world both the depth and breadth to identify, explore and intervene in various organizational contexts.

The final process that has engaged us is also the work being done on what is now being referred to as 'vertical development'. There is a great deal of research on the evolutionary paradigm of self and systems including Adult Development Theory (Robert Kegan, Jennifer Garvey), Ego Development (Susan Cooke-Greuter), Spiral Dynamics (Beck and Cowan) and AQAL[1] (Ken Wilber), all of which point to the idea of a continuing unfolding of the human self. We find several parallels and intersection points between the philosophical underpinnings of our model and the idea of human evolution and we are already looking at TAM from the evolutionary lens.

It is heartening that our tribe of TAM practitioners continues to grow and organizations which have been exposed to TAM continue to use them in various contexts and spaces. We look forward to your continued association and support as we continue the journey.

---

[1]AQAL stands for all quadrants, all levels, all lines, all states, all types.

Appendix 1

The Two Axes of Orientation

Having started out on our journey of discovering the pathways to individuated human beings and systems, our epistemological quest took us on many an uncharted road. Gareth Hill's work and subsequently the work of Cortlett and Pearson certainly provided our most valuable starting points, as did Jung's work on the Self and Mandalas with the 'Quaternity' principle.

One of those guiding posts—thanks in no mean measure to Hill—is the pairs of complementaries of the masculine and the feminine and the static and dynamic. In the following sections, we will delve first into the masculine–feminine complementarity and then to that of preference for stability or change. We will also describe where we have chosen to depart from Hill's classification.

Masculine–Feminine

There have been innumerable references to this complementarity. From the Christian Bible, we have the idea of Adam and Eve. The Tao refers to the non-duality of life (i.e., the idea of integration and wholeness, again) as represented by the interaction of *Heaven* (masculine) and *Earth* (feminine) and the *Tai-Chi* comprising the

homeostasis of *yin* and *yang*. The Sanskrit word 'Tantra' transliter-
ates as The Weft and Warp (*duality*) of the Weave (*non-duality*)—
as in the directions of the threads that go to make up the cloth we
wear—if one of these subjective pairs (dualities) did not exist,
neither would the cloth (*non-duality*). This is beautifully described
by Maffie—'the weaver then uses the weft-toting shuttle stick to
penetrate the shed and warp threads, giving birth to a cloth…'.

We are talking here of the archetypal patterns of 'feminine'
and 'masculine' which transcend gender. As mentioned by Ashok
Malhotra, the ideas of the feminine and masculine are both
socially defined constructs and bio-existential constructs. Taking
the socially defined view, males, females and intersex people can
display characteristics that are feminine and/or masculine.

To understand masculine and feminine better, we take a point
of view here from the idea of 'agency' and 'communion', one of
the basic dualities of human existence. It closely approximates
Rajagopalan's view of 'striving' and 'abiding' as a duality. We assert
that both the masculine and the feminine principles have an agentic
side and a communion side. This is not to be confused with Hill's
conceptualization of dynamic/static masculine and dynamic/static
feminine, as we will explain in another section. Agency and
communion are quite different from dynamic and static—both
agency and communion have dynamic (preference for change) and
static (preference for stability) qualities to them, which is the
nuance that we work with in Transformative Alignment.

As Malhotra[1] puts it, 'our agentic side propels us towards
autonomy, assertion, individuality and a sense of wholeness with
our selves'. In the masculine, agenticity appears in the form of being
'penetrative and assertive'. This quality of the masculine volitionally
enters spaces, territories and systems and makes its entry and
presence noticed. 'This is how it shall be', 'Get it done', 'Fight for a
cause, leave a legacy', 'Expand, grow'—these are some of the voices
that can be heard from the agentic/striving masculine. In the

---

[1]Malhotra, *Child Man*.

feminine, agenticity is 'expressive and generative'. Like the agentic masculine, the agentic feminine does not wait for permission—it sees a need to generate and regenerate life, and to express without restraint, and it does it. 'Let's make it whole again', 'Let's do it together', 'Let's express', 'Let's disrupt the existing order'—voices from the agentic feminine indeed!

On the other hand, the need for communion emphasizes our relatedness, our wish to belong and our need to merge ourselves into a larger entity. Masculine communion seeking exists in the form of being 'boundary maintaining/containing'. This masculine seeks to stay within the larger entity and helps by providing a container and a grounding quality. 'These are the traditions', 'Here are the resources for you to work with', 'Here is how you can solve this', 'Here is where we are and here are my insights on where to go from here'—some voices from the communion seeking or the abiding masculine. The corresponding feminine quality here is the 'receptive/nurturant' feminine. She receives life, protects it and offers back to the world. 'I protect and nourish you', 'Here is my guidance', 'Let's sit and wonder together', 'I love your thinking, how could you now express it' and so on—some voices from this feminine may be familiar to you.

Preference for Stability: Preference for Change

We have preferred to use the terms 'preference for stability' and 'preference for change' in place, respectively, of 'static' and 'dynamic' offered by Hill. The reason is that in mapping the TAM profile of a person (or a system), we are actually asking our respondents to state their preferences of how they prefer to normally live their lives: we are not exploring the conditions in which they exist.

Preference for stability is a relative preference to live with 'continuity', valuing the 'as-is' or 'as-has-been'. The existing scheme of things, traditions, customs, mores and practices are valued. Things are maintained and run. If things go off-kilter, they are restored. The givens are nourished and protected. They are fostered and perpetuated.

Preference for change is a relative preference to seek movement, transformation and newness. Expansion, pursuit, future focus and growth are sought. Newness is manifested. The old order is sought to be replaced. 'Current' is 'obsolete', and if things go off-kilter, they are mostly replaced.

More on Our Framework

As we have explained in the section 'Masculine–Feminine' earlier here, our explorations into the nature of 'masculine' and 'feminine' reveal what we believe to be two essential spectrums of these qualities, existing simultaneously. These are now illustrated here.

Penetrative Masculine	Receptive Feminine

Containing Masculine	Expressive Feminine

A first-level read might in a misleading way suggest to us that all penetrative masculine and all expressive feminine is dynamic. In similar vein, we might be misled to believe that all receptive feminine and all containing masculine is static. We believe differently.

Our explorations suggest to us that there is a 'stability-preferring' side to the penetrative masculine as well as the expressive feminine. Similarly, there is a 'change preferring' side to the receptive feminine as well as the containing masculine. Thus, our conceptualization leads us to eight basic patterns as follows:

The Penetrative—Masculine that prefers stability
The Penetrative—Masculine that prefers change
The Containing—Masculine that prefers stability
The Containing—Masculine that prefers change

The Receptive—Feminine that prefers stability
The Receptive—Feminine that prefers change
The Expressive—Feminine that prefers stability
The Expressive—Feminine that prefers change

Each of these patterns shows up in the 16 identities described in a unique way. We have touched upon these patterns briefly while describing the identities. A more detailed explanation of these energy patterns will perhaps need to be part of another book.

Appendix 2

TAM Self-assessment/TAM Self-certification

If you have read the whole book or even just parts of it, your interest is piqued and you want to explore more about yourself using the TAM framework, you can certainly do so.

All you have to do is send us your name and preferred email address to discoverthealchemist@gmail.com, with the subject header 'TAM-Self Assessment', and we will provide you further guidelines, options and instructions.

For those who may like to pursue certification in TAM-Self, please send an email to discoverthealchemist@gmail.com with the subject header 'TAM-Self Certification' and we will guide you through the certification process.

Bibliography

Ananthanarayanan, Raghu. *Totally Aligned Organisation: Aligning the Human Spirit to Organisational Endeavour.* Chennai: Productivity & Quality Publishing, 2008.

Arrien, Angeles. *The Tarot Handbook: Practical Applications of Ancient Visual Symbols.* New York: Tarcher Perigee, 1997.

Belohlavek, Peter. *The Unicist Theory, Its Applications and Scientific Evidences (Unicist Theory: The Nature of Things Book 1).* Argentina: The Unicist Research Institute, 2015.

Campbell, Joseph. *Hero with a Thousand Faces,* edition 3. California: New World Library and Joseph Campbell Foundation, 2012.

Cortllett, John G., and Carol S. Pearson. *Mapping the Organizational Psyche: A Jungian Theory of Organizational Dynamics and Change.* USA: Center for Applications of Psychological Type Inc., 2003.

Covey, Stephen R. *The 7 Habits of Highly Effective People: Powerful Lessons in Personal Change.* New York: Mango, 2017.

de Cervantes, Miguel. *Don Quixote,* UK edition. UK: Penguin, 2003.

Doyle, Arthur Conan. *The Memoirs of Sherlock Holmes.* UK: George Newnes Ltd., 1894.

Ernst, Chris, and Donna Chrobot-Mason. *Boundary Spanning Leadership,* edition 1. New York: McGraw-Hill Education, 2010.

Franz, Von, and Marie Louise. *The Problem of the Puer Aeternus,* edition 3. Toronto, Canada: Inner City Books, 2000.

Franz, Von, and Marie Louise. *Alchemy: An Introduction to the Symbolism and the Psychology*. Toronto, Canada: Inner City Books, 2015.

Frost, Peter J., and Sandra L. Robinson. The Toxic Handler: Organizational Hero and Casualty. *Harvard Business Review*, 74(4): 96–106, 1999.

Gladwell, Malcolm. *The Tipping Point*. London: Back Bay Books, 2002.

Green, Charles H. *Trust Based Selling: Using Customer Focus and Collaboration to Build Long Term Relationships*, edition 1. USA: McGraw-Hill Education, 2005.

Haynes, A. B., T. G. Weiser, W. R. Berry, S. R. Lipsitz, A. H. Breizat, E. P. Dellinger, T. Herbosa, et al. 'A Surgical Safety Checklist to Reduce Morbidity and Mortality in a Global Population', *New England Journal of Medicine* (29 January 2009). Available online at https://www.ncbi.nlm.nih.gov/pubmed/19144931

Hill, Gareth. *Masculine and Feminine: The Natural Flow of Opposites in the Psyche*. Boston and London: Shambhala Publications Inc., 2013.

Homer. *The Odyssey*. New York: Maple Press, 2013.

Johnson, Robert A. *He: Understanding Masculine Psychology*. New York: HarperCollins Publishers, 1989.

———. *She: Understanding Feminine Psychology*. New York: HarperCollins Publishers, 1989.

———. *Owning Your Shadow: Understanding the Darkside of the Psyche*. New York: HarperCollins Publishers, 2009.

Jung, Carl Gustav. *Man and His Symbols*. USA: Dell Publishing, 1968.

———. *Aspects of the Masculine*. London and New York: Routledge & Kegan Paul, 1989.

———. *The Four Archetypes*, edition 3. London and New York: Routledge, 2005.

King, Stephen. *Misery*, Reissue edition. London: Scribner, 2016.

Klein, Melanie. *Love, Guilt and Reparation and Other Works*, edition 1. New York: Free Press, 2002.

Krishna, T. M. *A Southern Music*. NOIDA: HarperCollins, 2013.

Lencioni, Patrick. *The Five Dysfunctions of a Team*. USA: AHA, 2000.

Maffie, James. *Aztec Philosophy: Understanding a World in Motion*. Colorado: University Press of Colorado, 2014.

Mahurkar, Uday. 'Blessed by the Plague'. *India Today*, 4 July 2005.

Malhotra, Ashok. *Child Man: The Selfless Narcissist*. New Delhi: Routledge, 2010.

Pascale, R., J. Sternin, and M. Sternin. *The Power of Positive Deviance: How Unlikely Innovators Solve the World's Toughest Problems*. USA: Harvard Business Press, 2010.

Rajagopalan, R. *Immersive Systemic Knowing: Rational Analysis and Beyond* (PhD thesis, Centre for Systems Studies, University of Hull, UK, 2016).

Williams, Kipling D., Joseph P. Forgas, and William von Hippel. *The Social Outcast: Ostracism, Social Exclusion, Rejection, and Bullying*. New York: Psychology Press, 2005.

Weblinks

Maqbool Fida Husain. 'Indian Art's Ambassador'. Accessed 9 June 2011. https://blogs.timesofindia.indiatimes.com/plumage/maqbool-fida-husain-indian-art-s-ambassador/

'This Is How Elon Musk Can Learn and Master Anything Quickly'. Accessed 14 December 2017. https://curiosity.com/topics/this-is-how-elon-musk-can-learn-and-master-anything-quickly-curiosity/

Chapter III, The Banking Practices of the Nattukottai Chettiars. http://shodhganga.inflibnet.ac.in/bitstream/10603/31094/10/10_chapter%203.pdf

'Decoding Infosys. Why Narayana Murthy and Vishal Sikka Were Not Made for Each Other'. http://www.firstpost.com/business/decoding-infosys-why-narayana-murthy-and-vishal-sikka-were-not-made-for-each-other-3997751.html

'Eleven Years After Plague Scare, Surat in Gujarat Is One of Cleanest Cities in India', Uday Mahurkar, https://www.indiatoday.in/magazine/states/story/20050704-eleven-years-after-plague-scare-surat-in-gujarat-is-one-of-cleanest-cities-in-india-788308-2005-07-04, July 2005.

'The Muse: A Releasing Your Unlimited Creativity Discussion Topic'. http://ryuc.info/common/creation_process/muse.htm

'Obsession, Danger and Absolutely No Sex: Why Every Woman Needs a Muse'. Accessed 30 June 2015. https://www.telegraph.co.uk/women/womens-life/11706461/Artists-muse-Why-every-woman-needs-one.html

'"Niti" or "Nyaya": The Real Injustice that Should Keep Us Awake at Night'. Accessed 8 April 2018. https://scroll.in/article/748345/niti-or-nyaya-the-real-injustice-that-should-keep-us-awake-at-night

'Demonetisation Effect: Digital Payments India's New Currency; Debit Card Transactions Surge to Over 1 Billion'. Accessed 27 May 2017. https://economictimes.indiatimes.com/industry/banking/finance/banking/digital-payments-indias-new-currency-debit-card-transactions-surge-to-over-1-billion/articleshow/58863652.cms

'Why Do Planes Crash? Expert Explains Five Most Common Reasons for Airliner Disasters, and only One in Ten Are Caused by Terrorism'. http://www.dailymail.co.uk/sciencetech/article-3600784/Why-planes-crash-Expert-explains-five-common-reasons-airliner-disasters-one-ten-caused-terrorism.html, 20 May 2016.

Ramrajya. Accessed 8 April 2018. http://www.mkgandhi.org/momgandhi/chap67.htm

'Collaboration Overload Is a Symptom of a Deeper Organizational Problem'. Accessed 27 May 2017. https://hbr.org/2017/03/collaboration-overload-is-a-symptom-of-a-deeper-organizational-problem

'Square Meals on Wheels'. Accessed 25 March 2017. http://www.newindianexpress.com/magazine/2017/mar/25/square-meals-on-wheels-1585119.html

'What Is a Mastermind Group? A Definition, Plus Articles, Classes'. Accessed 8 April 2018. http://www.thesuccess alliance.com/what-is-a-mastermind-group/

'"Diverge Before You Converge": Tips for Creative Brainstorming'. Accessed 17 February 2014. https://sloanreview.mit.edu/article/diverge-before-you-converge-tips-for-creative-brainstorming/

'Xi Jinping Heralds "New Era" of Chinese Power at Communist Party Congress'. Accessed 18 October 2017. https://www.theguardian.com/world/2017/oct/18/xi-jinping-speech-new-era-chinese-power-party-congress

'How Tech Companies Own Your Day'. Accessed 21 December 2017. https://www.bloomberg.com/graphics/2017-how-tech-owns-your-day/?utm_content=tech&utm_campaign=socialflow-organic&utm_source=twitter&utm_medium=social&cmpid%3D=socialflow-twitter-tech

'Nelson Mandela: Rebel, Warrior, Leader: And a Man Who Inspired a Nation and the World'. Accessed 7 December 2013. https://www.theguardian.com/commentisfree/2013/dec/07/observer-editorial-nelson-mandela

Sushanta Banerjee, http://sumedhas.org/media/The%20 Course%20of%20Self%20Reflexivity.pdf

'The Idyll-Maker Who Built Timbaktu'. Accessed 7 June 2014. http://www.newindianexpress.com/magazine/2014/jun/08/The-Idyll-Maker-Who-Built-Timbaktu-622350.html

Websites

www.auroville.org
www.bhoomicollege.org
www.brainyquote.com/authors/albert_schweitzer
www.pipaltree.org.in
www.rasikas.org
www.sumedhas.org
www.timbaktu.org

About the Authors

Kartikeyan V. is a leading Leadership and Organization consultant, coach and facilitator. With 20 years of experience in top management roles in human resources (HR) prior to his consulting, he has a significant appreciation of the challenges of the real world of executives working in volatile/dynamic contexts and structures. In addition, with his intimate engagement for over two decades with the 'process-work' movement in India, he imbues his work with a distinctive flavour of process-work technologies of understanding behaviour and the psychodynamics of systems. He has worked with and facilitated several teams from diverse industries.

Kartikeyan is a fellow of Sumedhas Academy for Human Context. He is also a trained flautist and has performed Karnatik music in several concerts. The Transformative Alignment Map (TAM) was born out of his dream of finding a space of correspondence between Karnatik music and the fields of the behavioural sciences and organization development (OD).

Rachna Nandakumar is a consultant in the areas of Strategic Human Resources and Organization Development. A human resource and learning professional with 15 years of experience, her primary areas of work have been in organization effectiveness, leadership development, change management, talent management and group facilitation. She believes very strongly in the spirit and potential of people and systems and works towards unleashing this energy and potential for increased organizational health where people are more productive, successful and fulfilled.

Rachna is a fellow with Sumedhas Academy for Human Context. She is certified in and administers several psychometric instruments as part of her consulting work. Rachna is also a trained dancer and continues to explore this art form. Rachna has published in *The Hindu Business Line* and in the journal of the National HRD Network, India.

Viswanath P. is the President and CEO of the Institute of Transformational Coaching LLC, an organization focused on building transformative, ecosystemic leadership. He is an experienced executive coach and leadership development professional with over 23 years of organizational experience across a diverse set of industries including IT, fast-moving consumer goods (FMCG), retail, power and manufacturing.

Vishy is a credentialed coach and a part of the Forbes Coaches Council. He works with senior leaders across the globe, spanning Asia, Middle East and the USA enabling them to lead successfully in times of increasing complexity and uncertainty. Vishy has also worked with several Fortune 500 organizations facilitating senior leadership retreats focused on strategy, culture building and leadership development.

Vishy is an avid trekker and has summited Mount Kilimanjaro and has been to the Everest Base Camp. He writes for *Forbes* and has been published in the *Hindu Business Line* and *Vikalpa*.